SHAKESPEARE SURVEY

ADVISORY BOARD

SHAKESPEARE SURVEY

AN ANNUAL SURVEY OF
SHAKESPEARIAN STUDY AND PRODUCTION

28

EDITED BY
KENNETH MUIR

CAMBRIDGE UNIVERSITY PRESS

CAMBRIDGE

LONDON · NEW YORK · MELBOURNE

Published by the Syndics of the Cambridge University Press
The Pitt Building, Trumpington Street, Cambridge CB2 1RP
Bentley House, 200 Euston Road, London NW1 2DB
32 East 57th Street, New York, NY 10022, USA
296 Beaconsfield Parade, Middle Park, Melbourne 3206, Australia

Library of Congress catalogue card number: 75–2720

ISBN: 0 521 20837 8

First published 1975

Shakespeare Survey was first published in 1948. For the first
eighteen volumes it was edited by Allardyce Nicoll under the
sponsorship of the University of Birmingham, the University
of Manchester, the Royal Shakespeare Theatre and the
Shakespeare Birthplace Trust

Printed in Great Britain
at the
University Printing House, Cambridge
(Euan Phillips, University Printer)

EDITOR'S NOTE

The central theme of *Shakespeare Survey 29* will be 'Shakespeare's Last Plays'. The theme of Number 30 will be 'Shakespeare from *Henry IV* to *Hamlet*' (the subject of the International Shakespeare Conference at Stratford-upon-Avon in 1976). Contributions on that or on other topics, which should not normally exceed 5,000 words, should reach the Editor (University of Liverpool, P.O. Box 147, Liverpool L69 3BX) not later than 1 September 1976. Contributors should leave generous margins, use double-spacing, and follow the style and lay-out of articles in the current issue. A style-sheet is available on request from Dr Ann Thompson at the above address.   K. M.

CONTRIBUTORS

N. W. BAWCUTT, *Senior Lecturer in English Literature, University of Liverpool*

RALPH BERRY, *Professor of English, University of Manitoba*

ROBERT ELLRODT, *Professor of English, University of Nice*

ANDREW GURR, *Senior Lecturer in English Literature, University of Leeds*

R. F. HILL, *Senior Lecturer in English Literature, King's College, University of London*

JOEL HURSTFIELD, *Professor of History, University College, University of London*

ARTHUR C. KIRSCH, *Professor of English, University of Virginia*

JACQUELINE E. M. LATHAM, *Principal Lecturer in English, Kingston Polytechnic*

D. A. LATTER, *Director of the British Council, Kaduna, Nigeria*

†PIERRE LEGOUIS, *Professor Emeritus, University of Lyons*

A. D. NUTTALL, *Professor of English, University of Sussex*

D. J. PALMER, *Senior Lecturer in English Literature, University of Hull*

RICHARD PROUDFOOT, *Lecturer in English Literature, King's College, University of London*

ERNEST SCHANZER, *Professor of English, University of Munich*

S. SCHOENBAUM, *Professor of English, Northwestern University, Illinois*

PETER THOMSON, *Professor of Drama, University of Exeter*

MORRIS WEITZ, *Professor of Philosophy, Brandeis University*

CONTENTS

PLATES

'RICHARD II' AND THE REALITIES
OF POWER

S. SCHOENBAUM

There is a scene in an Elizabethan play on the reign of Richard II – the play, anonymous and without title, of uncertain date and theatrical provenance, now commonly called *Woodstock* or *Thomas of Woodstock* – in which one of the caterpillars of the commonwealth enters the royal presence poring over a book. 'How now, what readst thou, Bushy?', asks the King. To which his favourite replies:

The monument of English Chronicles,
Containing acts and memorable deeds
Of all your famous predecessor kings.[1]

This book – is it Holinshed (a bit large for the purpose) or Stow evoked in a kind of surreal flash-forward? – holds examples, strange and wonderful, of treason and conquest applicable to Richard's own predicament. The information on which he eagerly seizes, however, is more prosaic. Bushy reads: 'Upon the 3rd of April 1365 was Lord Richard, son to the Black Prince, born at Bordeaux.' '1365...', muses the King. 'What year is this?' (This is one of those plays in which characters ask the year, presumably more for the spectators' benefit than their own; it is not dramaturgy of a Shakespearian order.) The year, it turns out, is 1387. Thus does it dawn on Richard that he has reached his majority. He can now claim his birthright, the throne of England, and set in motion the catastrophic sequence of events which will lead to his fall.

The episode illustrates the education of a prince and furnishes another instance – if one were needed – of the uses of literacy. The sequel in *Woodstock* properly reminds us of the caution we must exercise in making use of written memorials. Woodstock yields up the mace of his office of Lord Protector (an office that the historical Woodstock did not enjoy) with good grace, but not without glancing sceptically at the authority which the King has consulted:

And yet I think I have not wronged your birthright:
For if the times were searched, I guess your grace
Is not so full of years till April next.[2]

In truth our source-materials are often enough ambiguous, confused, or contradictory. A note of complaint is heard early. 'This tragicall example', William Baldwin remarks on Mowbray's 'tragedy' in *The Mirror for Magistrates*, 'was of all the cumpany well liked, how be it a doubte was founde therin, and that by meanes of the diuersity of the Chronicles: for where as maister Hall whom in this storye we chiefly folowed, maketh Mowbray accuser, and Boleynbroke appellant, mayster Fabian reporteth the matter quite contrary, & that by the reporte of good authours, makyng Boleynbroke the accuser, and Mowbray the appellant.'[3] What can a moral poet do? Leave such matters to the experts who have access to the documents, trust to the best authorities, and go about his proper business of discouraging vice and exalting virtue. For the modern scholar, deprived of the consolations of didacticism, the solution is not so straightforward.

[1] *Woodstock: A Moral History*, ed. A. P. Rossiter (1946), p. 98.
[2] *Ibid.*, p. 104.
[3] *The Mirror for Magistrates*, ed. Lily B. Campbell (Cambridge, 1938), p. 110.

I

I have turned to the reign of Richard II for the induction to my paper, and it is Shakespeare's play on Richard that is my subject here. It seemed an especially appropriate choice. In bodying-forth on the stage the *fons et origo* of the Wars of the Roses and the other tumultuous events that occupy Shakespeare through eight historical dramas, *Richard II* stands in much the same formal relation to the sequence as does the 'Introduction' (and first year) of the history of Henry IV in Edward Hall's vast chronicle of *The Union of the Two Noble and Illustre Families of Lancaster and York*. The deposition of a reigning monarch is (as events in America have lately reminded us) a fearful thing, intrinsically dramatic, immense in itself, and also immense in its consequences. It invokes great themes and issues: The Divine Right of Kings, the falls of princes, and the destiny of a nation, and invites us to meditate on the mysteries of historical causation, as a later poet did in his great sonnet on Leda and the Swan.

Such a subject has its disabilities too, though, for *Richard* cannot be reckoned one of Shakespeare's more neglected plays. It has been explicated by authorities with a more profound grasp of historical and philosophical contexts than may be claimed by the present writer, who has lately concerned himself with such unprofound (indeed unliterary) matters as the number of elm-trees in Shakespeare's Stratford, when brick first came into use as a building material in Warwickshire, and how a dramatist living in Bishopsgate ward managed to escape paying his rates. Anyway, isn't it an illusion, under the best of circumstances, to hope to say anything excitingly novel about one of Shakespeare's major plays? The excitingly novel has a way of being excitingly wrong, or tendentious, or beside the point. So Ernst Kantorowicz, in his celebrated study of the mystic fiction of the King's two bodies, applied to *Richard II* a point in medieval political theology of which I – and I dare say a number of others – had hitherto been ignorant; but I remain unpersuaded that the vast erudition brought to bear really illuminates Shakespeare's drama, pleasing as is an unexpected encounter with such recondite lore.

Of course an alternative to being excitingly off-base is to be correctly dull. It is not enough, especially in such a context, to reiterate pedestrian commonplaces with minor variations. The time is propitious for something a little bolder, for fresh breezes are blowing through scholarship on Shakespeare's English histories. In a recent review-article Professor Cyrus Hoy has likened the Shakespeare canon to a modern urban landscape – 'the tragic monuments have never lacked attention', Hoy observes, but 'the historical business sector has in recent years become something of a critical slum'.[1] This is perhaps to exaggerate a point for the sake of an ingenious metaphor; if the histories are a slum, then a number of able citizens have gone slumming. But it is true that the seminal contributions of Tillyard and Lily Bess Campbell established an orthodoxy, and accustomed a generation to view the two tetralogies as dramatic recapitulations of the Tudor myth of history, or mirrors of Elizabethan policy. Now we seem to have entered a revisionist phase, exemplified by the stimulating first chapter of Robert Ornstein's *A Kingdom for a Stage*. Tillyard has been enduring his knocks of late, and we are invited to take another, and different, view of the achievement of the history plays. Thus thesis breeds counter-thesis. This is well and good; it keeps the pot bubbling. Eventually, I expect, we shall look again at Tillyard, more disinterestedly, extrapolate what is of lasting value,

[1] Cyrus Hoy, 'Recent Shakespearian Criticism, Prefabricated and Authentic', *The Sewanee Review*, LXXXII (1974), 363.

and absorb it into the critical stream. Thus we have synthesis. It is what may be described as the Hegelian tendency in Shakespeare studies. Meanwhile Hoy is no doubt right to see the appearance of Ornstein's book as a liberating phenomenon.

These are large issues. My own objectives are more limited. I propose to look once again at two historical considerations that have been looked at often enough in the past: the matter of Richard, and the revival of a play about Richard II on the eve of the Essex rebellion. Finally I shall argue for a modest adjustment of interpretative emphasis as regards an aspect of Shakespeare's art that has been – dare I say it? – comparatively underestimated. My emphasis must be on *modest* and *comparatively*.

II

If Richard was not a popular king in his own time, he seems to have stirred a good deal of popular interest two centuries later. 'Certainly', Dover Wilson says in his introduction to the New Cambridge edition, '*Richard II* took London by storm when it first appeared'; also that Shakespeare's tragedy had become 'the talk of the town before December 1595'.[1] Dangerous word, *certainly*. The Chamberlain's men had no Henslowe to record for posterity the takings at the Theatre, and the age boasted no show-biz weekly to report the latest sensation in Shoreditch or on Bankside. If *Richard II* was the talk of the town in 1595, that talk has not been jotted down in any correspondence which has survived. Still, the play clearly made a strong impact. Three quarto editions issued from the presses in 1597 and 1598, and another two before Shakespeare's death. In August 1601 Queen Elizabeth made the famous remark, noted down by Lambarde, that 'this tragedy was played 40^tie times in open streets and houses'.

Interest in Richard and his reign was of long standing, as is evidenced by the rich mix of sources, possible sources, near misses, and analogues to Shakespeare's play. In addition to the usual English chronicles – Hall and Holinshed – there are no fewer than three French accounts, including the *Chroniques* of Jean Froissart. This last, Shakespeare very likely consulted in Lord Berners's translation. There is also, in the library of Gray's Inn, a narrative in Latin of 'The Deposition of Richard'. Daniel's *First Four Books of the Civil Wars between the Two Houses of Lancaster and York* deal at length with Richard, setting forth 'His Unkles pride, his greedie Minions gaine, / *Glosters* revolt, & death...', Bolingbroke's exile and return, and the usurpation. In *The Mirror for Magistrates* the first five of the 'sundry Unfortunate Englishe men' who deliver their laments are Richard and those around him. One learned investigator of the sources of Shakespeare's *Richard II* concluded, after duly weighing the evidence, that the playwright consulted no fewer than seven accounts.[2] The reckoning probably errs on the side of numerosity, but suggests the complexity of the task to which Professor Bullough has addressed himself with such superlative skill.

If anything emerges forcibly from the array of source-matter, it is the absence of consensus. Men and events are variously evaluated. In Dover Wilson's summation, 'two legends about the character of Richard II have come down to us from the fifteenth century: that of his supporters, which represented him as a saint and a martyr, compared his sufferings and death with those of Christ himself, while they accounted for his capture by an act of base betrayal; and secondly, that of the Lancastrians which depicted him as a weak,

[1] William Shakespeare, *Richard II*, ed. John Dover Wilson (The New Shakespeare; 1939), introd., p. ix.
[2] M. W. Black, 'The Sources of Shakespeare's *Richard II*,' *Joseph Quincy Adams Memorial Studies*, ed. James G. McManaway *et al.* (Washington, D.C., 1948), pp. 199–216.

cowardly, moody man who surrendered himself and abdicated of his own free will'.[1] This ignores, however, the shades between. Opinions also differ about the men around the protagonist. To the chronicler Grafton, Thomas of Woodstock was an 'honorable and good man miserable put to death, which for the honor of the King and wealth of the realme had taken great travayles'; but Daniel describes the same Woodstock as

> one most violent,
> Impatient of command, of peace, of rest,
> Whose brow would shew, that which his
>   hart had ment:
> His open malice & repugnant brest
> Procurd much mischiefe by his discontent.[2]

As with narrative, so with dramatic portrayals of the reign. Richard figures in several plays. 'Sir, findinge that you wer not convenientlie to be at London to morrow night', Sir Edward Hoby wrote to Sir Robert Cecil from his house in Cannon Row on 7 December 1595, 'I am bold to send to knowe whether Teusdaie may be anie more in your grace to visit poore Channon rowe where as late as it shal please you a gate for your supper shal be open: & K. Richard present him selfe to your vewe.'[3] Eminent authorities, Chambers among them, have assumed that Hoby is referring to a private performance of Shakespeare's *Richard II* for the delectation of the great, but Hoby doesn't mention Shakespeare, nor is it clear whether the play – if it is that – is old or new, or even whether the Richard alluded to was the second of that name, although likely enough it was. Such uncertainties should wonderfully encourage scholarly agnosticism. We are on safer ground in looking at the two extant plays (besides Shakespeare's) in which Richard appears, and the play about him witnessed by Simon Forman at the Globe.

Of unknown authorship and date, *The Life and Death of Jack Straw* (printed in 1593) limits itself to the Peasants' Revolt. The play is short, but few can have wished it longer. It has been attributed to George Peele, mainly (one guesses) on the unstated grounds that any play, mediocre or worse, from the early nineties that happens to be knocking around without an author had better be ascribed to George Peele. Still, the concept of Richard in *Jack Straw* holds interest. The young king is shown as an exemplary character, magnanimously dispensing free pardons to all but the ringleaders of unnatural rebellion; such compassion in a prince reminds the King's swordbearer of 'The gladsome sunne-shine in a winters day'.[4] It is not the only instance in the play of the sun imagery we associate with Richard.[5]

Another and less sympathetic Richard is presented to view in *Woodstock*. This headstrong youth neglects crown and kingdom as he gives himself up to 'wild and antic habits': aping foreign manners, feasting boon companions and hangers-on at Westminster Hall while the commons starve, extorting revenues with odious blank charters, and – ultimate irresponsibility – farming out his realm, at a fixed rent, to self-serving flatterers. The pejorative most frequently attached to him is

---

[1] Shakespeare, *Richard II*, ed. Wilson, p. lix.
[2] Samuel Daniel, *The First Fowre Bookes of the Civile Wars . . .*, in *Narrative and Dramatic Sources of Shakespeare*, ed. Geoffrey Bullough (1957–), III, 437.
[3] E. K. Chambers, *William Shakespeare: A Study of Facts and Problems* (Oxford, 1930), II, 320–1.
[4] *Jack Straw*, ed. Kenneth Muir and F. P. Wilson (Malone Society Reprints; 1957), l. 1014.
[5] See also:
> The Sunne may sometime be eclipst with Clowds,
> But hardlie may the twinckling starres obscure,
> Or put him out of whom they borrow light
>   (ll. 238–40).
In such an imagistic context figures of plant growth have propriety: '. . . commaund our wealth, / But loyall harts the treasure of a Prince, / Shall growe like graines sowne in a fertill soyle' (ll. 1194–6). The sun images are remarked by Irving Ribner, *The English History Play in the Age of Shakespeare* (rev. ed.; 1965), p. 74.

'wanton'. Eventually he becomes a 'wanton tyrant', although he is never seen as irredeemably committed to evil ways.[1] In contrast his uncle Gloucester, plain Thomas of Woodstock, represents the homely English virtues. It is distinctly a minority view of Woodstock that this playwright provides. Stage imagery reinforces the thematic point. The bearded elders contrast with the spruce, clean-shaven courtiers; Green at one point proposes making it high treason for any grey-beard to loiter within forty feet of the court gates. Woodstock's homespun clothing – he wears a country habit of English frieze – betokens the traditional values under assault. On the other hand, the king's favourites are fantastically tricked out in Polonian peaks, and jewellery chains that join knee with toe, and 'so toeify the knee and so kneeify the toe, that between both it makes a most methodical coherence, or coherent method'. Inevitably fashions, as men, collide: a foppishly attired courtier on horseback mistakes Woodstock for a groom, and offers him sixpence to take and walk the beast. One of Woodstock's virtues is thrift, and later he claims his sixpence – 'promise is a *promise*'. In the end he is conveyed to Calais, and there murdered at Richard's behest. The King in this play, unlike that of *Jack Straw*, is neither merciful nor just. When he experiences the twinges of conscience, and orders a reprieve, it comes, like Edmund's, too late.

The play on Richard II that Simon Forman saw on 30 April 1611 has not come down, but he has left a characteristic description of it in his 'Book of Plays'. Dr A. L. Rowse, who in Forman has found a biographical subject worthy of his mettle, does not doubt that this performance was of Shakespeare's *Richard*.[2] But Dr Rowse is not conspicuously given to doubt, and the play described by Forman differs in so many essentials from Shakespeare's that no theory of revision – always a dubious mode of rationalizing a conviction – can

reconcile the two. The play at the Globe seems to have covered the whole of Richard's reign, for Forman refers to the overthrow of Jack Straw as well as to the triumph of Bolingbroke (events separated by nearly twenty years). Whether the play is old or new Forman does not say. In it Gaunt is a secret contriver of villainy who sets Richard and the nobles together by the ears, his aim being to make his own son king. This Gaunt is the sort who, having consulted a wise man about the future of his house, and having got his answer, 'hanged him vp for his labor, because he should not brute yt abrod or speke therof to others'. Richard himself is not much behindhand when it comes to policy:

Remember also, when the duke [Gloucester] and Arundell cam to London with their Army, king Richard came forth to them and met them and gaue them fair wordes, and promised them pardon and that all should be well yf they wold discharge their Army, vpon whose promises and faier Speaches they did yt, and Affter the king byd them all to A banket and soe betraid them And Cut of their heades, &c, because they had not his pardon vnder his hand & sealle before but his worde.[3]

This episode eerily reminds us of the ruthless equivocation of Prince John at Gaultree Forest.

Forman is an unreliable reporter, capable of confusing what he has seen with what he has read.[4] Still, from the sum of the reports, playtexts, chronicles, and other accounts comprising the matter of Richard, it is clear that he could

[1] I cannot go quite so far as Robert Ornstein, who describes the Richard of *Woodstock* as 'thoroughly despicable and corrupt', *A Kingdom for a Stage: The Achievement of Shakespeare's History Plays* (Cambridge, Mass., 1972), p. 13.

[2] A. L. Rowse, *Simon Forman* (1974), pp. 13–14 and (transcript) pp. 305–6.

[3] I quote from the text in Chambers, *William Shakespeare* (Oxford, 1930), II, 340.

[4] The problems presented by a Forman account of a Globe performance (in this case of *Macbeth*) are expertly discussed by Leah Scragg, 'Macbeth on Horseback', *Shakespeare Survey 26* (1973), 81–8.

be variously represented: we have virtuous Richard, wanton Richard, and cunning Richard; the weak king, the politic king, the would-be despot. So too with others in the *dramatis personae*. Gaunt is patriot or self-seeker; Woodstock, a loyal peer or malevolent trouble-fomenter. Such latitude of interpretation should serve to discourage the historical critic from facile generalizations about how the Elizabethans assessed their past.

If for the scholar the contradictions in the sources are at times vexatious, for the artist they must have had a liberating effect, and invited him to explore the complexities of character and motive we in fact find in Shakespeare's Richard. My point is a corollary of one made by Ornstein in his recent book when he complains of 'the inherent bias of the historical method toward what is conventional and orthodox in Elizabethan culture, because any search for the "norms" of Elizabethan thought must lead to a consensus of truisms and pieties'.[1] Only here we do not even find the coveted norms.

III

Shakespeare's *Richard II* seems to have had several special performances in the author's lifetime. Sir Edward Hoby possibly refers to one in his letter already cited. Another took place on the high seas. In 1607 the *Dragon*, *Hector*, and *Consent*, bound for the East Indies, cast anchor off Sierra Leone. On 30 September William Keeling, captain of the *Dragon*, recorded in his journal, 'Captain Hawkins [of the *Hector*] dined with me, wher my companions acted Kinge Richard the Second'.[2] (On two other occasions the same thespians played *Hamlet*, once to the accompaniment of a fish dinner.) But the most celebrated revival of *Richard* was that mounted by the Lord Chamberlain's men at the Globe Theatre on Saturday, 7 February 1601. The circumstances are described by Augustine Phillips, the actor

who bore Shakespeare such affectionate regard that he bequeathed to him a thirty-shilling piece in gold. According to Phillips, some half-dozen men of position in the land – including the Percies (Sir Charles and Sir Jocelyn) and Lord Monteagle – had approached the players, offering them a reward of 40s 'to have the play of the deposyng and kyllyng of Kyng Rychard the second to be played the Saterday next'.[3] The actors hesitated, 'holdyng that play of Kyng Richard to be so old & so long out of vse as that they shold have small or no Company at yt', but in the end they consented. The purpose of the revival, as we all know, was to further sedition. At noon that Saturday the conspirators met for dinner, and afterwards repaired to the playhouse, where they applauded the downfall and murder of a king. 'So earnest hee was', Francis Bacon said of one, Sir Gilly Meyrick, 'to satisfie his eyes with the sight of that tragedie which hee thought soone after his lord should bring from the stage to the state, but that God turned it vpon their owne heads.' Meyrick was steward to the Earl of Essex. On Sunday the attempted coup took place. Shakespeare's troupe collected their £2. Essex and others were tried and executed. On the eve of the Earl's beheading the Lord Chamberlain's men acted before the Queen at Whitehall. We do not know which play; presumably not *Richard II*.

Most authorities agree that the performance bespoken by the conspirators was of Shakespeare's *Richard II*. It is not unusual to find this information given as a fact. We do well, however, to recognize that we are dealing not with a fact but an inference. Neither Phillips nor anyone else interviewed at the time mentions Shakespeare's name in connection with the event. Prosecutor Coke muddies the waters

[1] Ornstein, *Kingdom for a Stage*, p. 4.
[2] Chambers, *William Shakespeare*, II, 334.
[3] Chambers conveniently prints extracts from the principal documents (II, 27).

slightly when he speaks of 'the story of *Henry IV* being set forth in a play', but as Bolingbroke becomes king before the end of *Richard II*, that is accountable. There is of course no reason why there should not have been other plays on this interesting theme which, like the one seen by Forman, failed to achieve print: and the designation of the one acted on 7 February as 'old' opens up the whole vista of Elizabethan theatrical history. But the company in this instance was Shakespeare's, Phillips's description suits Shakespeare's *Richard II*, and no alternative possibility presents itself for consideration. So in what follows I shall assume the 'old' *Richard II* wheeled out for the Essex *putsch* was by Shakespeare, while not claiming more than that this is a plausible assumption.

To do so disposes of one problem only to raise another. Why *Richard II*? After all, the play hardly comes across as an inflammatory tract in favour of deposition and regicide. Richard in his sufferings is too sympathetic, and ultimately (at Pomfret Castle) heroic, while Bolingbroke in his triumph is too ambiguous. It seems an odd choice to rouse the rabble. Scholarly unease is understandable. 'I do not know the answer to the riddle', Lily B. Campbell confesses, and to Irving Ribner 'Shakespeare's relation to the Essex rebellion remains a puzzling problem which has yet to be satisfactorily settled'.[1] This may be so, but we do well to bear in mind that the revival in fact failed to kindle seditious sparks; if such was the conspirators' intention, it was one of many miscalculations. More likely, perhaps, that they were thinking of themselves rather than of the multitude, and sought by reviving a play about a successful deposition to buoy up their own spirits on the eve of the desperate adventure.

Yet might there not be another dimension, perilous to ignore and even more perilous to face? Many critics have fancied Shakespeare as moving about comfortably in the corridors of power, playfully taking the mickey out of the Sir Walter Raleigh set in *Love's Labour's Lost*, concocting a suitable wedding entertainment for the dowager Countess of Southampton with *A Midsummer-Night's Dream*, or advising King James on the respective merits of mercy and justice in *Measure for Measure*. The list might be extended, and there are recent additions. Such speculations, showing Shakespeare hob-nobbing with the mighty, represent what might be described as the Richard Ryan syndrome in Shakespeare studies. In his *Dramatic Table Talk* (in 1825) Ryan recorded an anecdote of Queen Elizabeth trying to catch Shakespeare's eye while he was acting at the playhouse, and resorting to the timeworn female ruse of dropping her glove; her favourite (we are told) picked it up and presented it to her, but not without first declaiming, 'And though now bent on this high embassy, / Yet *stoop* we to take up our *Cousin's* glove!' It is not what one would describe as a very probable story. The Ryan syndrome is nevertheless very prominent in Shakespeare studies; it has enlisted some choice spirits, and has illuminated the contexts for the plays if not always the plays themselves. Now Professor Richard Levin in several essays has been casting a cold eye on the whole phenomenon, to which he gives the term 'occasionalism'. Sceptical reappraisal along these lines is long overdue, and we do well to pay heed to Professor Levin's home truths.

But what of *Richard II*, which was used in Shakespeare's own day as a move in a power struggle? Here the connection is direct, not fancied. Might not Richard's reign (in the dramatist's conception) stand in an analogical relation to Elizabeth's reign, and animadvert obliquely – as censorship enforced – on actual

[1] L. B. Campbell, *Shakespeare's 'Histories': Mirrors of Elizabethan Policy* (San Marino, 1947), pp. 211–12; Ribner, *English History Play*, p. 155n.

persons and events? Of course the trouble with oblique commentaries is that they are oblique; we may miss what is there and find what is not. To his *D.N.B.* biographer the content of the Elizabethan historian John Hayward's *Life and Reign of King Henry IV* looks innocent enough of veiled allusiveness, and even a contemporary, Chamberlain, wondered what all the fuss was about.

Such considerations serve only to whet pursuit, and the trail, in truth, is not an utter blank. 'I am Richard II. know ye not that?', the Queen declared in Lambarde's presence, and she was not the first to make the comparison. As early as 1578 Sir Francis Knollys complained to Elizabeth's secretary that the Queen persisted in misliking safe counsel – in such circumstances 'who woll not rather shrynkingly...play the partes of King Richard the Second's men, then to enter into the odious office of crossing of her Majesties' wylle?' (To be one of Richard's men is to be a sycophant; there are other such references.) Knollys was related to the Queen, and also the grandfather of the Earl of Essex. The latter traced his descent from Anne, daughter of Thomas of Woodstock, the Duke of Gloucester, sixth son of Edward III – the same Thomas of Woodstock who had his life snuffed out at Calais by Richard's command. And were not Elizabeth's hands, like Richard's, stained with 'guilt of kindred blood'? 'The slaying of kindred here [i.e. in *Richard II*]...was probably intended to remind Elizabethans of the execution of Mary, Queen of Scots.' This suggestion was made almost half a century ago, by Evelyn May Albright, in what remains the most elaborate investigation of the Richard–Elizabeth analogy in relation to the play put on for the Essex conspiracy.[1] Miss Albright further notes that complaints about the influence of favourites, about oppressive taxes, and about the exaction of benevolences – all made in Shakespeare's *Richard II* – find their paral-

lels in agitation about Elizabeth's government. There is even a passing reference to 'the prevention of poor Bolingbroke / About his marriage'; and we all know how Elizabeth meddled in marriages. From such hints it is but an easy leap to interpreting York's speech in Act II, scene i – the speech about the consequences of Richard's seizure of 'The royalties and rights of banish'd Hereford' – as 'a warning to Elizabeth' concerning 'a popular favorite whom she is treating badly, and whose family also have been unfairly dealt with'. And who might that favorite be other than Essex?

This is heady stuff for which some evidence, besides the detection of covert allusions in Shakespeare's text, would be welcome. Such evidence has been offered in the form of Hayward's history of Henry IV, to which I have already referred. His book was published with a brief Latin dedication to Essex, in which the latter is extolled as the expectancy and rose of the fair state. Hayward's title is a misnomer, presumably prudential, for his history deals mostly with Richard's reign, not Henry's. That the work deliberately exploited the Elizabeth–Richard analogy was widely believed at the time; we hear of this 'seditious pamphlet' and 'treasonable book'. 'He selecteth a storie 200 hundred yere old', noted Sir Edward Coke, 'and publisheth it this last yere; intending the application of it to this tyme.'[2] Elizabeth, outraged, wanted Hayward executed, and were

[1] Evelyn May Albright, 'Shakespeare's *Richard II* and the Essex Conspiracy', *PMLA*, XLII (1927), 686–720. Her essay drew a rejoinder from Ray Heffner, 'Shakespeare, Hayward, and Essex', *PMLA*, XLV (1930), 754–80. Undaunted, she replied in 'Shakespeare's *Richard II*, Hayward's History of Henry IV, and the Essex Conspiracy', *PMLA*, XLVI (1931), 694–719.

[2] Margaret Dowling prints Coke's notes on Hayward's *Henry IV* in an important article, 'Sir John Hayward's Troubles over his *Life of Henry IV*', *The Library*, 4th ser., XI (1931), 212–24. For the passage cited, see p. 213.

it not for Bacon's discreet intervention, he probably would have been. As it was, not until after Elizabeth's death was Hayward released from prison to assemble the prayers and meditations of the enlarged *Sanctuary of a Troubled Soul*. Shakespeare and his fellows do not seem to have got into any trouble at all, which is odd if he was up to mischief similar to that for which Hayward was tried. Never mind; perhaps some neutral party, high up, intervened to get Shakespeare off the hook. Such a party has lately been suggested in the person of the Keeper of the Rolls; the same William Lambarde to whom Elizabeth made her famous protestation.[1]

What remains is to demonstrate that Hayward's *Henry IV* was one of Shakespeare's sources when he came to write *Richard II*. We are shown parallels as regards general ideas, groupings of ideas, echoes of words and phrases, the characterization of Bolingbroke, and a couple of specific episodes (Henry's repudiation of Piers of Exton, and Aumerle's supposed duplicity with Richard at Flint Castle). Some of these hold interest. There is a problem, however, and that is that Hayward's *Life and Reign of King Henry IV* was first published in 1599; three or four years after Shakespeare composed his play. Such a fact might ordinarily be deemed awkward, but there is a way round it, and that is to posit that the history circulated in manuscript for some years before being printed, and that Shakespeare saw and used it. Otherwise we might be tempted to account for the parallels as Hayward's borrowings from Shakespeare. There is nothing like a hypothetical manuscript to resolve an awkwardness of chronology. Only in this case the awkwardness remains, for Hayward is on record as saying that he had begun 'to write this history about a year before it was published, but had intended it a dozen years before, although he acquainted no man therewith'.[2] One might reckon that

such a statement would successfully discourage enthusiasm for the theory of Hayward's influence on Shakespeare, but this would be to underestimate scholarly ingenuity. In the phrase *although he acquainted no man therewith*, maybe *therewith* refers to the interval but not to Hayward's materials? I think not. Yet Ribner, in what is the standard study of the English history play in Shakespeare's age, can suggest that there is 'some possibility' that Shakespeare saw Hayward's *Henry IV* in manuscript – a manuscript that did not then exist.

Nor, although properly wary, does Ribner rule out the Albright thesis altogether. During the past year somebody has written that 'Shakespeare's connection with the Essex affair was all too obvious through his praise of the Earl in *Henry V* and his authorship of the deposition scene in *Richard II*', and he goes on to speak of Shakespeare's 'partisanship' for Essex.[3] It is one of many odd statements in a curious book. How many innocent spectators, standing at a play and caught up in the great issues of the drama, would pause to reflect on Essex's descent from Gloucester's line, or apply passing references to abuses of Richard's rule to the politics of the moment? I don't see Shakespeare as a seditious playwright involved, however peripherally, in a conspiracy against his monarch, any more than I see him as a darling of the Court, a sort of minister without portfolio, sagely advising his Queen, and later his King, on how to manage the affairs of state. I expect that he had his hands full writing his plays, acting in them and in those of others, and as 'housekeeper' advising his troupe about affairs in which we know he had a stake.

This is not to say that he failed to interest

[1] W. Nicholas Knight, *Shakespeare's Hidden Life: Shakespeare at the Law 1585–1595* (New York, 1973), p. 144.

[2] Quoted by Albright, 'Shakespeare's *Richard II*, Haywood's History...', p. 695.

[3] Knight, *Shakespeare's Hidden Life*, p. 143.

himself in the world of policy and power. That world was all around him. He found it chronicled in Plutarch and the Tudor historians. Machiavelli analysed it. Perhaps Shakespeare glimpsed it, as an observant bystander, when his company performed at Court, or were called upon to fulfil some ceremonial function, as when they attended upon the new Spanish ambassador and his train at Somerset House in August 1604. These opportunities he seized upon, not for political advantage by insinuating himself into the affairs of state, but imaginatively, for the purposes of his art, in which we find depicted the world of policy and power. Here, behind the scenes of public confrontation, as likely as not another drama – concealed or only obliquely revealed – is going on. In that drama the issues may be graver than those overtly bandied about. Such moments show Shakespeare's sophisticated grasp of the workings of *Realpolitik*. So it is in *Richard II*, especially in the big public scenes of the first act.

IV

'I cannot believe', Yeats wrote, 'that Shakespeare looked on his Richard II. with any but sympathetic eyes, understanding indeed how ill-fitted he was to be King, at a certain moment of history, but understanding that he was lovable and full of capricious fancy...'[1] 'What explains his failure to oppose Bolingbroke at all, his sudden collapse, as soon as the threat of deposition becomes real, into a state of sheer elegy, of pure poetry?' asks Mark Van Doren. 'The answer is simple. Richard is a poet, not a king.'[2] These views have much in common; they are expressed by poets with an understandable sympathy for poetical characters. But of course in a blank-verse play the characters, unless they be peasants, usually speak in numbers. Mainly criticism emphasizes Richard's weakness. The position has been lately put by Robert Ornstein in the book to

which I have already referred. 'The first scene of *Richard II* intimates the King's shallowness and weakness...' Or: 'Precisely why Richard chooses to halt the joust between Bolingbroke and Mowbray at the very last moment we do not know, but we recognize the characteristic theatricality of the gesture: here is the weakling's pleasure in commanding (and humiliating) men stronger than himself.'[3] Ornstein makes other remarks to the same effect, and together these restate, with more than usual eloquence and sensitivity, a dominant consensus. Now, one should very warily go about differing from views with widespread (even if less than universal) acceptance, for they are quite likely to be correct. So it is with some diffidence that I suggest that in Act I, in the council chamber at Windsor and at the lists in Coventry, Richard displays as much political acumen as weakness, that his behaviour is not capricious but calculated, and that he does not fail but achieves a success necessarily limited by the realities of his situation.[4]

[1] William Butler Yeats, 'At Stratford-on-Avon', *Ideas of Good and Evil*, in *Collected Works* (1908), p. 123.

[2] Mark Van Doren, *Shakespeare* (New York, 1939), p. 89.

[3] Ornstein, *Kingdom for a Stage*, p. 110.

[4] A view of these scenes very similar to my own is taken by Moody E. Prior in *The Drama of Power: Studies in Shakespeare's History Plays* (Evanston, 1973), which I had not yet seen when writing this paper abroad. Prior makes the point that 'Bolingbroke's challenge to Mowbray is in effect an oblique way of attacking the king' (p. 144), and he allows the advantages to Richard of Mowbray's banishment: 'The one man in whom is locked the secret of the murder of Gloucester is never to be in a position to worry the king again' (p. 145). Such a reading is indeed enforced as soon as one accepts as crucial Richard's complicity in Woodstock's murder. Prior and I do differ on a few details: he describes the murder as 'an old crime', although it took place only some six months before the events at Windsor Castle dramatized in I, i; and he takes a more qualified view than I of Richard's effectiveness when he concludes that this scene and I, iii, 'epitomize the uneasy unstable equilibrium which sustains the impressive façade of

It is no use trying to evaluate a man's strength or weakness without reference to the circumstances that determine the options he can exercise. Richard may prattle about Divine Right, but in his world power is wielded not divinely, but by men; those men in whose presence Richard goes through the rhetoric of public gestures. In the first scene Richard's manoeuvrability is limited by an episode from his past which has come back to haunt him. The past, whether in the form of an untoward incident on the road to Thebes or indiscreet conversations in the illusory privacy of the Oval Office, has a way of doing just that to men of exalted station. The problem for Richard, lovable poet and weakling, is that he is responsible for the murder of his uncle Gloucester, and everybody knows it. This fact Shakespeare chooses to treat indirectly, as befits the evasions of power struggles. Although Richard's embarrassment affects the conduct of all the principals, they remain silent on this score; it is rather as though the dramatist expected his audience to have made mental notes of *Woodstock*. No outside source is required once we get to Act I, scene ii, however, for there we have Gaunt referring, in the presence of Gloucester's widow, to correction lying 'in those hands / Which made the fault we cannot correct', and some lines later he declares:

> God's is the quarrel; for God's substitute,
> His deputy anointed in His sight,
> Hath caus'd his death.
>
> (I, ii, 37–9)[1]

This is plain enough about where the guilt resides, and should enforce retrospective revaluation of the preceding scene. It is extraordinary how many have failed to do so.

Well, in a way not so extraordinary. There is much to distract us at Windsor, and a little later at Coventry. The King sits in state with his nobles, attendants come on in armour, there are horses – or, as in the recent notable production by the Royal Shakespeare Company, hobby-horses – on which much of the whole action took place. Horses on the stage are a great distraction. But however we look at it, and however these scenes are staged, the pageantry of the chivalric tournament – for all the world like events depicted on a medieval tapestry – will leave a powerful impression.[2] Few producers can resist the temptation to make the most of the spectacle, and Shakespeare, dedicated professional that he was, has set it up that way. Nor does the declamatory mode, with its highflown rhetoric of subterfuge, make matters easier.

Despite the rhetoric, Richard is understandably nervous. When Bolingbroke and Mowbray greet their sovereign with fulsome wishes for many happy days, indeed years, he reacts suspiciously: 'We thank you both; yet one but flatters us...' He will not in fact be granted many happy days. In this scene Bolingbroke levels several charges against Mowbray, but the heart of the matter is the death of Gloucester, whose blood,

Richard's style of rule'. But mostly we agree; Prior's whole carefully considered discussion – which expresses what is still a minority view – should be read.

In another recent contribution, 'The Antic Disposition of Richard II', *Shakespeare Survey 27* (1974), 33–41, Lois Potter interestingly observes how in *Richard II* rhetorically elaborated language is associated with powerlessness, and brevity with strength; and how in the early scenes it is Richard (not Bolingbroke) who displays terseness. She notes too that even late in the play Richard shows flashes of his 'sharp-tongued, self-mocking and quite unresigned' self.

[1] I quote from the Peter Alexander text (London and Glasgow, 1951).

[2] The 'medievalism' of *Richard II* can, however, be overstressed; Nicholas Brooke is surely right when he suggests that 'The politics of the play were clearly contemporaneous; the jousting was Elizabethan; and the figure of Richard is far more significant to the play than a mere image of medieval man' (*Shakespeare's Early Tragedies* (1968), p. 109). Brooke has a number of acute things to say about the play.

like sacrificing Abel's, cries,
Even from the tongueless caverns of the earth,
To me for justice and rough chastisement.

(I, i, 104–6)

Why to Bolingbroke in particular? As the Abel reference suggests, because he is Gloucester's kin. But Richard is equally Gloucester's nephew, and moreover the chief guardian of justice in the realm. Yet he isn't calling out for any chastisement, for reasons of which everyone present is aware.

Mowbray defends himself as best he can. 'For Gloucester's death', he declares, 'I slew him not, but to my own disgrace / Neglected my sworn duty in that case.' This is obscure, deliberately so. What is he saying? He did not kill Gloucester with his own hands – 'slew him not' – but had others do the dirty work for him? What was his neglect of sworn duty? His responsibility for a royal life, A. P. Rossiter suggests, citing *Woodstock*: 'that allegiance / Thou ow'st the offspring of King Edward's house', as Woodstock puts it to Mowbray's counterpart in the anonymous play. Or was Mowbray's neglect his delay in performing the King's command? His dilatoriness, according to Holinshed, gave Richard 'no small displeasure'.

Bolingbroke's challenge, ostensibly directed against Mowbray, equally levels at the King. Unsurprisingly, Richard would like to forget about the whole thing as soon as possible, and so he tries to reconcile challenger and challenged. But matters have passed beyond the point of no return, under the circumstances a commission to investigate the charges is out of the question, and so the King sets up the trial by combat. In Act I, scene iii, we go through the full panoply of chivalric ceremony, until Richard casts his warder down. There follows the council session, with its verdict of a ten-year exile for Bolingbroke and lifetime banishment for Mowbray. Cunningly, Richard makes these proud men, seemingly so hopelessly at

odds with one another, swear never to patch up their differences,

Nor never by advised purpose meet
To plot, contrive, or complot any ill,
'Gainst us, our state, our subjects, or our land.

(I, iii, 188–90)

Bolingbroke's sentence is then reduced by four years.

This episode has generally been viewed as demonstrating Richard's vacillation and caprice: more prone to poetry than rule, the irresolute King falteringly exercises his authority. I believe, instead, that Richard brilliantly demonstrates his political skill under conditions of grave disadvantage. At a single stroke he manages to rid himself of two embarrassments: his aggressive cousin Bolingbroke, who represents a direct threat, and Mowbray, to whom he owes too much and who has outlived his usefulness. Had the joust taken place, and Bolingbroke triumphed, he would be still more dangerous. If, on the other hand, Mowbray came out on top, he would have an even greater hold on his monarch; the continuing presence of such men is rarely coveted. But why is Bolingbroke, less beloved, given the lighter sentence? One senses Richard's need to placate his court. Gaunt in particular is clearly uneasy, although (we learn) he has consented to the King's plan during the council we have seen represented by condensed stage time. In his book on *Shakespeare's Historical Plays* Sen Gupta suggests that it is out of pity for Gaunt, 'and not with an eye to the public... that King Richard reduces Bolingbroke's banishment from ten years to six'.[1] But Richard has little room for pity in this steely scene, and sentimental regard for Gaunt is later conspicuously absent during the deathbed interview. The seeming clemency of the reduced sentence is a gesture of politic magnanimity that costs Richard nothing – why worry about what will

[1] S. C. Sen Gupta, *Shakespeare's Historical Plays* (1964), p. 116.

happen in six years? – but serves as a sop to Gaunt.

The King and his retinue depart; the scene closes. Later we see Richard in private conference with his favourites. The masks are off. They mock 'high Hereford', their speech contrasting with the fraudulent rhetoric of the public scenes that have preceded. The King can now be himself.

In this reading of Act I of *Richard II* my aim has been to show that Shakespeare treats in a most sophisticated way the manipulation of power in a poker game where the stakes are exceedingly high. If Richard's triumph is shortlived, that is because he overplays his hand by confiscating Gaunt's estate immediately upon the Duke's death, a blunder which gives the wronged son a pretext for his return and direct confrontation with the King. It may be alleged that, even without this blunder, the King's manoeuvrings, however adroit, would have gained him only a temporary respite. Perhaps so, but that is speculation. It is, however, Richard's limitation that he never grasps the significance of Gloucester's death to his own tragedy.

V

The world with which I have been concerned – labyrinthine, remorselessly unsentimental, dangerous, and ego-centred – lurks everywhere in the Shakespeare canon. The power-seekers shrewdly ferret out the hidden points of vulnerability in their rivals, and work them over with the same impersonal cruelty as the prize-fighter in the ring aiming his blows at his adversary's bleeding eye. They dissimulate. They develop sudden politic cravings for strawberries. They stage elaborate little theatricals in which, appropriately costumed, they themselves perform in a bid to manipulate opinion. A father, playing crafty-sick, withholds military support from his son, abandoning him to defeat and death on the battlefield. A commander gives up pursuit of the demoralized enemy because he is conscious that by outclassing his general he courts disfavour. A duke eloquently promotes a royal match in order to rule the Queen, and through her the King and the realm. A ragged multitude, headed by a peasant with aristocratic pretensions, create a savage spectacle in the capital; the uprising seems spontaneous but is in fact manipulated from above by an ambitious peer in the expectation that, if his creature thrives, he will 'reap the harvest which that rascal sow'd'. But the possible examples are almost limitless. No playwright in this period treats such themes so often or with such complex variety.

Were I to choose an epigraph for my paper, it would be a familiar one. 'It is a strange desire, to seek power and to lose liberty', Bacon wrote in his essay 'Of Great Place': 'or to seek power over others and to lose power over a man's self. The rising unto place is laborious; and by pains men come to greater pains; and it is sometimes base; and by indignities men come to dignities. The standing is slippery, and the regress is either a downfall, or at least an eclipse, which is a melancholy thing.' From Bacon we expect such hard-won wisdom, but we are perhaps less prepared to find it so pervasively present in gentle Shakespeare. I am conscious that by these remarks I am placing myself in a vulnerable position, as I am only too well aware that I have but scratched the surface of a complex topic by treating it representatively. Still there may be something to be said for adding another Shakespeare to the list. The psychoanalysts have had a go at him; the Marxists too. Criticism has given us (amongst others) Shakespeare the practical professional, Shakespeare the theatre poet, Shakespeare the myth-maker, and Shakespeare the Christian gentleman. He also wandered imaginatively in the corridors of power, and what he recorded of the behaviour of men in those treacherous environs enables us to speak of Shakespeare the politic realist.

THE POLITICS OF CORRUPTION
IN SHAKESPEARE'S ENGLAND

JOEL HURSTFIELD

Carved on one of the exterior walls of the Kennedy Center in Washington we have a passage from a speech by the late President himself:

There is a connection, hard to explain logically but easy to feel, between achievement in public life and progress in the arts. The age of Pericles was also the age of Phidias. The age of Lorenzo de Medici was also the age of Leonardo da Vinci. The age of Elizabeth was also the age of Shakespeare. And the new frontier for which I campaign in public life can also be a new frontier for American art.

It may perhaps seem an ungracious and ungrateful act for one who spent one of the happiest periods of his life in Washington (during which many pleasant hours were passed in the Kennedy Center) to question the profound generalisation which the President delivered in this moving passage. Yet to the historian the belief that a great age in culture reflects the greatness of the men who govern is an assumption which may be flattering to the politicians but is at best unproven and at its worst conflicts with the evidence. I am in no position to comment as a scholar on either the age of Pericles or that of the Medici; but I have spent half my life studying the age of Shakespeare and I have often asked myself whether the greatness of Shakespeare's works mirrored the achievements of Gloriana or was in fact born out of the strains, the doubt and the despair which I find so marked a feature of the last years of Elizabeth and the early years of James I.

For the greatness of the Elizabethan era, in terms of its politics, was already passing when Shakespeare left Stratford for London to begin those two creative decades of his dramatic achievements. As it happened these years when Shakespeare flourished, roughly from 1590 until 1613, were also the years when Robert Cecil, that brilliant, deformed, ambitious man and powerful minister under Elizabeth I and James I, moved into a dominant position in government until, with an unparalleled concentration of power as Secretary of State, Master of the Wards and Lord High Treasurer of England, he died in 1612, not long before Shakespeare's return to Stratford.[1] (It has been claimed that Cecil took time off from his work to write Shakespeare's plays which shows, as every college dean is aware, that if you organise your office work properly there is plenty of time in the evening to write plays.)[2] I do not in fact know whether the two men ever met; but their co-existence in the same city at the same time – it is no more than that – provides us with the welcome opportunity to examine the nature of political power, and its corruption, through two different pairs of eyes, of a practising politician and of a dramatic genius.

But for my first insight into the nature of corruption I turn neither to Shakespeare nor Cecil but to Cecil's cousin, Francis Bacon. When, a few years ago, I was preparing my Shakespeare birthday lecture to be delivered

[1] Robert Cecil (1563–1612), son of William Cecil, Lord Burghley, became successively Baron Cecil, Viscount Cranborne and Earl of Salisbury.
[2] W. F. and Elizebeth Friedman, *The Shakespearean Ciphers Examined* (Cambridge, 1957), p. 6.

at the Folger I chose the attitude to liberty as my theme. And, since Francis Bacon had been my companion for so long, I naturally sought first for an essay 'Of Liberty'. I found that Bacon had never written one; and this negative fact was itself of significance. When I looked for an essay 'Of Corruption', I was no more fortunate; but I did read again his essay 'Of Deformity'. It was written in 1613, a year after Cecil's death, and everyone knew that its opening sentence referred to him: 'Deformed persons are commonly even with nature: for as nature hath done ill by them, so do they by nature, being for the most part (as the Scripture saith) void of natural affection. And so they have their revenge of nature.'[1] In saying, in essence, that Cecil was corrupt Bacon was expressing a widely held opinion of the time. Bacon believed, and so did most other people, that Robert Cecil was the architect and the operator of a politically deformed system whose effects could be felt throughout society.

In fact, I know of no major politician in the sixteenth century who was not believed to be corrupt; and we are therefore faced with three separate but related questions. What do we mean by political corruption? Secondly, were these men in fact corrupt? If they were, then were there certain conditions in Tudor England which favoured the growth of corruption until, in the next century, the whole squalid business could only be dealt with by the sustained opposition of the House of Commons, culminating in Civil War?

If we are in search of a definition our difficulty is that the word corruption can be used in many and diverse circumstances. We may, for example, speak of physical corruption, moral corruption, corruption in language, such as corrupt Latin or a corrupt text, corruption in the arts, and, what concerns us here, political corruption. When I first began research into corruption in its historical context I thought

that there might be some general principle which brought these various kinds of corruption within one framework. Do, for example, moral and political corruption always go together and fit into a common pattern of behaviour? I know of no 'villain' in Shakespeare's plays who is not as bad in his private life as in his public conduct. Mark Antony is corrupted by power and then by his blind passion for Cleopatra. The play *Hamlet* is about a corrupt King in a corrupt polity – 'Something is rotten in the state of Denmark' – but it is also about the moral corruption of a King and Queen:

> Nay, but to live
> In the rank sweat of an enseamed bed,
> Stew'd in corruption, honeying and making love
> Over the nasty sty.
>
> (*Ham.* III, iv, 92–5)

This was the charge made against the Court of James I: that it was corrupt both politically and morally.

Is there a link between moral and political corruption? If a man is unfaithful to his wife is he not also likely to be unfaithful to the state? I soon abandoned this line of inquiry when it became evident that the generalisation simply did not hold. Nearly all the British prime ministers who held office in the nineteenth century broke the seventh commandment; yet they included some of the most valiant and patriotic statesmen whose loyalty to their country was beyond reproach. On the other hand, one of the most corrupt politicians to emerge anywhere in the twentieth century has lived a blameless domestic life entirely free from even the breath of scandal. This lack of correlation between one kind of corruption and another within the same man indicates the immensely complex problem which corruption

---

[1] *The Works of Francis Bacon*, ed. J. Spedding, R. L. Ellis and D. D. Heath (1858), VI, 480. The punctuation has been modernised as in all citations in this paper.

presents to the historian, and it is as well, therefore, that in this paper I shall be concerned solely with political corruption, for which I shall offer a brief and provisional definition.

The word corruption means a condition of distortion and decay; while *polis*, and its adjective 'political', represent the state. If we consider the state to be a community of people joined together to preserve and enlarge the welfare of all its members, then we may define political corruption as the subversion of these interests for other ends, that is for one's private gain, or the gain of one's friends or of some other sectional group, or for some purpose contrary to the common welfare. I want to emphasise that financial reward need not enter into these matters though it often does. What is more important is power. Those who govern the state have had power conferred upon them. Political corruption, in a word, is the abuse of power. If this is so, it is worth noting that, in the sixteenth century, there was more political power around than previously and it was the subject of debate. For the century witnessed all over Europe a major redistribution of power, as well as its enlargement. It is possible to detect this at once by looking back from the sixteenth century to the structure of medieval society.

In medieval England, as on the continent, power was dispersed. It was distributed unevenly among different sources of authority. The average Englishman was very conscious of his local lord, or more likely his agents, the steward, the bailiff, the reeve. He would also, in some circumstances, feel the impact of the king through his representatives, the justices, the coroner, the sheriff, the escheator. But if he were lucky and the times were peaceful, he would not see very much of any of them. He would also be aware of the power of the Church, mostly through his parish priest or the nearby monastery, but he would hear something of a distant but supreme being, the Pope. Some

of these offices, secular and ecclesiastical, gave rise to dependent officials such as secretaries, clerks, deputies, surveyors and the rest. But power was diffuse and, away from such sophisticated centres as the papacy, administration was primitive and officials tended to be amateur.

The sixteenth century witnessed profound changes in England (as elsewhere) in the nature and function of government. The long struggle between the king and his baronage as to who should control law, government, war and administration, was drawing to a close and in the king's favour. This is not simply because the protracted blood-letting of the baronage in the French wars and then in the Wars of the Roses had left them too weak to resist royal pressures. More important, in many cases the economic bases of their power were diminishing and there was a relative shift in wealth to some sections of the urban and rural landed, commercial and industrial classes. But there was no total transformation of the social scene. As ever, members of the aristocracy obtained blood transfusions of commercial wealth; and some of the great territorial titles of medieval England were perfectly familiar in Tudor government and administration, though the men who bore them were of mixed or totally different family origins. None the less their territorial authority was shrinking. It is true that they were still saying in northern England that they knew no prince but a Percy, but the Percies were a waning force even in their native shire. The Elizabethan Duke of Norfolk could boast: 'I count myself, by your Majesty's favour, as good a prince at home in my bowling alley at Norwich as she [Mary, Queen of Scots] is though she were in the midst of Scotland.'[1] Half the justices of the peace in Norfolk were made at his choice. But he was the last Howard, Duke of Norfolk, who could exercise such authority. With his

[1] Cited in J. E. Neale, *Queen Elizabeth* (1934), p. 185.

execution in 1572 that power was fragmented and the Norfolk gentry disputed over their share of his patronage.[1]

But for the time being, the greatest residuary legatee of these powers was the Crown and it was the Tudors who set a term to aristocratic privilege and territorial franchise. What was accomplished in relation to the baronage was achieved in even greater measure in relation to the Church. The English Reformation carried through by Henry VIII and his minister, Thomas Cromwell, witnessed the greatest confiscation of land in English history; and with it went administration, royal supremacy and all the postures of Caesaro-papalism which flourished for a while in the person of Henry VIII. From the highest ecclesiastical dignitary to the humblest parish priest, all could be called upon to take the oath of supremacy or give up their office; and when the process was over the monarchy stood heir to the vast ecclesiastical apparatus which the medieval Church had taken centuries to erect. Nor should we wholly attribute this transformation to the effects of the Reformation. Even in those countries which, after a preliminary shudder of reform, returned to the old allegiance, the power of the Crown over the Church was none the less strong.

Meanwhile the representative assemblies, the estates, the cortes, the parliaments, one after another were being stripped of their powers. Even in England, in spite of the dramatic interventions of the House of Commons in affairs of state, usually unsuccessfully, its strength and prospects seemed nowhere nearly as good as later developments were to indicate.

One of the major consequences of these changes which I have briefly outlined was that the monarchy found itself with an unparalleled concentration of power in Church and State. And here was a government moreover which was assuming increasingly the role and functions characteristic of a modern state with all

the financial burdens which went with it. It was interfering far more than hitherto in the legal, economic and social life of its people, it was maintaining an elaborate and expensive royal court, a complex diplomatic machine, and was often called upon to fight appallingly costly wars. Two central consequences flowed from all this: the first is that the Crown needed a growing and enormously expensive bureaucracy; the second is that the Crown required immense sums of money if it was to govern efficiently, indeed govern at all. If we are to understand the nature of political corruption in Shakespeare's England it is essential to bear these prevailing conditions constantly in mind.

Tudor governments were trying to pursue the modern aims of a mature state with a ramshackle, medieval administrative machine and medieval financial resources to meet the mounting costs of government. And this task was made more complex and confusing by the irregular impulses of inflation, more severe than ever before. In time of war or other crises parliament would grant taxation to meet part of the difference between income and expenditure but, though given with a show of patriotic zeal, it was almost invariably less than was needed, took a long time to collect and a fair proportion of it was deflected into private pockets. Ill-supplied as it was, how then was the government to pay its extensive and extending bureaucracy?

The answer that was found was a relatively simple one and is perfectly familiar today in any underdeveloped country whose administration and economy are several centuries behind its style and its pretensions. Tudor governments made no attempt to pay their public servants realistic salaries because they did not possess the wherewithal to do so. They

---

[1] For a full discussion of the changing distribution of power in Norfolk see A. Hassell Smith, *County and Court: Government and Politics in Norfolk, 1558–1603* (Oxford, 1974).

left them to collect most of their own salaries from the public who used their services; and this practice extended down from the Lord Treasurer of England to his humblest menials. If you went to see them empty-handed you were wasting your time. It would be easy to describe these payments as bribes and condemn their recipients as corrupt. I would prefer for the present to call them gifts or gratuities and keep an open mind about it.

Some payments are, of course, easily identified as bribes, notably gifts to a judge, because Tudor judges were, like their modern successors, governed by a fourteenth-century statute which forbade them to take gifts before, during or after hearing a case.[1] That is why Francis Bacon would be correctly described as a corrupt judge. So were others who managed to get away with it. But what about Robert Cecil who, as Secretary of State, took substantial gifts from Spain and France and as Lord Treasurer took large sums from suitors? How much these various suitors gave we do not know but Hatfield House, which he built, still stands as a tribute to their generosity. And here is the difficulty. No man of his ability could have been expected to live on the nominal salaries of his offices. It was assumed and understood that he would obtain enough by the methods I have indicated to ensure a condition of life appropriate to a senior minister of the Crown. And how high a standard is that and at what point is he obtaining too much? How much is too much? This is a question which takes in the whole moral philosophy of the age, and I shall briefly return to it later.

If, for reasons I have indicated, it is legitimate to take £10 from a suitor, is it corrupt to take £100? We are up against the basic problem of an acquisitive society. 'True it is', said a Tudor preacher, recalling with some embarrassment Christ's parable about the camel and the eye of a needle, 'True it is that it is hard for a rich man to enter the kingdom of heaven; but it is not impossible.'[2] Less embarrassed was a seventeenth-century bureaucrat, Hugh Audley, who, according to one story, on being asked how much his post was worth, replied, 'It might be worth some thousand of pounds to him who, after his death, would instantly go to heaven; twice as much to him who would go to purgatory; and nobody knows what to him who would adventure to go to hell.'[3] We do not know Audley's ultimate destination; our only hint is that he was known to contemporaries as 'rich Audley'. 'To be honest as this world goes', says Hamlet to Polonius, 'is to be one man pick'd out of ten thousand.'[4] 'If I were...to punish those who take bribes', said James I, 'I should soon not have a single subject left.'[5]

If, however, gifts of money shed light on the problem of corruption, more instructive is the gift of office, that is the manner of appointment. The method by which a man is recommended for an office, or is in fact given it, is covered by the term patronage. There is nothing inherently evil in the system because it is essential in any developed society. When we recommend a student for a post, or advise a Foundation about a scholar's application, or serve on a committee to make an academic appointment, we are exercising the powers of patronage. It is the normal method by which honourable men go about their business. Within this system of patronage various checks and balances have been established to ensure a just evaluation of each candidate's claim to the appointment; and the governing criterion is the public interest, that is, we seek the best man for the post. So

[1] 20 Ed. III, c. 6.
[2] M. Maclure, *The Paul's Cross Sermons* (1958), p. 125.
[3] *The Way to be Rich, according to the Practice of the Great Audley* (1662), p. 12.
[4] *Hamlet*, II, ii, 177–9, cited in M. D. H. Parker, *The Slave of Life* (1955), p. 98.
[5] Cited in S. R. Gardiner, *History of England, 1603–42* (1883), III, 74–5.

much for the theory. One needs very little experience to discover that this is a criterion easier to define than to implement. For, cast on to the scales of judgement and unbalancing them are personal prejudice, favours remembered and needing to be repaid, pressures, weakness, prestige-massage, intrigue to preserve power and, quite simply, bad judgement. (I know of one such elector whose capacity to pick the wrong man amounts almost to genius and is without parallel since King James I.) But of all the risks inherent in the processes of patronage the most repulsive and dangerous is its use to build up a personal following, a body of men who will repay past favours by service, sometimes subservience, to their patrons. That is what is meant in the Tudor phrase, 'he is someone whom I may command'. If such hazards of the abuse of patronage dog any group of people engaged in making an appointment and may corrupt its processes, these dangers were incomparably greater in late sixteenth-century England. This is the system that Wolsey, at the time of his fall, is describing to Cromwell:

> No sun shall ever usher forth mine honours,
> Or gild again the noble troops that waited
> Upon my smiles. Go, get thee from me,
>   Cromwell;
> I am a poor fall'n man, unworthy now
> To be thy lord and master.
>   (*Hen. VIII*, III, ii, 410–14)

He does not mean morally unworthy.

The English patronage system of that period was monolithic. All public offices were held of the queen and appointments were made, either by her directly or by men whom she had appointed. That this created a dangerous situation she was well aware. For she must devolve the overwhelming majority of her appointments upon her ministers who would inevitably gain thereby influence, a following who would repay the fruits of office and authority with gifts, or subservience, or both. That

in fact happened, but the successful Tudors, Henry VII, Henry VIII and Elizabeth, usually managed to contain such patronage by balancing one senior minister against another, and breaking a minister if he seemed to be gaining a preponderance in political influence. Henry VIII for that reason destroyed in succession the power of Wolsey, Cromwell and the Duke of Norfolk. Elizabeth used more gentle processes to contain Leicester, Burghley, Walsingham, ensuring that there was always a rival minister equal to them in power. The ministers knew of these governing conditions and perforce accepted them. The Earl of Essex, at the end of her reign, refused to conform to them and she destroyed him.

A strong will, like that of Elizabeth I, could keep this delicate and elaborate system of patronage in reasonable working order. But to the suppliant who had to go cap in hand – or rather purse in hand – to a minister or one of his army of secretaries and assistants the situation was not only irksome and expensive, but also capricious, selfish and unjust. We have seen Francis Bacon's judgement of Cecil. Yet what Bacon said of Cecil had been said by Spenser a generation earlier of Cecil's father, Lord Burghley:

> O grief of griefs, O gall of all good hearts
> To see that virtue should despised be
> Of him that first was raised for virtuous parts,
> And now broad spreading like an aged tree,
> Lets none shoot up that nigh him planted be.[1]

Spenser's complaint, which he also makes elsewhere, is that Burghley, having created a monopoly of power, ruthlessly excluded everyone who was a potential threat to his authority. 'He that seeketh to be eminent amongst able men', wrote Francis Bacon in his essay 'Of Ambition', 'hath a great task; but that is ever good for the public. But he that plots to be the only figure amongst cyphers is the decay of a whole age.' In this Bacon put his finger on the

[1] Edmund Spenser, *The Ruins of Time*, ll. 449–53.

central issue, that patronage could easily decline into faction. 'I have spent my time, my fortune and almost my honesty', wrote Sir John Harington, Queen Elizabeth's godson, 'to buy false hope, false friends and shallow praise.'[1] Many believed that Burghley and later his son, Robert Cecil, were surrounding themselves with sycophantic second-raters. Hence the Court was corrupt, as Sir Walter Ralegh was to say in his indictment of the whole system in its politics, its religion, its laws, its culture, all of them based on a lie.

But this kind of thing had been said in Henry VIII's time by Skelton who poured scorn on the politics and administration under the dominance of Cardinal Wolsey.[2] And when, a little later, in 1536, there was a major rising in the shape of the Pilgrimage of Grace, the rebels again denounced the corrupt and overweening power being exercised by London, but now the principal object of their assault was not Wolsey but Thomas Cromwell.

The aphorism 'all power corrupts' is usually attributed to Lord Acton; but that was not what he said. His words were: 'Power tends to corrupt', which is a more tenable proposition.[3] Power has a built-in element which may corrupt its possessor but it does not always do so. There are many men who want neither to enlarge their power nor to perpetuate it. They treat it simply as a trust which they gladly yield up when their term is ended.

But why for others has it that fatal quality of corruption? Power is an addictive drug: the more some men take of it the more they need. And, as is commonly experienced with other addictive drugs, power creates an illusion. Power is never as great as it seems. The holder of the highest office in the state may see himself as the inspirer and saviour of his people but to some he may seem no more than a devious, ambitious man whose lust for wealth and power debases the high office he holds. Queen Elizabeth I's titles were The High and Mighty

Prince, Elizabeth by the Grace of God Queen of England, Ireland and France, Defender of the Faith, Supreme Governor of the Church of England by law established, etc. But she seemed to some who saw her as just a tetchy, vain old woman who had lived too long. James I, her heir to these sonorous titles, to which was added the unofficial one of the British Solomon, impressed some people as no more than a garrulous, pompous egomaniac of shambling gait and wandering eye.

> within the hollow crown
> That rounds the mortal temples of a king
> Keeps Death his Court; and there the antic sits,
> Scoffing his State and grinning at his pomp;
> Allowing him a breath, a little scene,
> To monarchize.
>
> (*Richard II*, iii, ii, 160–5)

James monarchised; but the gap between reality and illusion was wide.

I would state it as a generalisation that in every society, and under every form of government, whether autocratic or democratic, there is, over time, a progressive alienation of the governors from the governed. For a government has two objectives: to govern successfully and to preserve itself in power. In autocratic states it may do so for decades by the familiar processes of a heavy censorship, a strong propaganda machine, powerful controls over industry, trade, education, assisted by the use, or the threat, of force. This was true of the Tudor period when criticism of the government (though it was not autocratic) was under severe restraint and freedom of speech survived only in the interstices of authority.

This duality of power, this tension between fact and illusion, between the man as he is and

[1] John Harington, *Nugae Antiquae* as cited in L. C. Knights, *Drama and Society in the Age of Jonson* (1962 ed.), p. 270.
[2] John Skelton, 'Why come ye not to Court?'
[3] J. E. E. D. Acton, Lord Acton, *Essays on Freedom and Power*, ed. Gertrude Himmelfarb (1956), p. 335.

the panoply of his high offices, is clearly brought out in Shakespeare's play, *Henry V*, after the king's encounter with the common soldiers on the eve of battle. He has not been recognised but has been profoundly shaken by their frank comments on the selfishness of the governing classes including the king. He asks himself, therefore, the basic question of his authority: what qualities does a king possess which are not to be found in ordinary men? Is it ceremony, is it symbol – the sceptre, the crown, the mace – or is the whole thing a pompous sham?[1]

In effect, the king acknowledges the illusion of his authority yet he preserves it triumphantly for the whole war effort has been identified with another illusion, familiar enough in so many forms of government, namely that the person of the king, the survival of the nation and the will of God are united and identified in a common cause: 'God for Harry, England and St George.' The soldier who, in a moment of illumination, saw the king as no more than an ordinary man with a crown on his head can continue in his appointed role of dying nobly in battle, for he is dying for God, Harry, England and St George.[2] It was the achievement of Elizabeth I to identify the national awakening with herself and Christianity in the image created for her by John Foxe in his *Book of Martyrs*. In the case of James I his kingship was identified, not with nationhood, but with his personal vanity. If, then, in Shakespeare's *Henry V* we detect something of Elizabeth, it is in his *King Lear* that we detect something of James I.

Illusion exerts a double influence. It incites the holder of power (whether monarch or elected head of state) to enlarge his power so that the illusion can be made into reality. But the illusion also isolates him: he is different, he is greater than his fellow men. This is what we get from Julius Caesar in the last phase of his life.

> I am constant as the northern star,
> Of whose true-fix'd and resting quality
> There is no fellow in the firmament.
> *(JC,* III, i, 60–2)

Ordinary men, he says,

> are flesh and blood and apprehensive
> Yet in the number I do know but one
> That unassailable holds on his rank
> Unshak'd of motion; and that I am he.
> *(JC,* III, i, 67–70)

It is a nice piece of Shakespearian irony that, within minutes, all this bombast has been washed away in Caesar's blood.

The conflict between illusion and reality, exemplified in the fate of Julius Caesar, is re-enacted throughout Shakespeare's plays, in the experiences of Richard II, the three Lancastrian kings in their several ways, Lear and Coriolanus, to mention only the most striking cases. It is also to be found in some of the tragic historical figures like King Charles I and Napoleon I. For these men are driven by the passion to turn illusion into reality, to prove that the annointing is not simply the holy ritual of monarchy but really turns a man into a god. And it is this which drives men on sometimes to triumph, sometimes to destruction, and often to both. In any case, it calls for a single-mindedness and concentration of purpose which only few men possess. In short, a successful politician, whether monarch or subject, is a man who not only wills the end (we can all do that) but – and this is what separates him from the rest of us – who wills the means. And in politics the means may be elaborate, ruthless and corrupt.

Shakespeare's Richard III wills the means as well as the end. So does Lady Macbeth until her nerve fails. But the relationship between the end and the means is not a simple one. Coriolanus is destroyed not because he is corrupt but because he has failed to come to

[1] *Henry V*, IV, i, 234–66. [2] *Ibid.*, III, i, 34.

terms with the forces of corruption. He half realises this but he also believes that if he accepts office as consul, as his mother urges him, then the bond with the people will corrupt. In that extraordinary scene with Volumnia, when the pressures upon him are enormous and we can see him weakening, he suddenly reverts to his principle.

> I will not do't
> Lest I surcease to honour mine own truth,
> And by my body's action teach my mind
> A most inherent baseness.
>
> (*Cor.*, III, ii, 120–3)

Coriolanus has got through to the heart of the matter. If you use evil means to gain or retain authority you corrupt authority itself. Though not the wisest or most percipient of men, Coriolanus has seen the high price to be paid for the enjoyment of power and has refused to pay it.

Yet, in spite of the perils, the desires and the opportunities for power exercised a strong influence in late Elizabethan England; and it was in the 1590s that an always dangerous situation assumed critical dimensions.

The queen, of course, was growing old; but the significance of this may be exaggerated. More important, it seems to me, was that the very success of her reign produced a false confidence in her established ways. In a unitary state under personal rule the most dangerous time is when the head of the state has achieved a considerable measure of success. For nothing misleads like success. The queen had governed well for thirty years. She had won a spectacular victory against Spain. She was popular, and she was secure on the throne. The system worked, therefore – it was assumed – it would go on working. But there were serious weaknesses, too. Her very real achievement in balancing the pressures of the different claimants to power misled her into believing that her achievement would last. But the times were changing and so were the men involved.

Burghley was succeeded by his son, Robert Cecil, widely recognised as the most skilful politician of the age, whose accumulation of power was rapid at a time when there was no rival claimant of his stature, experience and resourcefulness. His father's rivals, Leicester, Hatton and Walsingham, were gone, to be succeeded in the struggle for power by the Earl of Essex. Here was a handsome and popular courtier, a brave soldier, a cultivated man. In short, he possessed all the qualities which Cecil did not possess. But he lacked other more essential qualities, a cool head, a balanced judgement, a rational assessment of an explosive situation. He was his own greatest enemy. He made a major blunder in thinking that the queen's show of affection gave him a special claim to authority in the state; and there he misjudged the queen in a way that his step-father, the Earl of Leicester, did not. To imagine that the queen would permit him to obtain power by force compounded his errors. In the late 1590s we can watch a marvellous lesson in statecraft as Cecil, increasingly supported by the queen, outmanoeuvred the earl. And he was hurt most in his continuing loss of patronage, the source from which he could support himself and maintain his followers. Faced with the almost complete attrition of his power he broke out of an intolerable situation by a clumsy, ill-organised rebellion which was easily snuffed out. With the fall and execution of Essex, Cecil found himself in the last years of the queen in a strong ministerial position without rival in the state. It marks also the end of the Tudor balancing of power, which was never restored in the next generation, and lesser men like Robert Carr, Earl of Somerset and George Villiers, Duke of Buckingham exploited the changed situation for personal ends.

These changes reflected others taking place within the monarchy. For we are witnessing the corruption of monarchy itself. Elizabeth I,

I have argued elsewhere,[1] came to believe, as her propagandists had proclaimed, that she was in fact a goddess. James I persuaded himself that kings were indeed gods subject only to God Almighty himself. Charles I succumbed to the illusion which Van Dyck has preserved for us in those majestic equestrian portraits of a king destined to become a martyr. And meanwhile amidst this haze of illusion the Stuart monarchy, increasingly isolated from reality, was crumbling. The first decade of the seventeenth century saw the open conflict between fact and illusion and it focused on Robert Cecil. It was, indeed, Cecil's decade. But new rivals were emerging and though they were not men of Cecil's stature they enjoyed influence of another kind. Elizabeth, it is true, was always attracted by handsome young men, and so was James I, if for somewhat different reasons. But though Elizabeth enjoyed the company of courtiers like Leicester, Hatton, Ralegh and Essex she gave them powers only commensurate with their political talents, not with their charm. Ralegh was never made a member of her privy council, and Essex and his dependants were strictly rationed with their jobs, gifts and influence. Under James the controls were removed: the Scottish friends of James were generously endowed with lands and office, and they and others systematically thwarted, for private ends, the efforts of Cecil to preserve a well-organised form of government. The Tudor system of appointments was being undermined and corrupted. Men were chosen for office not because of their competence for the work but because of irrelevant physical attractions and their ability to play upon and exploit the vanity of the king. The whole framework of political appointment was distorted and the system of government became a parody of itself. *Patronage was corrupted into favouritism.* This I think is the importance of James I's reign. And favouritism became a heavy charge upon the cost of government.

My case is that the Tudor system of government with its patronage, its gifts, its distribution of power, was not inherently corrupt though it was potentially so. By contrast the Jacobean system *was* corrupt because it sacrificed the national interest to the aims and vanities of James I and to the greed and ambitions of his minions, his friends and his dependants. James I's favouritism, a travesty of patronage, brought government into disrepute.

> The skipping king, he ambled up and down
> With shallow jesters and rash bavin wits,
> Soon kindled and soon burnt; carded his state,
> Mingled his royalty with cap'ring fools;
> Had his great name profaned with their scorns,
> To laugh at gibing boys.
>
> (*1 Hen. IV*, III, ii, 60–5)

In Bolingbroke's view Richard II had debased and corrupted his inherited crown; in the eyes of the parliamentary opposition James I had debased and corrupted his inheritance, the Tudor monarchy. The divinity which doth hedge a crown was an illusion, and the illusion was now threadbare.

What of James I's ministers? I have been reading the personal and political papers of Robert Cecil for more than a decade; and one of the unexpected side-effects of such an experience is that it forced me to turn away from a one-dimensional moral view of the Elizabethans, a view which would divide men into clear categories: corrupt men and honest men. Robert Cecil was in many respects a corrupt man who climbed to power by devious means, as many men have done, then and now.

> God knows, my son,
> By what by-paths and indirect crook'd ways
> I met this crown.
>
> (*2 Hen. IV*, IV, v, 184–6)

Yet in the end Cecil sacrificed his life in the service of his country. One does not need to

[1] See my forthcoming article, 'Queen and State: the emergence of an Elizabethan myth' in *Britain and the Netherlands*, v, ed. J. S. Bromley and E. H. Kossmann (The Hague, 1975 or 1976).

be a seventeenth-century Puritan to know that the road to the celestial city lay through a lusty mart.

From the beginning of James I's reign Cecil realised that the survival of effective government depended, in the first place, on curbing the king's extravagance and secondly, on increasing his income. In the first aspect of this programme Cecil failed. James's prodigality to his favourites could not be restrained by any of his successive finance ministers; and it was to the other aspect of the programme, the enlargement of the royal revenues, that Cecil bent all his energies.

Cecil had less than a decade in which to adapt the Tudor fiscal system to the necessities of a modern sovereign state. I cannot on this occasion rehearse in detail the measures in which he was involved: the improvement of land revenue by raising the entry fines; the increased profits from wardship; the new Book of Rates, the first for half a century, to increase the profits from customs; the impositions of 1608; and the tightening up of administration as a whole. But the pivot of the campaign was to be the ambitious – some said foolhardy – conversion scheme of the prerogative revenues which became known as the Great Contract. It was 1610; and Cecil, already a sick man, now embarked on it in the 'winter of my age'.[1] He was forty-seven.

It is not my intention to re-open either the seventeenth-century debate on the Great Contract, or the modern one.[2] In essence he would end many objectionable revenue sources in return for a parliamentary guarantee of an annual sum thereafter requiring no parliamentary consent. And everything now hinged on bringing it to completion. In ten years the parliamentarians had learned a good deal; and it did not require much percipience for them to see that in accepting the Contract they might be presiding over their own demise. Whether, therefore, in their elaborate, timeless discus-

sions with Cecil they had seriously aimed at an agreement it is impossible to say. To the king and his advisers these long delays, this close bargaining, disparaged the prerogative and offered scant prospects of reward. Only Cecil seemed to go on believing to the end; and when he failed he knew it was the end of his career. The parliamentarians imposed delay upon delay; the king's friends told him that Cecil was betraying the interests of the Crown; and finally James broke off the negotiations. Cecil had staked everything on what was perhaps the only unselfish act of his life; and he had failed.

Finally, there came the condemnation by the king. 'Your greatest error', James told him, 'hath been that ye ever expected to draw honey out of gall, being a little blinded with the self-love of your own counsel in holding together of this Parliament, whereof all men were despaired, as I have oft told you, but yourself alone.'[3] Only James could have so addressed himself to a falling minister; and yet he was right. Cecil had pursued a policy which was based on a contradiction. He, the great parliamentarian, was engaged in persuading a self-conscious, expansionist parliament to set a limit to its prospects and powers, to its right to consent, perhaps to life itself. And now he knew that he had failed.

Yet in 1611 Cecil once more set about the task of remodelling the administration out of the ruins of his plan and of his career. He was now forty-eight, an age when men may look forward to one or, if they are fortunate, two, of the best creative decades of their lives; for it is a time when vision joins hand with experience. If they sit in the seat of power then the prospects are dazzling. But at forty-eight Cecil

[1] *Proceedings in Parliament, 1610* (New Haven, Conn., 1966), ed. Elizabeth Read Foster, I, 4.

[2] For a discussion of the Great Contract see my *The Queen's Wards* (1958), pp. 317–25.

[3] *Ibid.*, p. 322.

was dying. The delicate frame, after more than two decades of unremitting public service, was at last yielding to the strain; and in May 1612 he died.

In the carrion politics of early Stuart England men had been eagerly awaiting the day. He was mourned by few save those who understood the pattern of his life; who saw that he had carried through the peaceful transition from the last Tudor to the first Stuart, at a time when half Europe thought England would be submerged in civil war; that he fought for social reform of which the Elizabethan Poor Law is his memorial; that he stood for an independent foreign policy, while after his death his king drifted under Spanish persuasion; that he tried to heal the divisions wrought by religious extremism. And yet he was a corrupt man. But only a few men knew that, though he grew rich in the service of the state, the service of the state came in the end to mean more to him than riches or career, or the applause of his contemporaries – or life itself. 'All our actions', Cecil had written years before, 'are upon the open stage and can be no more hidden than the sun. If we deserve ill we shall hear ill; or if the present time do flatter us yet, when our glasses are run (which cannot be long), that glory which maketh worthy men live for ever dieth with us; and our posterity shall be the heirs of our dishonour'.[1]

There is, however, a final paradox in this extraordinary story; and it concerns Cecil's whole approach to the government of the Tudor state. There were two outstanding statesmen in the sixteenth century who devoted the most important period of their lives towards making the government strong and efficient. One was Thomas Cromwell and the other was Robert Cecil. Both failed; and the causes of their failure may help us to understand the nature of the Tudor system of government. Between the Reformation and the Great Contract the Crown held the initiative in parliamentary and political affairs. But it was an initiative with limited powers of endurance. Two attempts were made, one at the beginning and the other at the end of our period, to make that temporary initiative permanent, to enhance the Crown's authority and to reduce the House of Commons to a lasting subordination. The first attempt was made by Thomas Cromwell with his Bill of Proclamations of 1539 (giving proclamations the force of law and therefore reducing the necessity for parliaments); the second by Robert Cecil with his Great Contract of 1610. Both men failed and for two principal reasons. In each case their monarchs never gave them their fullest support and in the end betrayed them: the one passed to the executioner's axe, the other to a consuming sickness of body. Secondly, in each case there were groups of men in the House of Commons who set too high a value on parliamentary government to barter it away for ministerial favour or illusory gain. There is indeed a tragic quality about the lives of both Cromwell and Cecil; for they were men who were much greater than their contemporaries, including the monarchs they served. But if we set great store by representative institutions and freedom of political expression, we do not see in Cromwell or Cecil sponsors of parliamentary liberty but powerful servants of the centralised state. They would have made England safe for the Stuarts, not for freedom and consent in government. While, therefore, we acknowledge the outstanding qualities of Cromwell and Cecil, we acknowledge also the contribution of those lesser men who, perceiving though dimly the consequences of strong centralised monarchical government, stubbornly preserved their parliamentary institutions at a time when they were being emasculated or extinguished on the continent of Europe. It is these lesser men, not Cromwell or Cecil, who should be counted

[1] R. Cecil, *An Answere to Certaine Scandalous Papers* (1606), sig. E. 2r.

among the founding fathers of the constitutional monarchy and the free institutions under which we live. For, though free institutions and free men are not incorruptible, the survival of their freedom depends on destroying the power and corruption of personal and selfish rule when it is entrenched in strong centralised institutions.

Cecil was the last man who might have saved the Stuart monarchy. With his death it became irrecoverable. Corruption was disseminated throughout its ministry and servants. A head of state with no sense of honour will draw to his ministry men equally barren of public responsibility and they will in the end undermine the whole system.

I have cited many instances of corruption, real and alleged, which we find in the politics and literature of the age. Yet the most powerful charge that society was corrupt through and through I have saved for the last. It was made long before the time of Shakespeare and is familiar to all students of the period. It is the voice of Thomas More in that astounding aside with which he interrupts his account of Utopia. 'When I consider and weigh in my mind all these commonwealths which nowadays anywhere do flourish so, God help me, I can perceive nothing but a certain conspiracy of rich men procuring their own commodities under the name and title of the commonwealth.'[1]

I am aware that a number of worthy scholars have sought to explain – or rather explain away – this erosive passage. But I am satisfied that the simplest explanation best fits the source. More, in creating his *Utopia*, had, as it were, stumbled on a community of people who, without being Christian, had managed to establish a just society. Early Tudor England, by contrast, with its enclosures and evictions, often safeguarded by the law, with its inequalities, injustice and war, was nominally Christian but, in fact, barbarous and corrupt, and so preserved by the law and the constitution. This is More's indictment of his own age. It was an acquisitive society and an affront to Christianity. The amount of money you took seems unimportant. It is the profit motive itself which is directly attacked. This is a larger question than that raised by the activities of James I and his friends but it embraces them too. It is a probing question about the foundations of western society which was to return again and again to torment the best minds of each generation.

I have attempted in this paper to show that the changing situation in the sixteenth and seventeenth centuries made available to politicians greater power than ever before. But the system of government remained personal and power itself was distributed through patronage. I have argued that patronage in itself was not corrupt unless those in power corrupted it for personal gain or for favourites, all at the cost of society itself. Patronage indeed was an essential process for distributing power in the intervening period of personal rule between the pluralist society of the Middle Ages and the democratic society of modern times. But the patronage system was always vulnerable because power derived from one central source, the monarch, and therefore too much depended on the person who wore the crown and the ministers he chose. But few men are wholly corrupt. If the historian, as he grows older, discovers both from his researches and the world he lives in that men are not gods, he learns also that they are not wholly devils. I know the historical sources better than the literary ones; and I have not, in the historical sources, ever found an Iago, an Edmund or a Richard III. The career of Robert Cecil exemplifies rather that corrupt men may sometimes in the end serve their country with great

[1] Thomas More, *Utopia*, ed. J. R. Lumby (Cambridge, 1885), p. 162.

devotion for, in their case too, the road to the celestial city lay through this lusty mart.

I have tried also to show that the two decades that Shakespeare spent in London were, as it happened, times when the forces making for corruption were increasingly manifest. I have not attempted in this paper to trace these features in Shakespeare's plays because I am aware that, like all other Elizabethan historians, I do not possess the technical equipment to do so. And I have only occasionally flirted with danger. But if I have briefly indicated some possible lines of inquiry to Shakespearian scholars then I have repaid a small fraction of my own debt to them.

I return finally to the first question raised, not by me but by President Kennedy. I have painted a dark picture of the second decade of Shakespeare's life in London, a time of political decline and decay yet when drama, poetry, the study of history, music, architecture flourished. The government at this time was moving on to no new frontier but stubbornly trying to defend an old one. I ask, therefore, whether the creative artist of the period owed more to the turbulence and uncertainties and vitality of the capital city of London than to the patronage he received at the royal Court at Westminster, outside its walls.

Yet, in fairness to President Kennedy's theory, I should like to bring to the witness box a contemporary who did sketch out an indirect relationship between the politics and the literature of the age. He is Arthur Wilson, the dramatist and historian, looking back on the reign of James I: 'Some parallel'd him to Tiberius for dissimulation, yet peace was maintained by him as in the time of Augustus; and peace begot plenty, and plenty begot ease and wantonness, and ease and wantonness begot poetry...'[1] It would have been nice if the quotation had ended there. It did not, and Wilson went on to show how poetry became a weapon for satirising the king and contributed to the collapse of the Stuart monarchy. We, therefore, turn back to one of the poets of that age as he comments, in a famous passage, on the patronage and corruption of late Elizabethan England, and in so doing answers the question raised by President Kennedy:

> Tell men of high condition
> That manage the estate,
> Their purpose is ambition,
> Their practice only hate.
> And if they once reply
> Then give them all the lie.[2]

Sir Walter Ralegh, courtier, poet, historian, parliamentarian, soldier, sailor, explorer, coloniser, one of the great creative artists of his time, never gained a secure footing in a corrupt system which in the end destroyed him at the will of a corrupt king subservient to Spain. In the process of destroying Ralegh, it was also destroying itself.

[1] Arthur Wilson, *Life and Reign of James I*, p. 792 as cited in *James I by his contemporaries*, ed. R. Ashton (1969), p. 18.
[2] Sir Walter Ralegh, 'The Lie', ll. 19–24.

LITERATURE WITHOUT PHILOSOPHY: 'ANTONY AND CLEOPATRA'

MORRIS WEITZ

Major claims have been made both for and against Shakespeare as a man of ideas – of his own time and for all time. These point to larger doctrines about the relation between literature and philosophy. In this paper I shall consider Shakespeare as a dramatist of ideas and his contributions to philosophy in literature.

Philosophy and Literature, Philosophy of Literature, and Philosophy in Literature have only one thing in common: each has been designated a non-subject. Of course this is a slight exaggeration, since it is true of the first two but not of the third. Philosophy and Literature is a piece of academic entrepreneurism, motivated by the mutual desire to make philosophy concrete and literature profound. It succeeds in neither. At best, it functions as a part of the history of ideas, using both literature and philosophy as reflecting mirrors of each other; at its worst, it is a series of distorting imitations of imitations, to borrow a phrase from the master.

Philosophy of Literature is a piece of philosophical imperialism, sponsored by the obsession that all disciplines have a philosophical dimension that awaits articulation and scrutiny. All that deserve examination, however, are those aspects of literature as an art that distinguish it from the other arts. Traditionally, aesthetics has regarded this problem of the differentia of literature as its proper domain. I see no need to recast or to reject this traditional role and discipline: there is nothing in philosophy of literature that is not already in aesthetics.

What about Philosophy in Literature? Is it a proper subject? According to a major tradition, from Plato to I. A. Richards, it is not. Philosophy and literature are radically distinct: the first aims at truth, the second, at falsehood or affective experience. Even Aristotle's compromise that poetry, though not pure philosophy, is at least better than history, is not much more than a left-handed compliment to the cognitive content of literature.

Having dealt with this issue of the legitimacy of philosophy in literature elsewhere, I do not wish to debate it here. Instead, let me dogmatically assert or reaffirm that they can be combined without the denigration of either. Indeed, it seems to me, that literature, in some cases, is able to convey a philosophy or truth that philosophy itself does not. Ancient Greek tragedy, for example, dramatizes what by implication is an ultimate, irreducible fact of human experience: that it is tragic. Plato recognizes the tragic but argues that it can be overcome by reason; Aristotle restricts the tragic to the stage, construing it only as a representation of the passage from happiness to misery, a passage that also reason can overcome. If we agree that the tragic, however variously conceived, is something irretrievable – a brute fact in the world – then surely Greek tragedy proclaims a philosophical truth that Greek philosophy does not. Greek tragedy, thus, is not only a clear case of philosophy in literature, it is also a striking victory of literature over philosophy in the pursuit of truth.

The rejection of Philosophy in Literature includes one aesthetically valid point that should be applauded, that literature must never be reduced to philosophy or to any nuggets of embroidered truth. This anti-reductionist insistence on the integrity of the individual literary work, however unfortunately conflated with the rejection of philosophy in literature, remains a solid contribution to literary criticism.

I understand by Philosophy in Literature two related doctrines: (1) that some works of literature contain philosophical ideas which are as integral to these works as any of their other constituents; and (2) that there is a place in literary criticism for the aesthetic articulation of these ideas. More particularly, I find it fruitful to ask of any work of literature: does it have any philosophical ideas? If it does, how do they get into the work? and what aesthetic contribution do they make to the work?

In asking the first question, one must distinguish between a philosophical theme and a philosophical thesis. For example, a novel, say *Anna Karenina*, may have many philosophical themes, among them, that we are not to blame, hence not to be judged, for what we do – a theme that is voiced by all the major characters; or that *laissez-faire* is the best philosophy of life, which is exemplified by Oblonsky. But it is not always clear that a philosophical theme, however much it is expressed, serves as the philosophical thesis; neither of these two themes, for example, can be read as Tolstoy's truth-claim about human life in *Anna Karenina*. In fact, the philosophical thesis, at least on my reading of the novel, is not even expressed on the printed pages of the novel but must be elicited from the plot in relation to the other elements. I am also aware of powerful arguments by aestheticians against the distinction between theme and thesis in literature. All of these arguments, I believe, rest on a confusion of the factual question, Are there philosophical theses in literature? with the normative ques-

tion, Ought we, when the plot, characters, dialogue, authorial interpolation, tone, and themes are described and explained in a certain way, to construe one or other of the themes as *a* or *the* philosophical thesis in the whole work? In regard to this normative question, it seems to me that there is no compelling reason for a negative reply and good reasons for an affirmative answer, provided we are able to accommodate false as well as true philosophical theses in those works that have or imply them.

My model for philosophical literary criticism is a form of the imagistic criticism of Shakespeare's plays. Traditionally – though the tradition is quite recent – the imagistic approach to Shakespeare displays the same conflict over reductionism as philosophy in literature, best seen in the work of Spurgeon and Clemen. Both of these critics explore the imagery of each of the plays. Miss Spurgeon, however, reduces the whole meaning of the play to its dominant image; Clemen, on the other hand, regards the imagery as but one aspect of each of the dramas, sometimes central, sometimes not but, in any case, as a contributing element to the whole drama, which cannot be reduced to any central element, including the imagery. For him, the play's the thing, not the imagery. So, too, for me, the literary work is central, not its philosophical theme or thesis, which may or may not be dominant in any particular work.

In a number of essays, I have tried – by way of examples, the only way philosophy in literature can vindicate itself – to practise philosophical literary criticism as a branch of literary criticism. Whether successfully or not, I have tried to show that Voltaire's *Candide*, Shakespeare's *Hamlet* and *King Lear*, Tolstoy's *Anna Karenina*, Proust's *À la recherche du temps perdu*, and Eliot's *Four Quartets* contain philosophical themes and theses; how these are brought into these works; and what aesthetic difference the theses make to the works.

This enterprise, I hope, justifies philosophy in literature, both in literature and in philosophy. In turning now to our present subject, *Antony and Cleopatra*, allow me to reiterate in the strongest terms that there is philosophy in (some) literature, consequently that philosophical criticism is as legitimate and enlightening as any other special branch of literary criticism. However – it cannot be overemphasized – this discipline is a part of literary criticism, not of philosophy.

Is there a philosophy or philosophical thesis in Shakespeare? Wholesale affirmative as well as negative answers have been equally disastrous. That Shakespeare presents a unified system of ideas about life and the world simply will not stand up to the diversity of the ideas in his plays. That Shakespeare has no philosophy, offers no profound claims about man, a view put forth by no less a poet and critic than Eliot, in his contrast of Dante as a poet–thinker with Shakespeare as a dramatist–poet, is also suspect when we turn to some of the individual plays. *Hamlet* and especially *King Lear* dramatize themes and proffer theses that in their profundity are not only philosophical but rival, as the writers of Greek tragedy did their contemporaries, the naive and pragmatic optimism of his age.

Without agreeing at all with Eliot about Shakespeare, I want to ask, in regard to literature in general and Shakespeare in particular, Can there be great literature without philosophy, that is, without a thesis about man or his world? It has long seemed to me that there can be. In this paper, I want to discuss this question – again by example – and, if I can, to persuade you that in the case of *Antony and Cleopatra* we have a great tragedy which contains a number of philosophical themes but no implied or elicitable philosophical thesis or universal claim. Thus, in the sense that *King Lear* may be convincingly interpreted as a philosophical drama with its dominant thesis

about man's worth in an indifferent world; or that *Hamlet* may be seen as a drama with its thesis about man's ability to raise all the important questions without being able to find any of the answers, *Antony and Cleopatra* is not a philosophical drama: it neither makes nor includes any general claim about man and his world. Rather it is a tragedy of two particulars who instance no universal applicable to all.

Among the distinguishable elements of *Antony and Cleopatra*, there are a number of ostensible philosophical themes, each beautifully explored by critics of the play. (Whether these themes are really philosophical or what is a philosophical as against a non-philosophical theme seem to me fruitless questions, resting as they do on the unwarranted assumption that philosophy is fixed and precise, a discipline that can be brought into a real definition, which it cannot.) There is, however, one philosophical theme in the play that, so far as I know, has not been given the scrutiny it deserves: the theme of generation and corruption, of coming into being and passing away, a theme as old as ancient Greek philosophy. This theme is richly unfolded in *Antony and Cleopatra*, so intensively that I would venture to call the play Shakespeare's 'pre-Socratic' tragedy.

Antony and Cleopatra is primarily a magnificent love story, full of exciting episodes, fascinating characters, marvellous, luscious poetry, and a traditional tragic theme of the rise and fall of great ones. Let us even grant that it is the Elizabethan–Roman version of the beautiful people, but without the not-yet Jet set.

What does such a *précis* leave out? For one thing, the multiple contrasts between earth and water, Rome and Egypt, Tiber and Nile, land and sea, Antony's victories on land, defeats at sea. Then, there are the epithets of melting Rome in Tiber, Egypt in Nile. Clemen especially has explored the sea-imagery of the play; Spurgeon, the vast expanse of the world. 'World', she shows, is as important in *Antony and Cleopatra* as 'nature' is in *King Lear*.

There is also the imagery of transformation that our summary account of the play leaves out. Here is Antony, preparing for his battle with Caesar, who will fight by sea, not land:

> I would they'ld fight i' the fire, or i' the air.
>
> (IV, x, 3)

This reference to the four elements is picked up toward the end of the play by Cleopatra:

> Husband, I come:
> Now to that name, my courage prove my title!
> I am fire, and air; my other elements
> I give to baser life.
>
> (V, ii, 286–9)

It is this theme of the transformation of the four elements, as it embodies the rhythm of nature, that I wish to concentrate on. In *Antony and Cleopatra*, there is much variation on one thing becoming another: the higher becoming the lower; and nature and her gaps of generation and corruption, as in Enobarbus' description of Antony's first sight of Cleopatra:

> and Antony
> Enthron'd i' the market-place, did sit alone,
> Whistling to the air; which, but for vacancy,
> Had gone to gaze on Cleopatra too,
> And made a gap in nature
>
> (II, ii, 214–18)

in contrast to Cleopatra's description of a world without Antony – the gap of former greatness:

> The crown o' the earth doth melt.
>   My lord?
> O, wither'd is the garland of the war,
> The soldier's pole is fall'n: young boys and girls
> Are level now with men: the odds is gone,
> And there is nothing left remarkable
> Beneath the visiting moon.
>
> (IV, xv, 63–8)

There is also in the play one thing becoming another, either in a normal, expected way or in an abnormal, unexpected way. Antony's description of the Nile expresses ordinary generation and corruption:

> The higher Nilus swells,
> The more it promises: as it ebbs, the seedsman
> Upon the slime and ooze scatters his grain,
> And shortly comes to harvest.
>
> (II, vii, 20–3)

The Nile, in its rises and falls, bringing feast and famine, is a perfect exemplar of one kind of normal, to be expected, passage in nature and life: out of the slime arises fertility; from fertility comes sterility, and the cycle is perennial. No surprises here.

There are many of these examples of normal, to be expected, generation and corruption in *Antony and Cleopatra*. In each, one thing brings forth its opposite. Here are some of them. Antony, to the first messenger from Rome:

> O then we bring forth weeds,
> When our quick minds lie still.
>
> (I, ii, 106–7)

Philo, opening the play by reflecting on Antony's change from warrior to lover:

> Nay, but this dotage of our general's
> O'erflows the measure.
>
> (I, i, 1–2)

Antony, on Fulvia's death:

> The present pleasure,
> By revolution lowering, does become
> The opposite of itself.
>
> (I, ii, 121–3)

Charmian, on Cleopatra's strategy for keeping Antony:

> Tempt him not so too far. I wish, forbear;
> In time we hate that which we often fear.
>
> (I, iii, 11–12)

32

Enobarbus, on Antony's bravura:

> and I see still,
> A diminution in our captain's brain
> Restores his heart.
>
> (III, xiii, 197–9)

Antony, on Enobarbus' desertion:

> O, my fortunes have
> Corrupted honest men.
>
> (IV, v, 16–17)

Cleopatra, in the Monument, after Antony's final defeat:

> our size of sorrow,
> Proportion'd to our cause, must be as great
> As that which makes it
>
> (IV, xv, 4–6)

and Cleopatra's reflection on the clown with the asp:

> What poor an instrument
> May do a noble deed!
>
> (V, 2, 235–6)

Besides these normal, to be expected, causally connected passages from one thing to its opposite, there are normal ones whose expectations do not occur. Two striking examples are the anticipated betrayals of Antony by Cleopatra that do not happen; and Antony's and Cleopatra's moves toward death that do not come off.

However, the really challenging examples of generation and corruption are these:

Enobarbus, on Cleopatra's powers:

> I do think there is mettle in death, which commits some loving act upon her, she hath such a celerity in dying. (I, ii, 139–42)

Here we expect dying and death to bring inaction; in Cleopatra, they create heightened action. Death does not become its opposite, it is its opposite.

Cleopatra, to Antony on his projected return to Rome:

> Riotous madness,
> To be entangled with those mouth-made vows,
> Which break themselves in swearing!
>
> (I, iii, 29–31)

A promise normally – some philosophers would say necessarily – embodies the intent to carry it out; here it is broken in its very utterance. The image is that of a vow that not only is not kept but becomes its opposite in the vowing.

Lepidus to Caesar and Antony, in attempting to reconcile them:

> When we debate
> Our trivial difference loud, we do commit
> Murther in healing wounds.
>
> (II, ii, 20–2)

The comparison of loud debate with murder is apt, the image of murdering in healing wounds is not, yet marvellously right as it yields the totally unexpected effect from a related cause. Healing does not cure, it destroys; one thing generates its opposite by being its opposite.

Enobarbus to Agrippa, on Cleopatra in her barge:

> On each side her,
> Stood pretty dimpled boys, like smiling Cupids,
> With divers-colour'd fans, whose wind did seem
> To glow the delicate cheeks which they did cool,
> And what they undid did.
>
> (II, ii, 201–4)

Enobarbus, again on Cleopatra:

> I saw her once
> Hop forty paces through the public street,
> And having lost her breath, she spoke, and panted,
> That she did make defect perfection,
> And, breathless, power breathe forth.
>
> (II, ii, 228–32)

Again Enobarbus on Cleopatra and the possibility of Antony leaving her:

> Never; he will not:
> Age cannot wither her, nor custom stale
> Her infinite variety: other women cloy

The appetites they feed, but she makes hungry,
Where most she satisfies.

(II, ii, 234–8)

Hunger normally leads to food and eating; too much food, to satiety. But the image here is that of a food that creates more hunger for it in the satiety of it. One thing generates its opposite in a very unusual, unexpected, yet totally convincing manner.

Enobarbus, this time to Menas, on Antony's marriage to Octavia:

But you shall find the band that seems to tie their friendship together will be the very strangler of their amity.   (II, vi, 117–19)

Ventidius to Silius, on Ventidius's victorious exploits:

I could do more to do Antonius good,
But 'twould offend him. And in his offence
Should my performance perish.

(III, i, 25–7)

Caesar to Antony, on Antony's marriage to Octavia:

Most noble Antony,
Let not the piece of virtue which is set
Betwixt us, as the cement of our love
To keep it builded, be the ram to batter
The fortress of it.

(III, ii, 27–31)

Octavia, on the strife between her brother, Caesar, and her husband, Antony:

The good gods will mock me presently,
When I shall pray, 'O, bless my lord, and husband!'
Undo that prayer, by crying out as loud,
'O, bless my brother!' Husband win, win brother,
Prays, and destroys the prayer, no midway
'Twixt these extremes at all.

(III, iv, 15–20)

Octavia, after receiving Antony's approval to go to Caesar:

Wars 'twixt you twain would be
As if the world should cleave, and that slain men
Should solder up the rift.

(III, iv, 30–2)

Enobarbus on Antony's bravado in defeat:

Now he'll outstare the lightning; to be furious
Is to be frighted out of fear.

(III, xiii, 195–6)

Antony, after his first defeat and before his final battle with Rome:

To-morrow, soldier,
By sea and land I'll fight: or I will live,
Or bathe my dying honour in the blood
Shall make it live again.

(IV, ii, 4–6)

Enobarbus, commenting on Antony's generosity after he deserts:

I am alone the villain of the earth,
And feel I am so most. O Antony,
Thou mine of bounty, how wouldst thou have paid
My better service, when my turpitude
Thou dost so crown with gold! This blows my
    heart.

(IV, vi, 30–4)

Antony, to Eros, after his final defeat:

Now all labour
Mars what it does: yea, very force entangles
Itself with strength.

(IV, xiv, 47–9)

Antony to Eros, begging Eros to kill him:

Come then: for with a wound I must be cured.

(IV, xiv, 78)

Cleopatra, as Antony is being lifted up to the Monument:

Here's sport indeed! How heavy weighs my lord!
Our strength is all gone into heaviness,
That makes the weight.

(IV, xv, 32–4)

Agrippa to Caesar, on the death of Antony:

And strange it is,
That nature must compel us to lament
Our most persisted deeds.

(V, i, 28–30)

Caesar adds:

> O Antony,
> I have follow'd thee to this, but we do launce
> Diseases in our bodies
>
> (v, i, 35-7)

and Cleopatra to Dolabella on her Antony:

> His legs bestrid the ocean, his rear'd arm
> Crested the world: his voice was propertied
> As all the tuned spheres, and that to friends:
> But when he meant to quail, and shake the orb,
> He was as rattling thunder. For his bounty,
> There was no winter in 't: an autumn 'twas
> That grew the more by reaping.
>
> (v, ii, 82-8)

There are probably more of these fascinating inverted images that I have missed. The list is long but since it is Shakespeare, it can hardly be tedious. Well now, to borrow from Miss Spurgeon's famous title, What do these unusual forms of generation and corruption tell us about the play? Can it be that there is at least one form of nature and life that grows from itself and becomes fully itself at the very moment it becomes its opposite? In that case, it is not the image of a Nile that begets fertility then famine but an image of a Nile that in its abundance of fertility destroys itself that is suggested by many of these examples of abnormal generation and corruption. One thing becomes itself, generates more and more of itself and, in so doing, generates its own destruction, not successively but simultaneously. In human beings, this kind of generation and corruption is the ascent to the rarified – fire and air – from the baser elements – earth and water – an ascent which transcends and destroys. Listen to Cleopatra again:

> Husband, I come:
> Now to that name, my courage prove my title!
> I am fire, and air; my other elements
> I give to baser life.
>
> (v, ii, 286-9)

Earlier she says of Antony:

> Be'st thou sad, or merry,
> The violence of either thee becomes,
> So does it no man else.
>
> (I, v, 59-61)

For all, except Antony and herself, moderation is in order. But excess – the ascent that is both life-fulfilling and death-fulfilling – is for them. Antony sets this theme at the very beginning of the play:

> the nobleness of life
> Is to do thus: when such a mutual pair,
> And such a twain can do't.
>
> (I, i, 36-8)

Contrast this with Ventidius's comment:

> and ambition,
> The soldier's virtue, rather makes choice of loss,
> Than gain which darkens him.
>
> (III, i, 22-4)

Is, therefore, one theme in the play that there is in Antony's love for Cleopatra a coming into being (the intensity of fire) of a love (the rarefaction of air) that destroys in its very perfection? It seems to me that it is, yielding one implicative claim in the play. But the claim is not universal; it holds only for 'such a mutual pair / And such a twain can do't'. It does not apply to Ventidius or to you or me: no undeniable feature of human experience is affirmed. All this theme provides philosophically in the play is a pre-Socratic setting, with the Empedoclean principles of love and strife as the sole forces of generation and corruption.

This theme of a form of generation and corruption that destroys itself in its perfection may not be central in the play but it does relate to a number of its elements: the contrast and unity of external and internal vastness; the infinite variety and ultimate enigma of Cleopatra; Antony's role as a middle-aged hero who has experienced the gap of boredom; and the human as well as demi-god in Antony and Cleopatra, both of whom create gaps in nature by their presence and absence. They are made, as all of us are, of earth and water – the baser elements. They, not we, however, can become fire and air, can transcend the normal rhythms of nature and life.

If there is anything to this theme that I have sketched, *Antony and Cleopatra* is not Dryden's 'All for Love or the World Well Lost' or Enobarbus' 'Don't lose your head when you lose your heart'. Rather, there is something unique: that there is in the world (to use an image whose banality Shakespeare would not have tolerated) a kind of perfume which in its loveliness suffocates. Without the suffocation, no loveliness: that is the full choice. The alternative is the gap of boredom. Antony in effect chooses a form of generation that destroys itself in its perfection; but it is his escape from what has become to him the gap of Rome.

Two final observations: however one responds to the theme I have set forth, the imagery on which I have based it does not confirm the traditional dichotomizing of the language of the play into the Roman and the Egyptian. The imagery of abnormal forms of becoming is shared equally by the stolid Romans and the sensual Egyptians, as well as by the Egyptianized Romans, Enobarbus and Antony. The imagery of the causally abnormal may not yield the major philosophical theme or thesis of the play; but neither can any reading of the play survive without including it. Nor – to close the critical gap between the explored imagery and the putative absence of any

philosophical thesis in the play – can any *philosophical* reading of the play survive with it. For the imagery of the causally abnormal, in its context of the vast varieties of generation and corruption, forecloses on any philosophical formula which, in effect, must needs reduce the variety to a uniformity required by a universal generalization. Unlike, perhaps, *Hamlet*, where the varieties of experience do suggest a philosophical thesis – that we can put all the great questions but can secure none of their answers – *Antony and Cleopatra* does not yield even this minimum resolution of coming into being and passing away.

That Shakespeare does not universalize this theme of a perfection that destroys can perhaps be seen in a final bit of irresistible philosopher's nonsense. If we project the plays of Shakespeare to mirror in some way the relation between the poet and the world he has created, as can be done with the *Tempest* and *Hamlet* and even *King Lear*, perhaps we can see in *Antony and Cleopatra* the same nobleness that, in its intensity and rarefaction – its fire and air – transcends the baser elements of language to create a mode of ecstatic perfection that fulfils without destruction. The vicissitudes and the grandeur of poetry, thus, make it, too, one among the infinite varieties of generation, a form unlike love that does not destroy itself in its perfection. The nobleness of the play transcends even the exclusive nobleness of its two main characters.

SELF-CONSCIOUSNESS IN MONTAIGNE AND SHAKESPEARE

ROBERT ELLRODT

The encounter of two master-minds is always impressive, but after surveying the collected evidence for the influence of Montaigne upon Shakespeare, I came to the conclusion that I could not break fresh ground in the field of source-hunting and that the assessment of Shakespeare's alleged debt only required the exercise of judgement – an unexciting prospect. I therefore rapidly turned from the sifting of parallels to a broader consideration of the ways in which the minds of the French essayist and the English dramatist had worked in self-scrutiny. This was bound to be a study in modes of self-awareness, not in self-revelation since I could not pretend to trace Shakespeare's elusive self. My present interest is not in the contents but in the forms of self-consciousness; not in ideas but in faculties of the mind. Ideas in a play need not belong to the author nor even be seriously entertained by him. But no character can be invested with mental faculties not possessed by his creator.

When you compare minds rather than ideas, proof of influence is unattainable. Besides, the gradual development of self-consciousness in Shakespearian drama certainly did not originate in the reading of Montaigne. However, if it could be proved that an acquaintance with the *Essays* preceded the writing or rewriting of *Hamlet*, it might account for the heightening and refinement of self-analysis in this tragedy and some of the next plays.

The only indisputable echo of Montaigne in the plays of Shakespeare was pointed out by Edward Capell in 1780.[1] Though Margaret Hodgen proved in 1952 that Gonzalo's de-scription of an imaginary commonwealth in *The Tempest* 'might well have been written in the same vein' though the *Essays* had never 'fallen into the hands of the English dramatist',[2] the verbal borrowings from Florio's translation are beyond doubt.[3] But no evidence of this type is available for earlier plays, though hundreds of parallels have been offered from Robertson to the present day.[4] I shall not say with the Montaigne expert, Pierre Villey, that 'a hundred ciphers still add up to zero':[5] if

---

[1] *Notes and Various Readings to Shakespeare*, II (1780), 63.

[2] 'Montaigne and Shakespeare Again', *HLQ*, XVI (1962), 23–42.

[3] Hodgen's conclusion is cautious: 'Did Shakespeare borrow directly from Montaigne? . . . it seems not unlikely that some indebtedness may have existed.' But certainty is afforded by the recurrence of such phrases as 'no kinde of traffike', 'no name of magistrate', etc (*Tempest*, II, i, 144–8; *Essays*, transl. Florio, I, xxx, Everyman edition (1910) used throughout, I, 220). A close parallel in thought and diction between Prospero's reconciliation speech and the essay 'Of Crueltie' has been pointed out by Eleanor Prosser in *Shakespeare Studies* I (1966), 261–4.

[4] G. C. Taylor has the fullest list in *Shakespeare's Debt to Montaigne* (Oxford, 1925) but the earlier *Montaigne and Shakespeare* of J. M. Robertson (London, 1897, rev. 1909) and the later *Shakespeare und Montaigne* of Susanne Türck (Berlin, 1930) have a different emphasis. For other studies see S. A. Tannenbaum's Elizabethan Bibliography No. 24, *Michel Eyquiem de Montaigne* (New York, 1942), pp. 37–46. All important studies published after 1940 are mentioned in my notes.

[5] Quoted by G. C. Taylor (*Shakespeare's Debt*) from *The Book of Homage* (I. Gollancz ed., 1916), but Villey's fullest study is 'Montaigne et les poètes dramatiques anglais du temps de Shakespeare' in *Revue d'histoire littéraire de la France* 24 (1917),

one is satisfied with probability, accumulation has some weight. But the contrast between Shakespeare's unsettled debt and Marston's or Webster's obvious borrowings is illuminating in F. P. Wilson's shrewd comment: 'his common place book was his memory and he is the very Midas of poets, transmuting all he touched'.[1]

The controversy over the alleged Shakespeare autograph in the British Museum copy of Florio's translation is inconclusive. Tannenbaum's persistent and, some say, perverse vindication of its genuineness has not convinced the British Museum experts.[2] Anyhow the Florio volume might have come into Shakespeare's possession at any time between 1603 and 1611 and even an early acquisition would leave the poet's acquaintance with Montaigne unexplained in earlier plays.

Shakespeare, of course, might have read the *Essays* in the original from the outset of his career. He may not have lived with the Mountjoys before 1602, but his friendship with the Quineys in Stratford and his early connection with Richard Field, together with the scraps of French dialogue in his plays, gave William Carew Hazlitt and the Countess of Chambrun among others fairly sound arguments for an emphasis on his French background. Which does not mean that we should endorse Hazlitt's tempting speculation when he writes:

These Quineys, who were mercers and vintners, and had relations with London, if not with the wine-growing provinces of France, notably Bordeaux itself, were persons of exceptional culture, and Thomas, who subsequently espoused Judith Shakespeare, was a most likely man to invest in one of the earlier Bordeaux editions of the *Essays* on their first appearance.[3]

The parallels so far pointed-out make an acquaintance with the original unnecessary

357–93. He is severe on Marston, who mainly borrowed apophthegms and witticisms for the sake of ribaldry, though 'la philosophie de "De l'honnête

et de l'utile" passe en bonne partie dans *Sophonisbe*'. Webster shows an interest in moral observations and in metaphors. Shakespeare's only certain debt is the *Tempest* passage, but Villey qualifies his scepticism in a short list of 'rapprochements plus probants, mais non décisifs'. It includes *Measure for Measure* III, i, 22–4 and *Hamlet* II, ii, 252–3. For all references to Shakespeare, lines are numbered as in Dover Wilson's Cambridge edition.

[1] In *Shakespeare Survey 3* (1950), 19. In the same volume (p. 6), however, C. J. Sisson asserted: 'The evidence is adequate that he gave close study . . . to Florio's *Montaigne*.' His confidence contrasts with Wilson's 'agnostic' attitude.

[2] See E. Maunde Thompson, 'Two Pretended Autographs of Shakespeare', *Library* (July 1917), 193–217, and S. A. Tannenbaum, *Problems in Shakespeare's Penmanship* (New York, 1927), ch. 9 (a revision of an essay in *SP* (July 1925), 392–411). W. H. Kelliher, Assistant Keeper of the British Museum, expressed in a recent letter to me the 'personal opinion' that 'Tannenbaum's arguments offer no serious challenge to Maunde Thompson' and that he even spoiled his case altogether 'by setting by the side of this signature [at plates 43, 44] another one, labelled spurious, that looks like the work of the same hand'.

G. C. Taylor apparently sought confirmation of authenticity in the fact that '*previous to the year 1780* [italics mine] Mr Patteson used to exhibit the volume to his friends as a curiosity on account of the autograph'. Since Capell's note on *The Tempest* only appeared in a volume issued 'From the Press of Henry Hughes . . . Feb. 21st, 1780', and attention had not been called earlier to a relationship between Shakespeare and Montaigne, the inference is that no one would have thought of forging Shakespeare's signature on the Florio volume: see G. C. Taylor in *RES*, 5 (1929), 317–19, and cf. Longworth–Chambrun, *Shakespeare Retrouvé* (Paris, 1947), p. 200. But the existence of the signature 'previous to the year 1780' seems to rest only on the assertion of Sir Frederick Madden in a letter dated 'Jan. 11, 1837'. The ink analysis suggested by Taylor has not been attempted for 'it would require a specimen of the manuscript to be detached'. To the horror of librarians I dare express the opinion that mutilation would be worth while for the sake of truth.

[3] In *Shakespeare* (London, 1902), p. 156. L. de Chambrun has emphasized the French culture of Thomas Quiney and Richard Field in her *Giovanni Florio* (Paris, 1921) and *Shakespeare: Acteur–Poète* (Paris, 1926). Cf. Kathleen Lambley, *The Teaching and Cultivation of the French Language in England during Tudor and Stuart Times* (Manchester, 1920).

since William Cornwallis, in his own essays written before 1600, praised a translation of Montaigne circulating in manuscript. Florio's translation, according to Frances Yates, was begun at least by 1598.[1] In the Southampton circle Shakespeare might have had easy access to the manuscript, early enough to account for the parallels in *Henry V*, *Julius Caesar* and *As You Like It*, unconvincing though I find them.[2] Still fainter are 'the traces of Montaigne' discovered by Warwick Bond 'at least as early as 1596'.[3] More serious parallels in ideas undoubtedly suggest that the influence of Montaigne upon Shakespeare, if it ever existed, was at its height in *Hamlet*, *Troilus and Cressida*, *All's Well that Ends Well*, *Measure for Measure* and *King Lear*.

In Taylor's study of Shakespeare's debt to Florio's Montaigne this 'one broad generalization' is supported by impressive lists of phrasal correspondences and a glossary of 750 words selected from Florio, words which do not appear in Shakespeare before *Hamlet*. This type of cumulative evidence to my mind is more impressive in word supply than in the supply of ideas when the ideas are commonplaces. Once more it would not imply imitation. For a poet words have an attraction in themselves: the most arresting may have been treasured in Shakespeare's memory and readily used on occasion. In his edition of *King Lear* Professor Kenneth Muir has judiciously sifted Taylor's evidence for this one play and a general survey only confirms his conclusion that it would be 'unreasonable' to deny the influence of Florio.[4]

The trouble is that source-hunters, from Taylor to Susanne Türck, invite scepticism in their eagerness to find evidence. Most correspondences in ideas are vague and inconclusive: analogues have easily been found in other writers, in the classics, and in collections of *loci communes*. The Duke's speech to Claudio in *Measure for Measure* had been assumed to

collect many of Montaigne's stoical comments on life and death: Alice Harmon easily showed that the correspondences may be 'due to a common knowledge on the part of Shakespeare and Montaigne of classical aphorisms'. But when she declares it 'more likely' than a direct relation between the two writers, she may commit herself too far since 'no one passage' she cites from other works 'can be pointed out definitely as Shakespeare's source'.[5] In some cases the Montaigne parallel, though not close

---

[1] *John Florio* (Cambridge, 1934), p. 213. Another translation had been entered to E. Aggas on 20 October 1595.

[2] For *Julius Caesar*, see A. H. Upham, *The French Influence in English Literature from the Accession of Elizabeth to the Restoration* (New York, 1908), pp. 529–30. Max Deutschbein has traced in Jaques traits from Montaigne in 'Shakespeare's Kritik an Montaigne in *As You Like It*', *Neuphilologische Monatsschrift*, v (1934), 369–85. Alois Brandl argued that the monologue of the King in *Henry V*, IV, i, followed almost step by step the argument of Montaigne's essay 'Of the Incommodity of Greatness' (*Shakespeare Jahrbuch* (1899), 314) and the parallel was expanded by Marcel May in *Revue Anglo-Américaine* (Décembre 1931), 109–26, but the resemblance is general. Sir Sidney Lee had compared Montaigne on 'feasts, banquets . . . [that] rejoice them that but seldom see them' with *1 Henry IV*, I, ii, 181–4 and Sonnet 52, 5–7, but there is no evidence of borrowing.

[3] In *Love's Labour's Lost* and *The Merchant of Venice*: see his interesting review of the second edition of Robertson's book in *MLR*, 5 (1910), 367.

[4] Arden Shakespeare, rev. ed. (1962), Appendix 6, pp. 249–53. Muir also surveys parallels in ideas offered by W. B. Drayton Henderson in 'Montaigne's *Apologie of Raymond Sebond* and *King Lear*' (*Shakespeare Association Bulletin*, 14 (1939), 209–25, and 15 (1940), 40–54) and wisely comes to the conclusion that 'it is difficult to go all the way with Henderson, some of whose views are rather fanciful'. Some are even definitely wrong. When Montaigne writes 'Let a Philosopher be put in a Cage . . .' (II, xxii, p. 314), he describes a situation not meant to give him an experience of paradise in prison as in the alleged Lear analogue ('Come, let's away to prison', v, iii, 7–15) but a very unpleasant experience of fear and dizziness.

[5] 'How Great was Shakespeare's Debt to Montaigne?', *PMLA*, 57 (1942), 1000.

enough to prove influence, is definitely closer than the new parallels offered.[1] Besides, Alice Harmon often disregarded the trend of argument. It is easy, indeed, to supply 'descriptions of the beauty of the heavens quite like those just quoted from Montaigne's *Essays* and from *Hamlet*'.[2] But a real analogue would be a passage expressing a mood in which 'this brave o'erhanging firmament' appears no other thing 'than a foul and pestilent congregation of vapours' (*Hamlet*, II, ii, 309–15). Such a mood does not appear in the *loci communes* cited. The contrast in Montaigne is between 'the majesty of the universe' and the vainglory of the 'miserable and wretched creature' which 'dareth call himselfe Master and Emperour of this Universe' (II, xii; p. 139). A different contrast, I admit, but the underlying irony in the *Essays* and in *Hamlet* at least discloses a kinship in spirit not traceable in the other analogues. Likewise, when Hardin Craig argued with admirable scholarship that Cardan's *De Consolatione*, not Montaigne's *Essays*, was Hamlet's book[2] he had to place twice an emphasis on thoughts which, to my mind, are irrelevant to the main line of argument. When Hamlet claims that 'conscience does make cowards of us all', whatever meaning may be attached to 'conscience', the line cannot mean that 'conscience tells us we are cowards', for it would imply that conscience works against our cowardice instead of making us cowards.[3] Moreover, Cardan argues that the remedy for the fear of death is virtue whereas Hamlet argues that the fear of death deters man from 'enterprises of great pitch and moment'. Even if we identified Cardan's virtue with *virtus*, the argument would remain different.

Craig saw Hamlet striving like Cardan to meet his trials with fortitude in accordance with the stoical maxims: 'man is but his mind, there are no ills in life but only in imagination' (p. 29). Whether this applies to the Prince who tells Horatio 'Thou wouldst not think how ill all's here about my heart' (V, ii, 210–11) is at least open to question. Besides, Shakespeare's emphasis in the last scenes is not on 'valiancy' nor on 'the pacient mind', but on the 'divinity that shapes our ends, / Rough-hew them how we will' (V, ii, 10–11). And here, in the very word 'rough-hew', is perhaps one of the least uncertain signs of Florio's influence: 'My consultation', he translated, 'doth somewhat roughly hew the matter... the main and chiefe points of the works, I am wonte to resigne to heaven' (III, viii, p. 171).

In judging of affinities the agreement of a great many minds through the ages deserves attention though our age does not believe in common notions. Sensitive readers of *Hamlet* have been persistently reminded of Montaigne, from John Sterling in 1838 to Harry Levin in *The Question of Hamlet*.[4] Even Stedefeld and

---

[1] E.g. the Montaigne parallel to *Measure for Measure* III, i, 22–4, given by Upham (*French Influence in English Literature*, p. 532) and accepted by Villey, rather than the passage translated from Seneca in *The Defence of Death* (Harmon, 'Shakespeare's Debt', pp. 1004–5).

[2] 'Hamlet's Book Cardan's *De Consolatione*', *HLB* (November 1934), 17–37.

[3] *Ibid.*, pp. 23 and 29–30. Cardan in 'his Christian moments' also holds up the prospect of 'heavenly joyes' (pp. 28–9), conspicuously ignored by Hamlet.

[4] In the *London and Westminster Review* (July 1838), 321, Sterling wrote: 'the Prince of Denmark is very nearly a Montaigne, lifted to a higher eminence, and agitated by more striking circumstances and a severer destiny, and altogether a somewhat more passionate structure of man'. Later critics have merely expanded this statement, whether striking the likeness with Robertson, Taylor and Türck, or the difference in passionate feeling and expression with Warwick Bond. To Harry Levin 'in introspection, [Hamlet's] mentor is Montaigne', whose philosophy and phraseology reverberate through the play. But, he adds, 'the Prince of Denmark cannot, like the country gentleman of Bordeaux, sleep soundly on a pillow of incuriosity' (*The Question of Hamlet* (New York, 1959), pp. 72–3). M. Deutschbein comes to the conclusion that Shakespeare agrees with Montaigne's 'Weltsicht und Lebensanschauung' on many points,

Jacob Feis in their vagaries, Robertson in his brilliant rashness, Susanne Türck in her frequent vagueness, agree with Taylor and more cautious critics on the extent of the influence, whether positive or negative.[1] I am not impressed by the number of alleged parallels – 100 to 170[2] – but by the closeness of some of them: half a dozen.[3] Hamlet, of course, often reacts in another way than Montaigne even when he seems to borrow his ideas from him and his words from Florio: 'Death may peradventure be a thing indifferent, happily a thing desirable...If it be a consummation of one's being, it is also an...entrance into a long and quiet night. We find nothing so sweet in life, as a quiet rest and gentle sleepe, and without dreames' (*Essayes*, III, xii; pp. 308–9). However, evidence for the influence of Montaigne is also found by Harry Levin in the atmosphere of the play, the attitude of questioning and doubt and 'a certain essayistic movement of thought'. If 'to raise all the important questions without obtaining the answers' is the philosophical characteristic.of *Hamlet*, it is also the distinctive trend of the *Essays*.[4]

My own conviction mainly rests on the unnoted fact that three *consecutive* essays in the Second Booke – 'We taste nothing purely', 'Against idlenesse, or doing nothing', 'Of bad means employed to a good end' – offer some of the closest parallels and may have suggested both the characters of Hamlet and Fortinbras.

The essay 'We taste nothing purely' – which also caught the imagination of Marston[5] – could explain Hamlet's behaviour as an avenger:

for the use of life and service of publike society, there may be excesse in the purity and perspicuity of our spirits. This piercing brightnes hath over-much subtility and curiosity...Therefore are vulgar and lesse-wire-drawne-wits found to be more fit and happy in the conduct of affaires. And the exquisite and high-raised opinions of Philosophy, unapt and unfit to exercise. This sharp vivacity of the spirit, and this supple and restlesse volubility, troubleth

our negociations. Humane enterprises should be managed more grosely and superficially, and have a good and great part of them left for the rights of fortune

– as Hamlet discovers on his way to England. But he has before plagued himself with 'sundry

but gives a new significance to the thoughts of Montaigne at some points and definitely opposes him at other points: 'Shakespeare's *Hamlet* und Montaigne', *Shakespeare-Jahrbuch*, 80–1 (1944–5), 70–107.

[1] G. F. Stedefeld in *Hamlet; ein Tendenzdrama Shakespeares gegen die skeptische und kosmopolitische Weltanschauung des Michael de Montaigne* (Berlin, 1871) argued that Shakespeare wrote Hamlet or 'the Drama of the Doubter' to free himself from the scepticism of Montaigne. J. Feis sought to demonstrate that the main traits of Montaigne's character were conferred on the Danish Prince to expose the superstitious notions and inconsistency of a Humanist who remained an adherent of Romanist dogmas: *Shakespeare and Montaigne* (1884), ch. 4.

[2] According to E. E. Schmid, 'Shakespeare, Montaigne und die schauspielerische Formel', *Shakespeare-Jahrbuch* 82–3 (1945–6).

[3] Parallels both in thought and phrasing:

Hamlet III, i, 60–5	Florio III, xii –III, 308–9
IV, iii, 19–24	II, xii–II, 155
V, ii, 10–11	III, viii–III, 171
V, ii, 218–20	I, xix–I, 89

Parallels in thought only:

Hamlet III, i, 83–8 }	
IV, iv, 40–3 }	Florio II, xx–II, 401–2

Hamlet's assertion of relativity, 'There is nothing either good or bad, but thinking makes it so' (II, ii, 252–3), can be traced to Lyly or Spenser, to Cardan, Baldwin or Nicholas Ling (see Robertson, *Montaigne and Shakespeare*, and F. P. Wilson, *Shakespeare Survey 3*, p. 19), but though the statement in *Politeuphia* (1597) – 'There is nothing grievous if the thought make it not so' – seemed to Wilson 'closer to Hamlet in wording and in date', one may still think with Robertson that in Hamlet it is no incidental or wayward utterance: 'we find the formula felt', as in Montaigne who devotes a whole chapter to the notion 'That the taste of goods or evils doth greatly depend on the opinion we have of them' (*Essays*, I, xl; cf. I, l; p. 343).

[4] Levin, *The Question of Hamlet*, p. 73; Morris Weitz, *Hamlet and the Philosophy of Literary Criticism* (Chicago, 1964).

[5] See *Plays of John Marston*, ed. H. H. Wood, II, 194 and 338.

subtill and sharpe considerations' and, like Simonides, 'doubting which might be the likeliest, he altogether dispaireth of the truth'.[1] This is the interpretation of Hamlet forced upon us not by the Romantics but by Shakespeare himself, unless we pretend the Danish Prince deceived himself about his own 'scruple' of 'thinking too precisely on the event' (IV, iv, 40–1). The same essay would have reminded him that *'Man all in all, is but a botching and party-coloured worke'* and convinced him that 'When I religiously confess my selfe unto my selfe, I finde the best good I have, hath some vicious taint'.[2] The cluster of Hamlet-like ideas is the more remarkable when the next essay supplies models for the fighting Prince, Fortinbras, arguing that a 'vertuous and coragious Prince' should 'manage his wars...by himselfe' (II, xxi; p. 403). And, to mingle the words of the poet and the essayist, a little further on, the invitation 'greatly to find quarrel in a straw / When honour's at the stake' (IV, iv, 55–6) might seem 'very strange and incredible; if we were not daily accustomed to see in our wars many thousands of forraigne nations, for a very small some of mony, to engage both their blood and life in quarrels wherein they are nothing interested' (II, xxiii; p. 412).

Should the reading of Montaigne have thrown 'the pale cast of thought' over Hamlet and perhaps Brutus, the case would be strengthened for a pervasive influence of the *Essays* in the tragedies and the problem plays. I shall not revive the extravagant claims of Philarète Chasles about the 'complete and sudden change' produced in the plays of Shakespeare by the thought and style of the *Essays*, nor Robertson's contention that Montaigne was 'the deep striking intelligence that first stirred him to philosophise'.[3] But I cannot agree that Florio's translation was only used as a 'storehouse' of ideas, images and phrases.[4] If Shakespeare did 'soak' his mind in the *Essays*,

as various critics have claimed, it was no doubt because they met his needs at the moment. What he may have owed to the formulated thought of Montaigne in his views on human nature or even his methods of characterization, has been fully explored by Paul Reyher, Max Deutschbein, Eduard Eugen Schmid and Robert Fricker in fairly recent studies.[5] I shall now concentrate on the change a reading of Montaigne could provoke in the experiencing mind. I introduce the concept of self-consciousness to approach the problem from a different angle and to reach the cause behind the effects. Doubt, irresolution, inconstancy in characters 'compact of jars', even self-dramatization and introspection, are related to different forms of self-consciousness.

I have been attempting for years to trace the emergence in European literature of a form of self-consciousness which implies a simultaneous awareness of experience and the experiencing self: it arises whenever a thought or emotion is perceived as *my* thought, *my* emotion in the very moment of experience. I cannot summarize the argument without distortion.[6] Yet

[1] *Essays* II, xx; II, 401–2.

[2] Cf. *Hamlet*, I, iv, 23–38; II, ii, 533–4; III, i, 122–30, and the general spirit of the play.

[3] *Montaigne and Shakespeare* (1909 ed.), p. 289. Philarète Chasles, a pioneer in comparative European literary history, set forth his thesis in *Etudes sur Shakespeare* (Paris, 1851), pp. 176ff.

[4] As E. R. Hooker maintained in 'The Relation of Shakespeare to Montaigne', *PMLA*, 17 (1902), 312–60.

[5] P. Reyher, *Essai sur les Idées dans l'oeuvre de Shakespeare* (Paris, 1947), pp. 420–45; Deutschbein, 'Shakespeare's Hamlet und Montaigne' (see n. 4 p. 40); Schmid, 'Shakespeare, Montaigne und die schauspielerische Formal', p. 103 (see n. 2 p. 41); R. Fricker, *Kontrast und Polarität in der Characterbildern Shakespeares* (Bern, 1951).

[6] I hope to correct and enlarge into a book a premature statement of my thesis in a not easily accessible article: 'Genèse et dilemme de la conscience moderne', *Revue de la Méditerranée*, 49–51 (1952), 293–306, 387–403, 543–60. There are analyses of different forms of self-consciousness in my *Poètes*

I have to put it thus. Greek thought saw itself outside itself: Plato in *Alcibiades* 132–3 invites the soul 'to look at a soul', not into herself, when she wishes to know herself, as the eye sees itself by directing its glance at the pupil of another eye. And when he came to look into himself the Platonist or Neo-Platonist, from Antiquity to the Renaissance, transcended himself in mystic introspection to reach the divine, the God *interior intimo meo*. Strictly Socratic self-knowledge had been pragmatic: know what you are capable of. Christianity turned it into 'know thy sins'. Medieval and Renaissance allegory, as C. S. Lewis has shown in the *Allegory of Love*, implied an awareness of the inner life and its conflicts, but it prolonged the objective apprehension of the passions as independent and warring forces. And statements by both Augustine and Montaigne show that the experience of self-division had long favoured a belief in the presence of several souls in one man.[1]

In the *Essays* of Montaigne Christian self-examination was laicized and stripped from the trappings of allegory. This was part of a general movement: a heightened sense of individuality and a sharper observation of the inner workings of the passions may be observed in many late Renaissance writers. Montaigne, however, was original in his *concentration* on the quest for self-knowledge – 'I dare not onely speake of my selfe: but speake alone of my selfe' (III, viii; p. 181) – in his *self-exhibition* – 'I greedily long to make my selfe knowne' (III, v; p. 69) – and the realization that the essence of his elusive self was bound to evade his inquiry. With Montaigne as with Donne the search for identity can only end in perplexity and leave us wondering with the poet at 'what we know not, our selves' (*Negative Love*).

As critics have observed, Shakespeare and Montaigne are at one in their acknowledgement of 'the inconstancie of our actions'. It was no new theme, and required no more than observation. But Montaigne gave it a new meaning through his self-consciousness. Gidian 'disponibilité' and Sartrian 'liberté' seem to be anticipated in statements that imply that our affections and our convictions are never so firmly rooted but we may discard them at any time to assume different affections and convictions:

'If I speak diversely of my selfe', he pointed out, 'it is because I look diversely upon myselfe' (II, i; p. 12). Which means that the contrarieties observed are not only found in the self as object, but also in the self as subject, the ego. They proceed from a mode of consciousness characterized by an ever-shifting point of view:

The blast of accidents doth not only remove me according to his inclination: for besides, I remove and trouble my selfe by the instability of my posture, and whosoever looketh narrowly about himselfe, shall hardly see him selfe twice in one same state. Sometimes I give my soule one visage, and some times another, according unto the posture or side I lay her in (II, i; pp. 11–12).

This goes beyond an observation of inconstancy or even a sense of relativity. Montaigne does not describe a succession of moods: he shows how he can throw himself into a mood. He takes in several aspects of his own self at a glance and chooses to emphasize one of them. 'All contrarieties are found' in the self, but 'according to some turne or removing' (*id.*; p. 12).

Métaphysiques Anglais (Paris, 1960, 1972), Pt I, Bk I, chs. 3–5; Bk II, ch. 1, sec. 2; Bk III, ch. 1, sec. 1, ch. 3, sec. 2; Bk IV, ch. 1, sec. 1, ch. 2, secs. 2–4; Pt II, ch. 5, sec. 1; ch. 6, secs. 2–3.

[1] *Essays*, II, i: 'This supple variation, and easie yeelding contradiction, which is sene in us, hath made some to imagine, that we had two soules, and others, two faculties' (II; p. 11). Cf. *Confessions* VIII, x: 'ego eram, qui volebam, ego, qui nolebam. Ideo mecum contendebam et dissipabar a me ipso, et ipsa dissipatio me invito quidem fiebat, nec tamen ostendebat naturam mentis alienae, sed poenam meae'.

When the inconstancy discovered in the conflicting impulses is traced to the conscious act of the mind, the consequence is dispersion or confusion. Before the modern novelists Montaigne knew that character does not exist:

Shamefast, bashfull, insolent, chaste, luxurious, peevish, pratling, silent, fond, doting, laborious, nice, delicate, ingenious, slow, dull, froward, humorous, debonaire, wise, ignorant, false in words, true-speaking, both liberall, covetous and prodigall. All these I perceive in some measure or other to bee in me, *according as I stirre or turne my selfe*; And whosoever shall heedfully survay and consider himselfe, shall find this volubility and discordance to be in himselfe, yea and *in his very judgement*. I have nothing to say entirely, simply, and with soliditie of my selfe, without confusion, disorder, blending, mingling... (II, i; p. 12; my italics).

The language is still substantialist but the intuition is eminently modern. Montaigne was only a shrewd observer when he asserted in another context: 'we are double in ourselves, which is the cause that what we beleeve, we beleeve it not' (II, xvi; p. 342). But at the back of his observation was the intense self-consciousness which later led analysts like Amiel and phenomenologists like Sartre to claim that we never believe enough in what we believe, never feel enough what we feel: 'on ne croit jamais à ce qu'on croit'.[1] When emotion and belief grow self-conscious they are removed from the perceiving mind in the mirror of consciousness and we realize we are playing a part. The hero of *Les Mains Sales* exclaims: 'You think I am in despair. Not at all. I am acting the comedy of despair.' This, I think, is the deeper intuition behind Montaigne's proclamation of inconstancy in terms of the traditional theatrical metaphor: 'We are all framed of flaps and patches and of so shapelesse and diverse a contexture that every peece and every moment playeth his part' (II, i; p. 14). What the modern philosopher describes as the insincerity commanded by the very structure

of consciousness, Montaigne – and John Donne as well – could only describe as inconstancy, but genuinely experienced through the free play of distancing irony and through the failure of their attempts at self-definition.

When the essayist writes 'I describe not the essence, but the passage' he describes a passage in the mind:

It is a counter-roule of divers and variable accidents, and irresolute imaginations, and sometimes contrary: whether it be that my selfe am other, or that I apprehend subjects by other circumstances and considerations...Were my mind setled, *I would not essay but resolve my selfe* (III, ii; p. 23; my italics).

This remarkable declaration gives us the full meaning of the title chosen. In his *Essays* Montaigne was essaying himself, exploring and trying out his possible selves in their multiplicity.[2] And he never resolved himself since he never could attain fixity, nor unity, never could define himself. Yet his aim, as elsewhere proclaimed, was to communicate his essential self: 'I write not my gests, but my selfe and my essence' (II, vi; p. 60). But though he sat complacently for his self-portrait, he only noted impressions: 'I describe not the essence but the passage' he declared in another essay (III, ii; p. 23). The contradiction is only removed if we recognize that the essence here is in the passage, that the universal being, 'l'estre universel', of Michel de Montaigne is best revealed through this calling in question of his own self, this hopeless yet incessant search for an elusive identity.

[1] *L'être et le néant*, 2e éd. (Paris, 1943), p. 110. Conversely Montaigne studies phenomena of self-persuasion in the 'Apologie of Raymond Sebond' (II, xii): 'Preachers know, that the emotion, which surpriseth them, whilst they are in their earnest speech, doth animate them towards belief' (II, p. 261).

[2] The common justification of the title is found in the statement: 'toute cette fricassée que je barbouille ici n'est qu'un registre des essais de ma vie' (III, xiii; Florio, III; p. 339: 'a register of my lives-Essayes'), 'essais' meaning 'expériences' (note to the Pléiade edition of the *Essays* by A. Thibaudet, p. 1211).

The Renaissance mind slowly broke away from the prevailing objectivity of the Ancient and Mediaeval mind in the apprehension of the inner life. Elizabethan drama at large and Shakespearian drama in particular evidence this momentous change. Again in rough outline, I shall say that the characters move from sheer self-assertion or self-dramatization to subtler forms of self-consciousness. Thus will the dramatic monologue, originally directed at the audience, turn into a genuine soliloquy, an image of the living mind.

Self-assertion, as one knows, became a common feature among Machiavellian characters. From Machiavelli's proclamation in Harvey's epigram – 'I alone am wise, I alone live and triumph for myself'[1] – to Richard III's 'I am my selfe alone' (*3 Henry VI*, v, vi, 83) and the Bastard's 'And I am I, how e'er I was begot' (*King John*, I, i, 175), there is little progress in the depth of self-consciousness. When the assertion of personal identity and will power is in the Stoic strain, as in later drama and satire, it is fraught with moral earnestness, but need not imply self-analysis.

Though the first person singular is prominent in such statements, in early plays the characters insistently resort to the third person when expressing their thoughts and feelings. Hamlet will do so once, but not in a soliloquy: only to distinguish between his true self and Hamlet 'when he's not himself' (v, ii, 231–5). With Greene and Marlowe the constant use of the third person is, of course, rhetorical, but it does suggest a kind of self-projection into a dramatic figure, as if the character saw himself outside himself – the primary pattern of self-consciousness, distinctly objective and almost impersonal.[2] That it is an early stage in the development of self-consciousness is, I think, confirmed by child psychology.

The evolution begins with Greene and Marlowe. In *James IV*, probably Greene's last play, the rhetorical use of the third person is far less obtrusive.[3] Marlowe will never discard it, as Mortimer's last words show;[4] but the monologues of Faustus, unlike Tamburlaine's lyrical speeches, are not spoken to the audience. Yet, between the soliloquies of Hamlet or Macbeth and those monologues, dramatically vivid though they are, there is the difference between 'pensée pensante' and 'pensée pensée', to borrow a distinction from Gabriel Marcel. The first soliloquy is not a train of associations connecting thoughts and images as they arise in the thinking mind. It is solidified thought with a clear logical pattern; the insistent and premeditated symmetry extends to details. Besides, the monologue is a short-cut and a summary, compassing a gradual realization of the fruitlessness of all arts and sciences, a conviction that could only have been borne in upon Faustus after years of study. The last soliloquy is an image of an experience that could actually be lived through by the mind in this way, though an 'hour' is contracted into minutes for the sake of dramatic concentration. The mind moves freely and its associations are imaginative or emotional rather than logical. Irregularities in syntax and prosody convey

[1] *In Gratulationum Valdinenses* (1578), quoted by Michel Poirer in *Christopher Marlowe* (London, 1950), p. 49. Cf. his attack on Nashe for admiring only 'his wondrous selfe' (*ibid.*, p. 58, note).

[2] In Greene's *Alphonsus, King of Arragon*, the main characters constantly express themselves in the third person: Alphonsus, ll. 260, 266, 372, 421 ('What thoughts *Alphonsus* casteth in his mind'); Carinus, 114, 167; Belinus, 279, 461, 470, 517, 561; Albinius, 186–207, 242, 258; Medea, 854, 875, 1664, etc. In *Frier Bacon and Frier Bongay* see Bacon, ll. 217–21, 256, 316, 567–71, 617, 1340, but also Margaret, 1016, 1021, 1062, 1514, 1521–2.

[3] Almost confined to Ateukin, a descendant of the Vice, e.g. ll. 342, 1294. But the King and Ateukin in their speeches and monologues address themselves in the traditional, 'objective' way, as if speaking to a 'persona': 'But, wretched King . . .' (ll. 184–201; cf. 274–96, 433).

[4] *Edward II*, ll. 2632–4; cf. l. 2333, and *Faustus*, ll. 1427, 1430, 1445, 1456.

intense emotion. Yet Faustus does not pass beyond egotism and self-dramatization to subjective self-analysis, and earlier in the play the Good and Bad Angels were even more objective than the two souls in one breast of the Ancients.[1]

Shakespeare started where Marlowe left off. After the First Part of *Henry VI* he dropped the third person in self-expression, apart from special occasions, like Caesar's boasting, solemn vows or moments when it emphasizes, as in Troilus, the exemplary value of a character.[2] Self-dramatization was used in ever subtler ways. No hint from Montaigne was necessary since Richard III and Richard II already prove born actors, forever performing parts, creating or improving occasions for a display of histrionic talent.[3] Peter Ure found it unsafe to suppose that Richard II, 'because he continually takes the centre of the stage... necessarily enjoys playing a part' (*Richard II*, Arden ed., p. lxxix). But Richard himself says 'Thus play I in one person many people' (v, v, 31). When he tells his followers 'let us sit upon the ground / And tell sad stories of the death of kings' (III, ii, 155–6) or asks the Queen: 'Tell thou the lamentable fall of me, / And send the hearers weeping to their beds' (v, i, 44ff.) he laments his fate by projecting himself into a story, past or future, as an object of contemplation and pity in a collective experience. Hamlet's injunction to Horatio – 'in this harsh world draw thy breath in pain / To tell my story' (v, ii, 346–7) – is not essentially different, but in the experience of his concern to let 'a wounded name' live behind him the tone is more private.

The soliloquies in the earlier plays involve a certain amount of self-analysis. Gloucester, after addressing the audience in his monologues of self-definition in both *Henry VI* and *Richard III*, will address himself in a repentance soliloquy which is no longer a projection of himself into a *persona*. He apparently allows

us to enter his consciousness and flashes on us the equation of character and ego: 'Richard loves Richard; that is, I am I' (*Richard III*, v, iii, 177–206). But his debate with himself, formalized in objective questions and answers, is a construction of experience and ends in allegory.[4] We seem closer to Hamlet with Richard II. Yet when the king in prison peoples his little world with 'thoughts' he declares begotten by the 'father' soul on his female brain (v, v, 6–10) like many sonneteers he still seems to contemplate 'thought outside itself' in the ancient and mediaeval way. He narrates what his thoughts 'plot' or how they 'flatter themselves' like 'silly beggars' (v, v, 18–30). To borrow a distinction from the terminology used for the study of the novel, he still gives us 'summary' rather than 'scene'.[5]

The evolution from rhetoric and objectivity towards more spontaneous forms of self-awareness is perceptible in the comedies as in the histories. Proteus in *The Two Gentlemen of Verona* (II, vi, 1–30) still justified his treachery and deluded himself in Petrarchan dialectics of logical rather than psychological complexity. Berowne in *Love's Labour's Lost* (III, i,

---

[1] *Faustus*, ll. 1419–69 and 623–8, 691–5.

[2] *Julius Caesar*, III, i; cf. Brutus in II, i, 58; *Troilus*, III, ii, 168–99.

[3] As generally noted for Richard III; on Richard II see G. Bonnard, 'The Actor in *Richard II*', *Shakespeare-Jahrbuch* (1952), 80–101.

[4] I dissent from W. Clemen's analysis (*A Commentary on Shakespeare's Richard III* (Gottingen, 1957; tr. 1968), pp. 218–22) on this one point, though I agree 'Richard appears to speak at the very moment of experience'.

[5] The development of self-consciousness should also be traced in the novel or romance. It was slow. Jean Rousset has recently pointed out the limitations of the introspective monologue in the French romances of the seventeenth century: 'Le XVIIe siècle se borne à essayer ce nouvel instrument si propre à l'exploration sur le vif d'une sensibilité sans en dégager les virtualités introspectives . . .' ('Le monologue romanesque à la recherche de lui même', *Mouvements Premiers, Etudes critiques offertes à Georges Poulet* (Paris, 1972)).

178–207), the Bastard in *King John* (II, i, 587–97, particularly 586–92) dispel illusions, see clearly into their own hearts, and the lively spontaneity of their soliloquies is unprecedented. The same dramatic vividness obtains in the monologues of *Henry IV* (Pt 2, III, i, 4–31) and *Henry V* (IV, i, 245–301), but the Kings address Sleep or Ceremony as the Bastard had railed on Commodity: no introspection is required.

Julius Caesar may seem to mark a decisive advance: over Brutus steals the pale cast of thought. But the main part of his monologue is deliberative – to kill or not to kill – and when he describes his state of mind as an insurrection (II, i, 63–9) the point of view remains objective. Hamet and Macbeth will convey what this insurrection feels like in their very language; Brutus only defines it as it might have been defined in a moral treatise.

What is new in Hamlet's soliloquies is not the self-analysis, though more extensive than ever before, whether under the influence of Montaigne or not. There are also precedents for the dramatic immediacy, though never before had we been allowed to 'enter the stream of consciousness' with greater truth.[1] In the first monologue – 'O, that this too too sullied flesh would melt…' (I, ii, 129–59), we watch the flotsam and jetsam of the mind heaving with the ebb and flow of emotion and the thought moves from the feeling to the cause or object of feeling. At other times, no doubt, the personal experience will be generalized but it often was in Montaigne as well.

Because of the immediacy of his self-consciousness Hamlet is capable of irony directed at himself in the very moment of passion. In the Hecuba soliloquy (II, ii, 553ff.), at the pitch of his fury against Claudius and against himself, he suddenly realizes what is histrionic in his frenzied attempt to unpack his heart with words: 'Why, what an ass am I…' (l. 596). With due diffidence I am tempted to add that he discovers, like the hero of Sartre, that he has been acting the comedy of indignation. After all, what moves Hamlet to admire and envy the deep tragedian is not the player's capacity for action but his ability to act so as to 'force his soul so to his own conceit'. A dream of passion – grief for Hecuba – acquires, through his acting, the fulness, roundness and reality of grief in itself, grief self-subsistent and aesthetically satisfying, not the kind of grief Hamlet can feel for his father in shreds and patches of intermittent passion. Are words really used by Hamlet to lash himself into action or mainly to whip up his own emotions? Did he earlier reject 'the trappings and the suits of woe' (I, ii, 86), will he later parody the ranting of Laertes over Ophelia's grave (V, i, 268–77) because his own emotions are too deep for words or out of an intuition that no self-conscious emotion is fully genuine? He himself seems capable of feeling only in fits and outbursts, which might account for his procrastination, his callousness to Ophelia, his strange coolness after causing disasters.[2]

This may be to consider it too curiously. What is certain is that Hamlet's brooding introspection does not achieve, but defeats, self-knowledge. Like Montaigne he is uncertain about his own motives, about the true cause of his delay:

> Whether it be
> Bestial oblivion, or some craven scruple
> Of thinking too precisely on th'event
> …I do not know.
>
> (IV, iv, 31–43)[3]

[1] As H. Levin and other critics have noticed.

[2] After killing Polonius – a disaster if he still loved Ophelia – and after Ophelia's burial in his dialogue with Horatio and Osric.

[3] Cf. the Montaigne passages quoted on pp. 41–4. Granville-Barker had observed that Hamlet 'does not reach self-understanding . . . The baffled "I do not know . . ." is his last word on the matter' (*Prefaces to Shakespeare* (Princeton, 1947), I, 253–4). This does not mean that Hamlet's 'ignorance of himself' contrasts with the self-knowledge achieved by other

Professor Muir has noted it: 'It is a curious paradox that the one intellectual among Shakespeare's tragic heroes should be least able to know why he acts or fails to act.'[1] Could it not be a universal paradox, at least with intellectuals? Self-consciousness so exercised is apt to dissolve character and motive, as the literature of the modern age shows.

To prick illusions only requires gifts of observation but an interest in the exposure of self-delusion is a sign of self-consciousness in the writer, as evidenced by Montaigne and by later moralists, either in the vein of the *Essays* or in the Puritan or Jansenist vein. Frances Bolen in her recent study of *Irony and Self-Knowledge in the Creation of Tragedy* fails to distinguish between the 'mystery of self-deceiving'[2] and the blindness of Othello or Gloucester, who allow themselves to be deceived, or the blindness of Lear who is deluded about others, about the nature of man; or about the character of a king.[3] The workings of self-consciousness as a reflexive act are better illustrated by Troilus or Angelo.

Both Troilus and Cressida are conscious of a self-division. The introspective self-awareness of Troilus, already perceptible in his anticipation of sensual delights (III, ii, 17–28, 34–8), is best displayed in his inward apprehension of his lover's unfaithfulness: 'this is, and is not, Cressid' because

> Within my soul there doth conduce a fight
> Of this strange nature, that a thing inseparate
> Divides more wider than the sky and earth.
>
> (v, ii, 147–9)

When Cressida earlier said

> I have a kind of self resides with you,
> But an unkind self that itself will leave
>
> (III, ii, 147–8)

the experience was not original, yet a vivid self-awareness seems to be denoted by the insistence on 'self' and by the recurrence in the play of such compounds as 'self-admission', 'self-assumption', 'self-affected' (II, iii, 164, 123, 236). Incidentally, I think that the sudden and massive appearance of those compounds in late sixteenth-century and chiefly in seventeenth-century English is not mainly due to imitation of Greek compounds in *auto*, as the O.E.D. suggests, but to the heightened self-consciousness of the writers.[4]

In the first soliloquy of Angelo the very process of self-awareness, as Dodds already noticed, is shown 'in the moment of becoming conscious'.[5] The agony of his divided mind forces upon him the question: 'What dost thou? or what art thou, Angelo? (II, ii, 173).

tragic heroes, as Frances Bolen argues in *Irony and Self-Knowledge in the Creation of Tragedy* (Salzburg, 1973), p. 216. What Lear and Othello discover is not really their true selves but their errors, and a higher truth. Unlike them, Hamlet cannot know himself though he looks into himself from the beginning.

[1] *Shakespeare's Tragic Sequence* (1972), p. 88.

[2] The phrase I use is the title of a treatise by Daniel Dyke (London, 1614), a follower of Augustine and a predecessor of La Rochefoucauld. The book is one of the landmarks in the development of religious and moral self-consciousness in the seventeenth century.

[3] *Irony and Self-Knowledge*, ch. 5. See n. 3, pp. 47–8.

[4] The only compounds recorded in *O.E.D.* before 1580 are: self-like (1556), self-liking (1561), self-love (1563), self-minded (1530), self-murder (1563), self-opinion (1579), self-praise (1549), self-same (1407), self-soothing (1571), self-wise (1561). Some fifty new compounds could be listed for the period 1580–1600. The large number of such compounds in translations is linguistically explainable, but Sidney's insistent use and creativeness may not be merely rhetorical: his mind willingly turned in upon himself.

The more philosophical compounds appear in the seventeenth century: self-centred, self-confidence, self-conscious, self-content, self-delusion, self-determination, self-essence, self-examination, self-experience, self-interest, self-knowledge, self-preservation, self-respect, self-righteous, self-sufficiency, etc.

[5] W. M. T. Dodds, 'The Character of Angelo in *Measure for Measure*' in *Discussions of Shakespeare's Problem Comedies*, ed. R. Ornstein (Boston, 1961).

This is the living confirmation of Isabella's earlier remark on

> proud man...
> Most ignorant of what he's most assured –
> His glassy essence
>
> (II, ii, 119–21)

And Angelo's new self-awareness allows him to probe into the depth of what might have been a subconscious association: in this man, whose love of purity is genuine, sexual desire is aroused by the purity embodied in Isabella, but this desire seeks to foul the body whose very purity it covets.[1]

It seems to be generally agreed that *Hamlet*, *Troilus and Cressida* and *Measure for Measure* are more consonant with the spirit of Montaigne than any other play, despite the number of parallels in *King Lear*.[2] Out of the three plays two are tragi-comedies and *Hamlet* in its intellectuality has affinities with the so-called problem plays. The full tragic response calls for a heightened consciousness of identity – evident in Lear, Othello or Macbeth – not for the kind of self-consciousness that may dissolve identity. Shakespeare the tragedian had to part company with Montaigne.

He had another reason for doing so. Unlike the French essayist he was not self-centred. He could create self-conscious characters but not confine his attention to them. His sonnets, in which he is said to have unlocked his heart, seldom show him self-absorbed in a brooding self-examination as Petrarch and Sidney often are. He only confesses his 'sin of self-love' to merge his self in his friend: 'Tis thee (my self) that for my self I praise' (Sonnet 62). His mistress, like his friend, takes him from himself: 'Me from my self thy cruel eye hath taken' (Sonnet 133): 'Do I not think on thee when I forgot / Am of my self?' (Sonnet 149).

The dream sonnets may seem to be introspective, but the image of the friend is still the only object for his eyes, for 'when I sleep, in dreams, they look on thee' (Sonnet 43; cf. 113). The sonnets in which attention is focused on the poet are few and they are sonnets of self-expression or self-contemplation rather than self-analysis.[3] When the poet–player deplores he has made himself 'a motley to the view' he sees himself as seen through others' eyes (Sonnet 110; cf. Sonnet 117). The self-contemplative sonnets 'That time of year thou mayst in me behold', 'No longer mourn for me when I am dead' (73, 71) are descriptive or meditative, but not introspective. Complexities of the inner life are often handled in the objective manner of traditional amorous allegory:

> Mine eye and heart are at a mortal war (46)
> Betwixt mine eye and heart a league is took (47)
> Thou blind fool, Love, what dost thou to mine
> eyes (137)
> My love is as a fever, longing still
>
> .   .   .   .   .   .
>
> My Reason, the physician to my Love (147).

When 'Th' expense of spirit in a waste of shame / Is lust in action' (Sonnet 29), we have the result, not the process of self-examination.

Whether written before *Hamlet*, as I incline to think, or completed later, Shakespeare's sonnet sequence makes the introspective soliloquies of the plays all the more remarkable.

---

[1] Note the undercurrent of sexual meaning in the images – carrion, pitch our evils – and the obsessive recurrence of the word 'desire' (ll. 171, 174, 178).

[2] Cf. Taylor's statistics and his comment: '*Measure for Measure, All's Well, Troilus and Cressida* – all written at just about the time when one would expect Montaigne's influence in thought, if ever, to set in – do to a remarkable degree show a definite departure in thought and general spirit from the thought and spirit of the preceding plays' (*Shakespeare's Debt to Montaigne*, p. 39).

[3] Besides the poems cited in the text see Sonnets 29, 117, 146. The dialectics of Sonnets 119, 148 and 149 hardly required deep searchings into the heart.

The rare parallels between the sonnets and the *Essays* of Montaigne so far mentioned seem to me utterly unconvincing: see the notes of S. Bercovitch in *Explicator* 27/3 (November 1968), 22, and D. Hamer in *Notes and Queries*, 214 (1969), 129–30.

Selfless or self-surrendering in their passionate devotion or scornful passion, the sonnets invite again a question that may tease us out of thought. Would Shakespeare have endowed Hamlet or Angelo with so vivid a self-consciousness if he had not read Montaigne? Rather than raise a question that cannot be answered, we may at least assert that the dramatist in his creation of such characters followed Hamlet's advice to the players and did 'show the very age and body of the time his form and pressure'. This heightening of self-awareness was a process in which many minds were engaged by the end of the sixteenth century.

© ROBERT ELLRODT

'MEASURE FOR MEASURE': THE BED-TRICK [1]

A. D. NUTTALL

Helena won Bertram by a trick; in response he submitted formally to the contract, told his bride how he despised her and fled, preferring the grim visage of war to Helena's fair face; she pursued him and, by another trick, won him once more, and at last acquainted him with the felicity he seemed unable to perceive for himself.

Claudio got Juliet with child before their marriage contract had been solemnized, and so became liable to the biting laws of Vienna. Isabel conceded the viciousness of his act but interceded on his behalf to Angelo. Angelo in return made Isabel an offer: 'Submit to my lust and your brother lives.' The Duke suggested that Mariana, whose contract with Angelo had not been solemnized, should secretly take the place of Isabel in Angelo's bed. Isabel welcomed this suggestion. And so the knot of the comedy is untied.

Both of these stories, told thus in the barest language, are already tense and uncomfortable, *before* we endow the agents with any richness of character or psychological depth. I therefore reject the view that *all* our disgust in watching or reading these plays arises from an illicit, post-romantic urge to psychologize the agents. At the same time, it is equally clear that if we do allow the agents any richness of personality, the disgust becomes *more* acute.

First a confession of faith, or, rather, of conviction: I believe that it is in general surprisingly difficult to impart to any important Shakespearian figure a subtlety of character and psychology greater than that already given him by the dramatist. I allow exceptions to this rule: Lysander and Demetrius seem to

me virtually without depth. But take Cordelia in the first scene of *King Lear*. The persons of the play tread before our eyes an ancient and beautiful measure of pre-personal fairy-tale: an old king and three daughters of whom two are wicked and the third good. And yet, as soon as Cordelia says, 'I cannot heave my heart into my mouth', she acquires inner complexity, and the situation implicitly assumes all the tensions which can impede relations between parents and even the best children.

In *Measure for Measure* the part of Isabel is given a sexual resonance which, though it may prepare us for her marriage to the Duke, is subliminally subversive of her status as virgin-martyr. The whole play, of course, unites an elegant intricacy of plot with the greatest possible inconsistency of ethical principle. I have described it elsewhere as a minuet performed to a sequence of discords.[2] But when Isabel in the splendid simplicity of her charity and the glimmering complexity of her desires, having denounced Claudio's vice, seems almost to *relish* the acting of a parallel offence by Mariana and Angelo – 'The acting of it gives me content already'[3] – our discomfort is made more vivid because we sense dimly that we have been offered a psychological explanation which we are yet not authorized to accept.

---

[1] With regard to the legal questions discussed in this essay, I have deliberately chosen to address myself to Ernest Schanzer's interpretation ('The Marriage-Contracts in *Measure for Measure*', SS, XIII (1960), 81–9) rather than to S. Nagarajan's '*Measure for Measure* and Elizabethan Betrothals', (SQ, XIV (1963), 155–9).

[2] '*Measure for Measure*: Quid pro Quo?', *Shakespeare Studies*, IV (1968), 231–51.

[3] III, i, 250.

But here I encounter a technical difficulty. I have assumed so far that this union of Claudio with Juliet on the one hand and that of Angelo with Mariana on the other are, morally and legally, parallel. However, it is sometimes suggested that Elizabethan law substantially distinguishes them. By far the best account I know of the legal background to *Measure for Measure* is Professor Schanzer's article in *Shakespeare Survey* for 1960. Professor Schanzer – Henry Swinburne *Redivivus* – goes to work like an Elizabethan lawyer and offers us a legal analysis of great – perhaps too great – clarity: Claudio is joined to Isabel by what was called a *de praesenti* contract, Angelo to Mariana by a *de futuro* contract. This is a distinction of canon law and rests entirely on the tense used in affirming the contract: i.e. if one says, 'I take thee, Juliet' (present tense), that is a *de praesenti* contract, but if one says 'I shall take thee, Juliet' (future tense), that is a *de futuro* contract. The curious co-existence in Claudio's speeches of a sense of innocence with a sense of guilt is explained by the dual character in law of an unsolemnized *de praesenti* contract. It is both valid and illegal. That is to say, parties who have made a *de praesenti* affirmation are, even without any witnesses, without consummation and without solemnization, validly and indissolubly married. Claudio is married to Juliet. At the same time it was laid down that to contract such a marriage without public solemnization was illegal and contrary to the moral law.

A *de futuro* contract, on the other hand, is more like what we call 'engagement'. It does not constitute marriage but only an undertaking to marry. In certain circumstances it can be dissolved. If, however, the parties to a *de futuro* contract have sexual intercourse the relation between them is converted *ipso facto* into full and valid matrimony. Thus the Duke is a pious bawd: in bringing two together he creates lawful matrimony.

Such, according to Professor Schanzer, is the distinction between the two espousals in *Measure for Measure*. Claudio's is *de praesenti*, Angelo's is a sworn *de futuro* contract converted into matrimony by consummation. But I am not sure what weight Professor Schanzer attaches to the distinction. My own reaction falls into two parts. First, I have some doubt whether this technical distinction is discernibly present in Shakespeare's play. Secondly I think that even if we concede that it is present, the moral parallelism I assumed between the two contracts is unimpaired.

Let us take the first stage first. Neither of the phrases *de praesenti* and *de futuro*, nor any explicit contrasting of present and future contracts, occurs anywhere in the play.[1] The distinction, if it is to work in our responses, must therefore be supplied by the audience. But in that case the audience must be presumed to have a fairly vivid prior sense of the distinction since it must spontaneously apply it to the events of the play without any direct cue, so to speak, from the dramatist. The phrase *per verba de praesenti* does occur, of course, in *The Duchess of Malfi* (I, i, 478). But to my ear the tone of the Duchess's remark does not suggest that she is referring to matters so familiar as hardly to need mentioning. She says:

I have heard lawyers say a contract in a chamber
Per verba de praesenti is absolute marriage

In fact the old distinction of the canonists proved too fine-grained for the courts and *a fortiori* that which magistrates and jurists had difficulty in applying clearly can hardly have been immediately perspicuous to the man in the

---

[1] The word 'pre-contract' *does* occur, at IV, i, 70, where the Duke says that Angelo is Mariana's 'husband on a pre-contract' and at I, ii, 140 Claudio says that Juliet is 'fast my wife'; the space between these two passages, however, is too great for this to count as a 'contrasting'; moreover the possible clarifying force of 'pre-contract' is in any case dulled by the presence of the term 'husband' (not fully appropriate to a *de futuro* party) in the same phrase.

street. Rudolph Sohm cites a number of cases in which practically the same form of contract was held at one time to constitute *sponsalia de praesenti* and at another *de futuro*.[1] In the *Liber Officialis*[2] of St Andrews we have a case for the year 1522 which by Ernest Schanzer's account ought to be unambiguously *de futuro* – the party concerned said, 'I promytt to yow Begis Abirnethy that I sall marry yow and that I sall never haiff ane uther wiff and thereto I giff yow my fayth.' But this case is described in the record as BOTH *de futuro* AND *de praesenti* (*tam verba de futuro quam de praesenti*). Martin Luther was sufficiently interested in the distinction to vent his ridicule on it on more than one occasion. He observed that in the German language the difference between future and present is often obscure.[3] The same point is made by Henry Swinburne in his *A Treatise of Spousals* (1686, but written a century before). He notes that to 'the vulgar sort' 'I will take thee, Mariana' can mean either 'I, in the future will take thee' *or* 'I willingly take thee here and now'. The matter is resolved, says Swinburne, by the intention of the speaker.[4] Meanwhile, in Shakespeare's play, a great and positive gulf is in any case opened at once between the legal practice of Vincentio's Vienna and James's England. The consummation of an espousal before matrimony may have been an offence in strict law but there was never any question of a death penalty. This is *story-book* law.

But, for the sake of argument, let us grant that Shakespeare's audience did draw the distinction Ernest Schanzer expounds; what then? In *All's Well that Ends Well* we can assert at once that every modern audience misunderstands the moment (II, iii, 171) when the King tells Bertram to take Helena by the hand and 'tell her she is thine'. He is ordering Bertram to marry Helena *on the spot*. By line 176 the King assumes that the two are married, though Bertram has in fact said only 'I take

her hand', and not 'I take thee'. The tension is much greater than is usually supposed. But our main concern is with *Measure for Measure*. Professor Schanzer explains that the intercourse of Claudio and Juliet, though it occurs within marriage, is illegal and immoral because it precedes the solemnization. Exactly the same thing is true of Angelo and Mariana. The union of Mariana and Angelo, like the union of Juliet and Claudio, is wrong because it is clandestine. Swinburne in his treatise is clear that this particular charge of irregularity is quite as applicable to *de futuro* parties as it is to *de praesenti*: 'The Law doth forbid all persons to make *secret* contracts of spousals or matrimony.'[5] An excellent account of the matter

---

[1] *Das Recht der Eheschliessung* (Weimar, 1875), p. 135, n. 51. See also G. E. Howard, *A History of Matrimonial Institutions* (Chicago, 1904), I, 344.

[2] *Liber Officialis Sancti Andree: Curie Metropolitane Sancti Andree in Scotia Sententiarum in Causis Consistorialibus que Extant*, 'presented to the Abbotsford Club by Lord Medwyn' (Edinburgh, 1845), 'Johnsoune and Eldare, 5th May, 1522', p. 21. The case is cited in E. Friedberg, *Das Recht der Eheschliessung* (Leipzig, 1865), p. 58 and in Howard, *Matrimonial Institutions*, I, 344.

[3] See Howard, *Matrimonial Institutions*, I, 340–1. He quotes: 'they have played a fool's game with their *verbis de praesenti vel futuro*. With it they have torn apart many marriages which were valid according to their own law, and those which were not valid they have bound up . . . Indeed, I should not myself know how a churl . . . would or could betroth himself *de futuro* in the German tongue; for the way one betroths himself means *per verba de praesenti*, and surely a clown knows nothing of such nimble grammar as the difference between *accipio* and *accipiam*; therefore he proceeds according to our way of speech and says: "I will have thee", "I will take thee", "Thou shalt be mine". Thereupon "Yes" is said once without more ado.' The passage, which is from *Von Ehesachen*, can be turned up in *Luther's works*, ed. J. Pelikan and H. T. Lehmann, vol. XLVI (Philadelphia, 1967), 273–4, but the translation there provided is seriously misleading.

[4] *Treatise of Spousals*, p. 62. He adds, more practically, that the most obvious sense must always be upheld for any words uttered.

[5] *Treatise of Spousals*, p. 194. Swinburne uses

can be found in Francis Douce's *Illustrations of Shakespeare* (1807): speaking expressly of sworn espousals *de futuro* (that is, Angelo's situation) he observes that the parties 'were not permitted, at least by the church, to reside in the same house, but were nevertheless regarded as man and wife independently of the usual privileges'.[1] So now the Duke begins to look a little less pious and a little more of a bawd.

One part of Ernest Schanzer's article suggests to me that he also views the two acts of intercourse as morally parallel; that is, the place where he says that Isabel must be ignorant of the matrimonial bond between Claudio and Juliet, since otherwise it would be impossible to account for her censoriousness in the one case and her complaisance in the other. I agree as to the contradiction and reject the proffered resolution. It seems to me extraordinarily strained to say that Isabel, throughout her great debate with Angelo, argues from a false premise. *Nobody* in the play disputes the overwhelming strength of the *legal* case against Claudio. On all hands the plea is not for equity but mercy.

And so I reaffirm the first thesis of this paper, which is that the stories of *Measure for Measure* and *All's Well that Ends Well* are essentially and systematically disquieting, and that our disquiet is exacerbated by the presence in the plays of psychological complexity.

But now I come to my second thesis, which is that the plays are also fairy-tales; the endings are genuine eucatastrophes, the forgiveness is experienced as real forgiveness and the concluding matrimony as joy. Some years ago I wrote an essay on *Measure for Measure* in which I stressed the element of vertiginous scepticism which can be discerned behind the main movement of the play.[2] I was careful to insist, however, that it was an under-movement only, and – herein actually distressing some of my more iconoclastic friends – that

the resolution, though threatened, was not overturned into cynicism by what had passed in the shadows behind the main action. This I think was always Shakespeare's way. He gave the dark gods their head, and yet love always remained love, forgiveness forgiveness (except perhaps in *The Tempest*) and marriage marriage.

My real quarry in this essay is the EITHER/OR thesis: the thesis that Shakespeare must be *either* a psycho-dramatist *or* a purveyor of folklore. It seems obvious to me that he brought the two modes together, quite deliberately, in a strange and quickening relationship. He could easily have smoothed the conclusion of *All's Well*. Remember how in Sidney's *Arcadia*, when Parthenia is restored under another name to Argalus, Argalus persists in fidelity to Parthenia's other, dead self.[3] Shakespeare could easily have shown Bertram as vowing, after the supposed death of Helena, that he could never marry again. Instead he went out of his way to show Bertram entirely willing to love another young woman altogether only minutes before he is joined indissolubly to Helena. What is the effect of this in the theatre?

Why, it makes the audience *smile*. I grow more and more convinced that the brilliant acceleration of the end of *All's Well* is entirely the product of deliberate art, and that the sense of joy against all expectation, against all sense, against everything and yet still joy, so far from being achieved *in spite of* the psychological depth of the drama, would actually have been impossible *without* it. Shakespeare was neither

spousal in contradistinction to *matrimony*; cf. p. 64 (where he is talking about rustics who are in doubt whether their contract was *de futuro* or *de praesenti*): 'If the one party should say, that he did intend to contract spousals and not matrimony . . .'

[1] *Illustrations of Shakespeare*, I, p. 114.
[2] See p. 51, n. 2.
[3] In Ponsonby's Quarto of 1590, I, vi, p. 32 *verso*; in *The Prose Works of Sir Philip Sidney*, ed. A. Feuillerat (Cambridge, 1912), I, 50.

a medieval man nor a late Victorian but a great poet of the Renascence. And at that word we may remember how often the greatest paintings and sculptures of the Renascence work by uniting the new achievements in realism with what seem at first sight the least tractable iconographic subjects. The *pietàs* of Michelangelo derive from carvings in which the figure of Christ is made unrealistically tiny so as to fit on his mother's lap. 'If that were done realistically', they might have said, 'the figure of Christ would sag dreadfully to either side of the mother's knee.' 'Why then', says Michelangelo, 'I will let it sag, and at the same time I will give you more majesty and pity than you ever saw before.'

The New Arden editor of *All's Well that Ends Well* is right when he says that the second half of the play is concerned with things working out under pressure of forces other than the personal.[1] But I add: Shakespeare wanted it to be felt as pre-personal. In straight fairy-tale the pre-personal character is not *awkwardly* vivid as in Shakespeare because it is uncontested; there is no tension between pre-personal and personal because there is no personal. No doubt the pre-personal factor isolated by Shakespeare is indeed something very ancient, a way of viewing the marriage contract which we are perhaps beginning to lose. Today we tend to think of marriage as drawing all its substance from the texture of personal relationship between the husband and the wife. For Shakespeare marriage has its own substantial reality. In *As You Like It* an unhappy personal relationship is actually promised[2] to Touchstone and Audrey, and yet their marriage also is marriage and matter for joy. I have said that today we think differently, but I am not sure that is true when one attends a wedding. To misquote Tolstoy, all married couples are different, but all weddings are the same. And if research into the history of law teaches us anything, it teaches us this same

thing. There is a moment of mystery in the law of *de futuro* espousals. In spite of all the strictures against clandestine marriage, when the man lies with the woman sin is in a manner converted into virtue by the mere performance.

Dostoevsky has a fiercely negative parody of this strange logic – which one might describe as the anticipation of the ordinary serial order of *causality* by *entailment* – in Smerdyakov's casuistry near the beginning of *The Brothers Karamazov*:

Once I'm taken prisoner by the enemies of Christians who demand that I should curse the name of God and renounce holy baptism, I'm fully authorised to do so by my own reason, since there wouldn't be no sin in it at all...For as soon as I says to my torturers 'No, I'm not a Christian and I curse my true God', I become, by God's high judgement, immediately and especially anathema, accursed and excommunicated from the Holy Church, just as if I was a heathen, so that at that very instant, Sir, not only when I says them words, but just as I thinks of saying them, so that before even a quarter of a second has passed, I'm excommunicated. Isn't that so, Mr. Kutuzov, Sir?...Well Sir, if I'm no more a Christian, then I can't be telling no lies to my torturers when they ask me whether I'm a Christian or not, for God himself has stripped me of my Christianity on account of my intention alone...[3]

This to most men living before 1700 (and they would understand it very well) would sound like the logic of Hell, for it cuts man off pre-emptively from God. But the same logic, when in the very act of carnal intercourse it transforms Angelo and Mariana into man and wife before God, pre-emptively links man with God – and this, for all the worries about the lack of public solemnization and so on, may have carried in some strange way the smell of Heaven about it.[4]

[1] (1967), p. xxxii.   [2] v, iv, 185–6.
[3] *The Brothers Karamazov*, I, iii, 7, in the Penguin translation by David Magarshack (1958), I, 149–50.
[4] Once more, however, the legal point seems not to have been generally known. In the eleventh chapter of Deloney's *Jacke of Newberie* (1626) a knight deludes a maid-servant 'with hope of marriage', she becomes

Marvellous sweet music...But of course there are harsher chords, if we wish to listen for them. Elizabethan marriage held at its centre a high mystery, but at the same time it seems plain that the ease with which it could be contracted had trivialized it. The disparity between the absolute, indissoluble character of the bond and the casualness with which it could be formed must always have been too much to hold in one's head. Think what it must have been like for a man alone with a reminiscent conscience: 'Here am I, having lived with my Maudlin these fifteen years and three fine children, and my true wife is that wench whose name I have forgot, whom I married under a hay-rick in my seventeenth year – and her with a man and eight children of her own, they tell me.' But this fellow is safe from everything but his conscience and the wrath to come. People would swear themselves married and then unswear themselves again.[1] In Act III of *All's Well* Mariana warns Diana not to trust the oaths of soldiers.[2] We must understand that she is talking not of girls who think they are engaged, but girls who suppose themselves *married*, and may *be* married though the world and the husband will never after acknowledge the fact. The modern audience is at a loss; on the one hand we see old Capulet in *Romeo and Juliet* arranging a marriage for his daughter with a casual celerity which shocks us,[3] and on the other marriage itself is so absolute. The Jacobean sense of marriage must have been a curious compound: an imperative at once inescapable and muted by habit and expediency. Here we all are in merry Middle Earth and yet always, at the same time, we tread either in Heaven or in Hell.

To this infinite variety, to this illimitable divide Shakespeare is faithful. We must not take from him the humanity of his characters, the magic of their fortunes or the mysterious felicity of the end; we must not be ungrateful to that plenitude.

pregnant and reminds him of his 'promise' but he rejects her. At this, Jack, the good angel of the story, brings the two together, *not* by pointing out that they are married already (this is never mentioned) but by tricking the knight into a solemnized marriage with the girl he had wronged. See *The Works of Thomas Deloney*, ed. F. O. Mann (1912), pp. 64–8.

[1] Compare the passage from Luther's *Tabletalk* quoted in Howard, *Matrimonial Institutions*, I, 344: 'Now the Pope and Jurists say that marriage can never be dissolved. What happens? The wedded people fall out and separate. So they come to me in the Cloister, or wherever an official can be found and swear themselves apart; then they marry again.' Luther goes on to explain how the parties later, smitten in their consciences, apply to 'swap back again'.

[2] III, v, 17f.   [3] III, v, 15–20.

© A. D. NUTTALL 1975

SHAKESPEARE AND THE DOCTRINE OF THE UNITY OF TIME

ERNEST SCHANZER

Anyone who sets out to discover Shakespeare's attitudes towards the ideas of his time, his thoughts and feelings about them, must soon come to realize that he is pursuing a will-o'-the-wisp, which will leave him 'swallowed up and lost, from succour far'. 'Others abide our question. Thou art free...' But there is one idea of his time where Shakespeare, I believe, for once abides our question; where, when we ask and ask, he smiles, yet is not still, out-topping knowledge, but, on the contrary, allows us some very palpable and consistent glimpses of his feelings about it. That idea is the doctrine of the unity of time.

This doctrine, buttressed by the supposed authority of Aristotle, was grounded on the critics' desire for the utmost verisimilitude, for making the least possible demands on the audience's powers of imagination. The ideal play was therefore held to be the one in which the time of its action is co-extensive with the time taken by its performance. But it was generally agreed that up to twelve or even twenty-four hours could be conceded, provided the extra hours fell in the intervals between the acts.

First formulated in Italy towards the middle of the sixteenth century as one of the rules of drama, the doctrine of the unity of time assumed the status of an inviolable law after Castelvetro, in his commentary on Aristotle's *Poetics*, first published in 1570, had joined it with the unities of place and action, which were a logical inference from it. It began its tyrannical reign, first in Italy and then in France, in the last quarter of the sixteenth century. In Spain it met with a good deal of opposition, and in England it would have been largely ignored by writers for the public stage, had it not been for the authority of Sir Philip Sidney and later of Ben Jonson.

All this is well known. But Shakespeare's attitude towards the doctrine of the unity of time has, as far as I am aware, been scarcely discussed, partly, perhaps, from a conviction akin to that which made Dr Johnson remark in his *Preface*: 'Whether Shakespeare knew the unities and rejected them by design, or deviated from them by happy ignorance, it is, I think, impossible to decide and useless to inquire.'[1]

Shakespeare began as he ended his career as dramatist with a comedy which satisfied the critics' demand for unity of time in its more stringent form. The action of *The Comedy of Errors* extends from mid-morning to the late afternoon, covering some six hours or so. Though time is much referred to throughout the play, and appears in various emblematic guises, there is nowhere in the text any sign that Shakespeare was in the least concerned with the neo-classical doctrine. The unity of time in this play arose out of the peculiar needs of the plot, which requires an exceedingly short duration in order to be viable. It is simply not possible for two pairs of identical twins let loose in the same town and constantly mistaken for each other not to become aware of the truth after the lapse of a few hours. There is no sign

[1] *Dr Johnson on Shakespeare*, ed. W. K. Wimsatt, Penguin Shakespeare Library (Harmondsworth, 1969), p. 72.

in *The Comedy of Errors* that Shakespeare was adopting the unity of time out of deference to the demand of the critics, but neither is there any sign that he was making fun of this demand.

Shakespeare's first explicit allusion to the doctrine is found in *Love's Labour's Lost*. When at the end of the play the four lovers find their hopes deferred by their ladies' imposition of a year's period of testing, Berowne remarks,

> Our wooing doth not end like an old play:
> Jack hath not Jill. These Ladies' courtesy
> Might well have made our sport a comedy

(a comedy, that is, in the medieval sense of a story that begins in trouble and ends in joy).

> *King.*
> Come, sir, it wants a twelvemonth and a day,
> And then 'twill end.
> *Berowne.*   That's too long for a play.
> (v, ii, 882)

One of the main concerns of *Love's Labour's Lost* is the ridicule of various forms of pedantry, of men's attempted adherence to stringent, self-imposed rules and restrictions. Hence Berowne's mocking glance at the rule of the unity of time is in keeping with the spirit of the whole play. Ironically, *Love's Labour's Lost* happens to be one of Shakespeare's plays where he came closest to satisfying the demand for unity of time and place. But, as with *The Comedy of Errors*, this is due not to the critics' prescription but to the nature of the story he dramatized.

We have to wait until the writing of *Hamlet* for Shakespeare's next explicit reference to the doctrine of the unities of time and place. One might have expected such a reference in the choruses of *Henry V*. But instead of an explicit allusion, we get in these choruses an indirect reply to the simple-minded realism of the neo-classical critics through Shakespeare's insistence on the capacity of the audience's imagination to bridge space and time.

> For 'tis your thoughts that now must deck our kings,
> Carry them here and there, jumping o'er times,
> Turning th'accomplishment of many years
> Into an hour-glass.
> (*Prologue*, ll. 28–31)

The explicit reference to the doctrine of the unities of time and place in *Hamlet* is found in Polonius's description of the actors:

The best actors in the world, either for tragedy, comedy, history, pastoral, pastoral–comical, historical–pastoral, tragical–historical, tragical–comical–historical–pastoral, scene individable, or poem unlimited. Seneca cannot be too heavy nor Plautus too light. For the law of writ and the liberty, these are the only men   (ii, ii, 392–7)

Commentators are divided about what is meant by 'scene individable, or poem unlimited' and by 'the law of writ and the liberty'. But the majority are agreed that 'scene individable' means a play which observes the unity of place, or of time and place, and 'poem unlimited' means a play that does not heed any such limitations; while 'the law of writ and the liberty' means plays composed according to strict rules of dramatic composition and those that show complete freedom from such rules. Shakespeare places his reference to the doctrine of the unities in a context of mockery. First Polonius's pedantic classification of drama is laughed at, then the critics' pedantic insistence on the rules. By using the phrase 'the law of writ and the liberty', which, as Dover Wilson has pointed out, are 'terms defining the jurisdiction of the Sheriffs in and about the city of London...quibblingly applied to types of drama',[1] Shakespeare expressed his irreverent, mocking attitude to the neo-classical rules.

[1] See his edition of *Hamlet* (Cambridge, 1934), p. 181.

In *Pericles*, the play in which, together with *The Winter's Tale*, Shakespeare came nearest to providing the *corpus vile* against which Sidney and Ben Jonson inveighed, with a time-gap of fourteen years between Acts III and IV, there is no explicit reference to the doctrine of the unities of time and place. Instead we have in the choruses of Gower, much as in the choruses in *Henry V*, the insistence on the power of the audience's thoughts to annihilate time and abolish distance.

> Only I carry winged time
> Post on the lame feet of my rhyme;
> Which never could I so convey
> Unless your thoughts went on my way.
> (IV, 47–50)

> Thus time we waste, and long leagues make short;
> Sail seas in cockles, have and wish but for't;
> Making, to take our imagination,
> From bourn to bourn, region to region.
> (IV, iv, 1–4)

It is in *The Winter's Tale*, with its gap of sixteen years between Acts III and IV, that we are given Shakespeare's most extensive direct comment on the doctrine of the unity of time. He hit upon the witty device of making Father Time himself appear upon the stage and, in admittedly rather cryptic language, defend Shakespeare's extreme contravention of the rule of the unity of time in this play, by making him point out that all such 'laws' are of no permanent validity, but merely a passing fashion, subject to time.

> Impute it not a crime
> To me or my swift passage that I slide
> O'er sixteen years, and leave the growth untried
> Of that wide gap, since it is in my power
> To o'erthrow law, and in one self-born hour
> To plant and o'erwhelm custom. Let me pass
> The same I am, ere ancient'st order was
> Or what is now receiv'd. I witness to
> The times that brought them in; so shall I do
> To th'freshest things now reigning, and make stale
> The glistering of this present, as my tale
> Now seems to it.
> (IV, i, 4–15)

This is similar in spirit and matter to what Ben Jonson, some twelve years earlier, made his spokesman, Cordatus, say in the *Induction to Every Man Out of His Humour*. Cordatus argues that, since the laws of Comedy, including that of the unity of time, did not exist from the beginning of time, and the whole history of ancient comedy, of which he gives a thumbnail sketch, consisted of a series of innovations:

> I see not then, but we should enjoy the same licence, or free power, to illustrate and heighten our inuention as they did; and not bee tyed to those strict and regular formes, which the niceness of a few (who are nothing but forme) would thrust vpon us.[1]

This attitude towards 'the laws of comedy' is, by the way, not contradicted by what Ben Jonson says some thirteen years later in the Prologue to *Every Man In His Humour* where, in lines evidently based on a passage in *Don Quixote* in Thomas Shelton's translation (published 1612), he lists among 'th'ill customes of the age'

> To make a child, now swadled, to proceede
> Man, and then shoote vp, in one beard, and weede,
> Past threescore yeeres.[2]

Here, as in the chorus at the end of Act I of *The Magnetic Lady*,[3] it is the extravagant excesses of romantic drama that he ridicules, as Sir Philip Sidney had done some thirty years earlier in the famous passage in his *Apology for Poetry*. Such ridicule is quite compatible with Jonson's refusing to be bound by the stringent rule of the unities in *Every Man Out of His Humour*, in which a week or more elapses in the course of the action.

Shakespeare, after having written in *The Winter's Tale* his play which contravened most grossly the rule of the unity of time, went on in *The Tempest* to produce his play which

---

[1] *Ben Jonson*, ed. C. H. Herford, P. and E. Simpson (Oxford, 1925–52), III, 437, ll. 266–70.
[2] *Ibid.*, III, 303, ll. 7–9.
[3] *Ibid.*, VI, 527–8, ll. 16–26.

5-2

fulfilled it most completely. With an action extending over a little more than four hours, from shortly before two until shortly after six o'clock in the afternoon, it came as near as any play in that age to the ideal of a time of action which is co-extensive with the time of performance. It also contains, I suggest, Shakespeare's most extended mockery of the critics' demand for unity of time.

The analogy between Prospero and the dramatist – not just Shakespeare the dramatist but any dramatist – has been often observed. Prospero designs, and in the course of the play stage-manages, two dramas. The one, concerned with Ferdinand and Miranda, is a romantic comedy, according to the medieval formula for comedy: a story that starts in trouble, ends in joy, and centres on love. The other drama, concerned with the three men of sin, Alonso, Antonio, and Sebastian, is not a romantic comedy, but it is also a comedy in the medieval sense. Like Dante's *Commedia*, it moves from *Inferno* through *Purgatorio* to what was designed by Prospero as a kind of *Paradiso*, from the Hell of the shipwreck through the purgation of Acts III and IV to the intended forgiveness and reconciliation at the end. Now both these dramas are not easily and naturally confined within the space of a few hours. The passage of at least a day or two rather than of a couple of hours between the first meeting of Ferdinand and Miranda and their betrothal would have seemed more natural, especially as it is part of Prospero's design to test through his vexations the quality of Ferdinand's love for his daughter. Still more does the lapse of a good deal of time seem needed in the other drama designed by Prospero, the drama of the purgation and regeneration of the three men of sin. And yet at various points in the play Shakespeare shows Prospero to be obsessed by the need to finish the action before the afternoon is up. 'What is the time o'th' day?', he asks Ariel towards the beginning of the play. 'Past the mid season', Ariel replies. 'At least two glasses', says Prospero (in other words, it is at least two o'clock in the afternoon). 'The time 'twixt six and now / Must by us both be spent most preciously' (I, ii, 239–41). At the beginning of Act III Prospero is still in the same hurry:

> I'll to my book;
> For yet ere supper time must I perform
> Much business appertaining.
>
> (III, i, 94–6)

Towards the end of the play Prospero is as preoccupied as ever with finishing his plot before evening. Act V opens with Prospero and Ariel.

Prospero.
> Now does my project gather to a head;
> My charms crack not, my spirits obey; and time
> Goes upright with his carriage. How's the day?
Ariel.
> On the sixth hour; at which time, my lord,
> You said our work should cease.
Prospero.   I did say so,
> When first I rais'd the tempest.
>
> (V, i, 1–6)

Shakespeare provides no real explanation why Prospero is so anxious to finish the action before the end of the day. There is Ariel's demand for freedom, but this is not tied to any particular time, and, besides, is not made until after Prospero's declaration that 'The time 'twixt six and now / Must by us both be spent most preciously'. There is the auspicious star mentioned by Prospero at the beginning of the play,

>   and by my prescience
> I find my zenith doth depend upon
> A most auspicious star, whose influence
> If now I court not, but omit, my fortunes
> Will ever after droop.
>
> (I, ii, 180–4)

But this is not phrased so as to make one infer that the star's favourable influence is confined to a few hours. I believe Shakespeare is making fun of the doctrine of the unity of time by depicting Prospero in the role of the harassed designer of the plot, who is obliged by the critics' demand to bring his action to a close by a certain hour of the day, and so has to keep his eyes riveted to the clock. I am not at all suggesting that this is a major concern of the play, or that it is the reason why Shakespeare adopted the intensive structure for it. But I think it is the reason why he confined the action to a little over four hours rather than to the several days which would seem more appropriate to the plot.[1]

We have seen various ways in which, in the course of his dramatic career, Shakespeare expressed his sense of the absurdity of the neo-classical demand for unity of time: through

Berowne's explicit mockery; through associating it in the figure of Polonius with other forms of pedantic absurdity; through the device of making Father Time himself disparage it as a passing fashion; and finally, and most amusingly, through making Prospero enact before the audience's eyes the harassment of the plot-designer who is committed to its observation. It was Shakespeare's last thrust in his scattered skirmishes against that bloated, tyrannical upstart, the doctrine of the unity of time.

[1] In his article on 'Time and *The Tempest*' (*JEGP*, LXIII (1964), 255–67) James F. Robinson discusses the play in relation to the neo-classical critics' demand for unity of time. But he does not suggest that Shakespeare may be making fun of their doctrine.

© ERNEST SCHANZER 1975

'CORIOLANUS' AND THE BODY POLITIC

ANDREW GURR

The incidents in *Coriolanus* which reflect the Midlands riots of 1607 and the parliamentary quarrels of 1606 are well known.[1] Less obvious perhaps is the place of these topical echoes of contemporary troubles in the larger orchestration of the play. Topical references on their own do little more than date the play, in both senses of the word.

A fresh look at the belly fable and how Shakespeare sets it out at the beginning of the play might help to clarify where the food riots and the jibes at Yelverton and Hyde as tribunes of the people fit in the larger pattern. Both topical events raised questions of power and authority by posing the problem of sectional interests in a commonwealth which was clearly less than organically united. Through his presentation in *Coriolanus*, I think, Shakespeare was exposing some basic anomalies in the belly fable's cognate concept, the body politic, which shaped traditional thinking about authority in the state.

The body politic had a long and respectable history, traceable back to Plato and Aristotle.[2] Its substantive medieval version was the one analysed by Kantorowicz,[3] the legal fiction of the king's two bodies, one the private flesh and one the politic body which never dies. In Tudor times Henry VIII promoted the more metaphysical idea of the whole state as a corporate organism, symbolised in parliament with the king as head and lords and commons as 'members', a concept which became the dominant one in the course of the century. Corporate sovereignty, the supreme authority of *rex in parliamento*, was written into the chief statutes of the Reformation Parliament. The preamble to the Act of Appeals (1533)

claimed that 'this Realm of England is an Empire...governed by one supreme Head and King...unto whom a body politick, compact of all Sorts and Degrees of People...been bounden and owen to bear a natural and humble Obedience' (Act 24 Hen. VIII, xii). Sir Thomas Smith's Elizabethan account of the peculiarly English 'mixed' form of government endorsed the Henrician preambles. His statement that 'the most high and absolute power of the realme of Englande, consisteth in the Parliament' was slightly less radical than it sounds now since 'Parliament' to him was the inclusive head and torso of king in parliament. It was sovereign because it was representative. Like the Roman *centuriatis*, it

> representeth and hath the power of the whole realme both the head and the bodie. For everie Englishman is entended to bee there present, either in person or by procuration and attornies, of whatever preheminence, state, dignitie, or qualitie soever he be, from the Prince (be he King or Queene) to the lowest person of Englande. And the consent of the Parliament is taken to be everie mans consent.[4]

Consciously or not, the Tudor emphasis on the Aristotelian version of the body-politic concept reflected a shift in thinking about the state as a national unit,[5] and a broadening of the

---

[1] E. C. Pettet, '*Coriolanus* and the Midlands Insurrection', *Shakespeare Survey 3* (1950), 34–42; W. G. Zeeveld, '*Coriolanus* and Jacobean Politics', *MLR*, LVII (1962), 321–34.

[2] Cf. D. G. Hale, *The Body Politic* (The Hague, 1971).

[3] E. H. Kantorowicz, *The King's Two Bodies* (Princeton, 1957).

[4] Sir Thomas Smith, *De Republica Anglorum*, ed. L. Alston (Cambridge, 1906), p. 49.

[5] Henry's elevation of the body-politic concept had several causes, not least the need to establish a new

basis of authority. It was now important to be able to say that the actions of government went forward with the consent of the whole nation. The body politic was the appropriate means of conceptualising this interpretation of the process of government and the source of authority to govern.

The concept which Elizabeth's successor held in 1603 was in direct conflict with this. For his Scottish coronation in 1567, the guardians of the young James minted a set of coins which showed on the reverse an unsheathed dagger, and the motto *Pro me si mereor in me*. George Buchanan, James's tutor, gave the story behind the motto in his *Rerum Scoticorum Historia* (1582). In translation it reads

Even in those times in which the Roman republic was oppressed by the most cruel tyranny, when by accident any virtuous man was made emperor, he considered it his highest glory to acknowledge himself inferior to the people, and liable to the empire of the law. Trajan, when, according to custom, he delivered the sword of justice to the prefect of the city, is said thus to have addressed him, Use it for me, or against me, as I shall deserve.[1]

The adult James would never have allowed such a motto (for his English coronation the motto was *Exsurgat Deus Dissipentur Inimici*). He agreed that the sword of justice was the chief instrument of rule and its use the chief test of a monarch's quality, but he never agreed with Buchanan and the other early Monarchomachs that it could properly be used to check the monarch himself. To James this was the most important theoretical issue of his time. It was the main stem of his troubles with his first parliament.

The question it raised was where sovereignty was located. Thanks to the body-politic concept sovereignty was not an issue under the Tudors. Smith did not use the word. So long as king and parliament were thought of as one and indivisible, sovereignty was everywhere and nowhere. James made it an issue by his insistence that he was the law-giver, and therefore himself above the law. If the king makes and gives authority to the law, the king has sovereign power, and constraints on his exercise of power have only moral backing, not legal. If on the other hand laws make and protect kings, sovereignty rests with the legislative body.

When James came to the throne of England he brought with him a long list of his own writings proclaiming that sovereignty rested in the person of the king, and that laws took their authority from him. In his *Trew Law* (1598) he had argued that in Scotland kings had existed before there was any parliament or any law. 'And so it follows of necessity, that the kings were the authors and makers of the laws and not the laws of the kings.'[2] The judiciary in England, long accustomed as they by then were to thinking of the law as the source of authority for government and the king, stood to their defences. 'The law protecteth the king', said Coke to James in 1608, echoing Hooker's *Lex facit regem*.[3] James made

basis for title and for sovereignty in the wake of the English Reformation. Certainly it marked a general enlargement of thought about the state. Henry's reign was the time when, according to Elton, 'a self-contained national unit came to be, not the tacitly accepted necessity it had been for some time, but the consciously desired goal'. G. R. Elton, *The Tudor Revolution in Government: Administrative Changes in the Reign of Henry VIII* (Cambridge, 1953), p. 3.

[1] *A History of Scotland*, trans. J. Aikman, 4 vols. (Glasgow, 1827), II, 602–3. Shakespeare's Henry V echoes Trajan when he hands the rod of justice back to the Lord Chief Justice in 2 *Henry IV*.

[2] *Political Works*, ed. C. H. McIlwain (Cambridge, Mass., 1918), p. 61.

[3] *Of the Laws of Ecclesiastical Polity*, VIII, ii, 13: 'I cannot choose but commend highly their wisdom by whom the foundations of this commonwealth have been laid; wherein though no manner, person or cause be not subject to the king's power, yet so is the power of the king over all and in all limited, that unto all his proceedings the law itself is a rule. The axioms of our regal government are these: *Lex facit regem*: the king's grant of any favour made contrary to the law is void. *Rex nihil potest nisi quod jure potest*.'

him go on his knees to beg forgiveness,[1] but the common-law men in parliament were unabashed. James had to back down over Cowell's *Interpreter*, which claimed that civil (Roman) law, and consequently the king, took priority over common law. Where ultimate sovereignty lay, in the king or in parliament's laws and law-making authority, was an issue which formed one of the steps up to Charles I's scaffold.

Since Austin's nineteenth-century formulation of the concept of sovereign authority as a question of jurisprudence it has not been easy to see it as something diffused in the will of the people, whether that will is expressed through the 'natural' consensus of a supposedly organic body politic, through Rousseau's General Will or Proudhon's militancy of the ballot box. The law's need for a court of final appeal, an ultimate authority beyond whose desk the buck does not pass, authoriser of the ballot itself, a need which Austin voiced, is a recurrent constitutional problem. It appeared in the aftermath of Watergate (President Ford in his inaugural address proclaimed 'our long national nightmare is over. Our Constitution works. Our great republic is a government of laws and not of men'). It is there, too, in the constitution of, for instance, Kenya, framed largely at Lancaster House, and which explicitly makes the President above the laws he gives his authority to. The influence of jurisprudence in such cases may give hindsight an unnaturally strong light to read the Jacobean sovereignty issue by. The question whether the law protected the king or vice versa was an oversimplification then as now. Law-making, as G. R. Elton pointed out,[2] is a dynamic process, not a normative one, and it is important to separate legislative power from judicial, the dynamic function from the interpretative. The Tudors failed to make such a distinction, understandably enough since common law was thought to be based on natural law which was immutable. This in the long run was perhaps the main cause of the difficulties the seventeenth-century lawyers got into.

What James's challenge to sovereignty did begin to make clear was the unfitness of the body-politic concept. From roughly this time on, and long before Hobbes turned it into a mechanical monster, the concept became more and more unpopular. In the early part of James's reign, though, it was still widely used, and Shakespeare's deployment of it in *Coriolanus* shows among other things that it was still current coin. But its anomalies were becoming clearer, and one particular use of it, in 1606, may have influenced Shakespeare's decision to dramatise it in the way he does.

Edward Forset's *Comparative Discourse of the Bodies Natural and Politique* (1606) was only one among several contemporary accounts of the story of Menenius and his belly fable. What makes it a possible stimulus to the writing of *Coriolanus* is its extended use of the body-politic concept, and more specifically its challenge to the traditional idea of dispersed sovereignty which it offered. Forset, with one eye on James's theory, took issue with Hooker's version of the body and the role of law in it. To Hooker the 'very soul of a politic body' was 'the law of a Commonweal'. The moral laws of nature were the obvious candidate to identify with the human faculty which regulated moral and social conduct. But equally, since the soul was the mark of God's finger on man, it was the obvious seat of sovereign authority. Certainly it was a better proposition than the head, which ruled by simple reason rather than the right reason sanctioned by God in the soul. Forset openly took issue with this. The law he demoted to the equivalent of simple

[1] Cf. Roland G. Usher, 'James I and Sir Edward Coke', *English Historical Review*, XVIII (1903), 664–75.
[2] Introduction to J. N. Figgis, *The Divine Right of Kings* (New York, 1965), p. xxx.

reason, and in its place as the soul of the politic body he put the royal prerogative. 'In man the soule ruleth by reason', he wrote, 'and in the State the Soveraigne governeth by lawes; which may no lesse aptly be termed the soule of sovereignty, than reason is said to be the soule of the soule.'[1] The law, he suggests, is merely the faculty by which the soul governs the body, and obedience is due to the ruler, not to the instrument of rule. So glossed, the body-politic metaphor confirms the divinity of sovereign power in the king, since 'in the creating of man, God is said to have breathed into him the soule, whereby the puritie and dignitie thereof is much extolled above that lump of mowlded earth his body'.[2] Princes are God's gift to man.

The body politic was an ideal rather than a reality, of course. Like the moral laws of nature it existed uneasily in a theological limbo between *is* and *ought*. But its character as an ideal in no way impaired its domination as the shaping conceit, the basic means of conceiving the state and political power. Only when its interpretation came into dispute, as it did when Forset set about modifying Hooker, did it begin to need displacing, like a Kuhnian paradigm. In 1607 the Midlands riots over food and prices emphasised the unreality of the idea of the commonwealth as a harmoniously concordant organic entity. And later that year Shakespeare started *Coriolanus* with a riot over corn which Menenius held in check with his story of the belly and the mutinous members. The presentation of the fable and its deployment in the play show Shakespeare's sensitivity to the tilting of the political paradigm.

Forset's version of the belly fable is worth quoting here, because although it is similar in detail and moral to the versions in Sidney, Camden, and North's Plutarch, its emphasis makes a little clearer the kind of adjustments Shakespeare made to his version. In his preliminary epistle to the reader, Forset out-

lines the body-politic concept, and then goes on to say:

This similitude was both fitly and fortunately enforced by *Menenius Agrippa*, who being imployed in the appeasing and persuading of the seditious revolting commons of Rome, did by a very tale of this proportionable respectivenes of the parts in mans body, and the mutualitie of kindnes and ayd afforded from each to other, so sensibly shew them their errour, that surseasing their malignant envy wherewith they were inraged against their rulers (whom they accounted as the idle belly that swallowed the labors of their hands) they discerned at the last, that their repining against, and their pining of that belly, whence was distributed unto them their bloud and nourishment, necessarily tended to their owne destruction; and were thereupon forthwith reclaymed into their bounds of obedience.[3]

Forset's account in the first place unwittingly underlines the anomalies in the body-politic concept by linking it with the belly fable and making the point from that fable that the 'revolting commons' saw their rulers as the belly, not the head. The point is acknowledged in *Coriolanus* when the First Citizen enlarges on Menenius's similitude with his own list,

> The kingly crowned head, the vigilant eye,
> The counsellor heart, the arm our soldier,
> Our steed the leg, the tongue our trumpeter...
> (I, i, 113–15)[4]

a catalogue of the body militant which starts, as in orthodoxy it should do, with the head as ruler, not the belly.

Shakespeare further altered his version of the belly incident with two changes from his sources which bear more weightily on the concept than this anatomical question. By cutting two citizen mutinies down to one, eliminating the riot over usury, and transferring

[1] Edward Forset, *A Comparative Discourse of the Bodies Natural and Politique* (1606), sig. B2v.
[2] *Ibid.*, sig. B2r.
[3] *Ibid.*, Epistle to the Reader.
[4] Quotations from the play are taken from the text of Peter Alexander, *The Tudor Shakespeare* (1963).

the belly fable incident from the usury riot to the food riot, he tightened up the parallel with the Midlands food riots and gave the belly metaphor a more precise relevance. One mutiny with one motive, the shortage of corn, and a fable which was more appropriate to food than to usury, was a change combining topical point with structural economy.

The second change was a more subtle one. Forset's version of the incident omits a detail which comes out in several of the other accounts, the fact that Menenius was popular with the citizens because he was a former pleb himself. Livy tells us he was 'dear to the plebeians as being one of themselves by birth'.[1] In Shakespeare the citizens listen to him because they think he is 'honest', and 'hath always loved the people', but no mention is made of anything which might moderate his total commitment to the patricians and 'noble Senate'. He describes himself, in fact, as a 'humorous patrician' to the mutineers. Plutarch's version makes him a genial diplomat, a peace-maker. Shakespeare presents him rather differently.

The central point of Menenius's fable is that the storehouse-belly gives out its food: 'The strongest nerves and small inferior veins / From me receive that natural competency / Whereby they live.' It is an extraordinary demonstration of his contempt for his hearers and his faith in verbal smokescreens that he should offer this defence of the Senate to citizens whose whole complaint (thanks to Shakespeare's amalgamation of the two riots) is that the Senate is refusing to distribute its stores. 'Suffer us to famish and their storehouses crammed with grain' is their grievance. Menenius is not offering a rationale of the state as a single natural organism so much as conducting a cynical delaying action until help in the form of his fellow patrician Caius Martius arrives. His real view of the grain question comes out when with Martius's soldier arm to support

him he exultantly says 'Rome and her rats are at the point of battle.' Rome is the Senate and patricians to Menenius, its citizens the vermin which infest the Senate's grain stores. Caius Martius Coriolanus is the city rat-catcher.

All three of Shakespeare's alterations to the belly fable come together by means of this third change, which makes Menenius a wholly partisan figure in the patrician faction. Forset's linkage of the belly fable with the body politic, the focus on the food supply question and the cynicism of Menenius the patrician all in their different ways emphasise faction, the partisanship of a headless state cloven in two by disputes over the basic necessities of life. The political realities of Rome are almost a parody of the idea of the body politic.

This was democratic Rome in its early days as a republic (a word the Elizabethans translated as 'commonwealth'). We are reminded that Coriolanus himself received seven wounds in the battle to expel the tyrant Tarquin. The tribunes' main charge against Coriolanus is that he threatens their 'liberties' by wanting for himself 'a power tyrannical'. For this one play Shakespeare reached back about as far as he well could in Roman history from the time when the rule of the Caesars was turning Rome back once again into a monarchy. The republic according to most Elizabethan commentators was characterised as a time of transient governors and civil strife. As Grenewey describes it in the *Proeme* to his 1598 translation of Tacitus,

The citie of Rome was in the beginning governed by Kings. Libertie and the Consulship *L. Brutus* brought in. The Dictators were chosen but for a time: the *Decemviri* passed not two yeeres: neither had the Consularie authoritie or the Tribunes or the souldiers any long continuance: nor *Cinna* nor *Sillaes* dominion: *Pompey* and *Crassus* quickly yeelded

[1] Quoted in G. Bullough, *Narrative and Dramatic Sources of Shakespeare*, 8 vols. (1957–74), V, 461.

to *Caesars* force: *Lepidus* and *Antonie* to *Augustus*: who entitling himselfe by the name of Prince, brought under his obedience the whole Romane state, wearied and weakened with civill disorders.[1]

Faction and a nearly headless state are also the main ingredients of Shakespeare's mixture.

On the face of it, choosing a republic for the exhibition of anomalies in the body-politic concept would seem to create more difficulties in making the analogy fit than it solves by its aptness for the parody. The same awkwardness seems to apply to the second set of topical equivalences which Zeeveld noted, between the Roman tribunes and the defenders of common rights in the English House of Commons.[2] Those who sarcastically called Yelverton, Hyde and the others in James's first parliament of 1604–7 tribunes of the people were making a point which depended on divided political allegiances. In the play the tribunes stand for 'the old prerogative' (III, iii, 14), and they issue their decrees 'I' th' right and strength o' th' commons'. 'Commons' here need mean no more than the plebeian faction, of course, but when the tribunes describe the citizens' statutory rights as

> Your liberties and the charters that you bear
> I' th' body of the weal
>
> (II, iii, 179–80)

they are unequivocally echoing Coke, Chief Justice of Common Pleas, who upheld Magna Charta as the great written record of common rights. There is an unmistakable echo of the contemporary debate in a context which strictly limits any extension of the parallel.

This limitation, the headless state, prevents any easy parallel between Senate and consuls on the one hand and Lords, and beyond them James and his ministers, on the other. The mutual hostility between Senatorial gentry and many-headed multitude may reflect political polarities in seventeenth-century England, as the Midlands riots suggest they do. But factions

in a headless state, where consuls chosen from the Senate and elected by the people govern for a single year in a lifetime, are a very different matter from factions polarising and disputing sovereignty in a monarchy. Moreover, as McIlwain noted,[3] the parliamentary dispute was, in this first decade of the century, more a lawyers' quarrel than a political schism. The parallels are constricted in a way which seems almost a warning not to stretch them too far.

What Shakespeare seems to have done is to take two quite separate contemporary events and link them through the body-politic concept so that they independently confirm the fallaciousness of the organic analogy. The state he depicts is the converse of the organic city which Paul described in 1 *Corinthians*, which, said Paul (and after him most of the sixteenth-century commentators), is a body unified by the power of love. In republican Rome hatred is the normal condition, of the citizens to the greedy Senate, of Menenius to Rome's rats, of Coriolanus to that incompetent commander 'general ignorance'. Only necessity holds the balance against hatred, as the servants in their dialogue in IV, v make clear:

> 2 [*serv*] . . . as war in some sort may be said to be a ravisher, so it cannot be denied but peace is a great maker of cuckolds.
> 1 [*serv*]. Ay, and it makes men hate one another.
> 3 [*serv*]. Reason: because they then less need one another.
>
> (IV, v, 233–9)

War is what makes the citizens need the patricians, who are, as Menenius puts it, 'the helms o' th' state' (I, i, 75), warriors as well as

---

[1] *Ibid.*, v, 144–5.
[2] It is perhaps worth noting that long before 1606 Smith had drawn a parallel between the tribunes and the members of the English House of Commons, when he wrote 'all that ever the people of Rome might do either in *centuriatis comitiis* or *tributis*, the same might be doone by the parliament of Englande'. *De Republica Anglorum*, p. 49.
[3] James I, *Political Works*, p. lxxxviii.

steersmen. Where the Senator of III, ii urges peace on the old organic grounds, 'lest our good city / Cleave in the midst and perish' (ll. 27–8), Menenius sees unity as a matter of dress rather than body, and discord as a torn garment which 'must be patch'd / With cloth of any colour' (III, i, 252–3). This reversal of the Pauline vision was the political setting in which Coriolanus was expected to exchange the casque for the cushion, to plead resentfully for the 'voices' of the multitude (another of Shakespeare's elaborations), and to convert a talent for war into a talent for policy at a time when men, according to the servants' paradox, most hate one another. The tragedy starts from political realities.

© ANDREW GURR 1975

'TITUS ANDRONICUS', III, i, 298–9

PIERRE LEGOUIS

And make proud Saturnine and his emperess
Beg at the gates, like Tarquin and his queen.

No editor so far seems to have investigated the source of the vehicle in this comparison. Yet Shakespeare, if it be he, as generally admitted, who wrote the scene, surely had in mind an incident in early Roman history as understood in his age. Now the obvious *auctor* for it would have been Livy and we shall begin with him. His first book, *ad finem* (1, 60.1–2), tells how Tarquin (Lucius Tarquinius Superbus), having heard, at his camp before Ardea, of the rising in Rome consequent upon Lucrece's suicide, set out to quell it, but 'Tarquinis clausae portae, exsiliumque indictum[1] (the gates were closed to Tarquin and exile notified to him).' The gates are here all right but no mention is made of the begging.

So let us try another historian, hardly less honoured and trusted by the men of the Renaissance, Dionysius of Halicarnassus. His history of early Rome had already been translated more than once from the original into a more widely accessible learned language, so that Shakespeare could read him with his 'small Latin' without resorting to his 'less Greek'.[2]

Now Dionysius, in his Book IV, *ad finem*, tells of Tarquin's fruitless ride from the camp before Ardea to Rome, and the Latin translation reads thus:[3]

At rex Tarquinius, quum ex nuntüs ex urbe profectis, qui forte antequam portae clauderentur effugerant, hoc solum audisset, a Bruto concionem populari oratione detineri et cives ad libertatem vocari...magna contentione laxatis habenis equitabat, ut defectionem anteverteret. Sed quum portas clausas offendisset, et armis plena propugnacula, quanta maxima potuit celeritate castra repetebat, gemens et de miseriis sui conquerens.

(After hearing from the messengers who had chanced to escape from the city before the gates were closed no other news than that Brutus was holding an assembly, making a demagogic speech and inciting the citizens to freedom, King Tarquin rode full tilt to forestall the rebellion. But when he encountered closed gates and battlements packed with armed men, he returned to his camp, groaning and lamenting his misfortune.)

This narrative is, as usual with Dionysius, more prolix than Livy's, but it is also more lively and picturesque. The closing of the gates is mentioned twice; the frustrated king returns whining, which sorts well with begging.

Shakespeare, however, seems to have also had in mind the later development of the conflict between Tarquin and the Roman people. Envoys came to Rome in the name of

---

[1] We use what seems to have been the best edition in Shakespeare's time, *Titi Livii Patavini Historiae Romanae ab Urbe condita, libri XLV Lutetiae, Apud Michaëlem Somnium* ... MDLXXII.

[2] Yet Thomas W. Baldwin, in *Shakespeare's Small Latine and Lesse Greeke* (Urbana, Illinois, 1944), I, p. 121, does not consider it impossible that Dionysius Halicarnassus might have figured in the curriculum of the grammar-school at Stratford-on-Avon.

[3] We use what must have been the most accessible edition by 1593–4, the generally agreed date of *Titus Andronicus: Dionysius Halicarn. Antiquitatum Rom. Libr. XI. Ab Aemilio Porto Recens et post aliorum interpretationes Latine reddidi et notis illustrati Cum indice locupletissimo, et Henrici Glareari Chronologia* (Parisiis, 1588). Another edition, *Dionysii Halicarn. Antiquitatum rom. libri undecim ab Aemilio Porto latine redditi doctissimorumque virorum* (*H. Stephani et I. Casauboni*) *annotationibus illustrati* (Lugduni, apud F. Fabrum, 1592), may however have reached Shakespeare in time if the London booksellers were very alert. For convenience sake we give the references now in use.

the expelled king and his sons, ostensibly seeking to recover their private property. Livy puts it succinctly (II.3.5): 'legati ab regibus superueniunt, sine mentione reditus, bona tantum repententes (envoys came from the kings, not mentioning their return, but merely demanding their property).' This request would have proved successful but for the discovery of the royalist conspiracy that those envoys had been fostering among a number of young aristocrats, including Brutus' sons. The incensed republicans reversed their decision to return the property and, instead of confiscating it for the state, gave it up to the plebs to plunder (II.5.2): 'ut contacta regia praeda spem in perpetuum cum his pacis amitteret (so that after seizing the property of kings as plunder they should abandon hope of ever making peace with them).' Hearing this consummation, Tarquin went about *supplex* among the cities of Etruria. He represented himself as *egentem*. He succeeded in stirring the people of Veii and Tarquinii against the Roman republican leaders who, he said (II.6.3): 'bona sua diripienda populo dedisse, ne quis expers sceleris esset (had given his property to the populace to plunder, so that no one should be free from guilt).' War ensued.

Dionysius tells this part of the story somewhat differently. He places Tarquin's supplication to the Etruscan cities before the royalist conspiracy in Rome. The expelled king reminds the inhabitants of Tarquinii of his former beneficence; then (V.3):

Postremo autem questus est de suo infortunio, quod uno die magna felicitate spoliatus, erro et omnium rerum necessarium indigens cum tribus filiis ad eos, qui olim suo imperio paruissent, confugere coactus fuisset.
(Lastly he complained of the misfortune that had overtaken him; he had fallen in a single day from great happiness, and had been forced to become a fugitive, deprived of all necessaries, and flee for refuge with his three sons to his former subjects.)

To an ill-disposed reader 'deprived of all necessaries' may smack of the beggar. But the people of Tarquinii were moved to compassion by that speech; and they, not he as in Livy, sent envoys to Rome: yet their real aim is much the same. Indeed they first asked that he should be allowed to come to Rome and clear himself before the Senate and then before the *concio*, but this request was at once rejected by Brutus, who however encouraged the envoys to present a more measured one, *aliud mediocre* (V.5).[1] Whereupon they, after a last argumentative flourish, gave up Tarquin's restoration and came to business:

a vobis aliud, quod instum est, petemus. . . ut videlicet regi restituatis bona quae avus eius ente habuerat, qui nullam rem vestram aut vi aut dolo possederat, sed iure hereditatis ad se devoluta et a patre relicta acceperat et ad vos transtulerat. Satis enim illi erit rebus suis receptis, in alio aliquo loco beate vivere, nullum vobis negotium facessenti.
(We make another request of you, a reasonable one. . . to restore to the king the property that formerly belonged to his grandfather, who had not gained possession of anything of yours either by force or by subterfuge, but had inherited it from his father and transferred it to you [i.e. moved it to Rome when he settled there]. It will be enough for him to recover his property and to live in comfort in some other place, making no trouble for you.)

The Senate's favourable decision and its reversal after the disclosure of the royalist conspiracy are told as in Livy, but again at greater length.

Later, Lars Porsenna, king of Clusium in Etruria, with whom the Tarquins had sought refuge, was persuaded by them that monarchy would not be safe anywhere if Rome were allowed to remain a republic; so he waged war against that evil precedent. But, impressed by the attempt on his life by Mutius (Scaevola), Porsenna only made a half-hearted request for

[1] A marginal note however prefers, as a translation for the phrase τῶν μετρίων, another adjective, *aequum*, adopted by the more recent translators.

the restoration of the Tarquins, which was at once rejected. He repeated it for the last time the next year, with no more success. And, to get rid of the worry, he invited the Tarquins to seek another place of exile. This is Livy's story.

But Dionysius is much more fully informed. His Porsenna came out so warmly to the Tarquins' assistance that

promisisset se a duobus alterum effecturum, vel eos suis civibus reconciliaturum, ut in patriam redirent, et regnum recuperarent: vel, recepta eorum bona, quibus fuerant spoliati, se epsis redditurum
(he had promised that he would achieve one of two things: either reconcile them [i.e. the Tarquins] with their citizens, so that they should return to their country and regain their regal title; or that he would recover the property that had been forcibly taken from them and restore it to them [an alternative unmentioned by Livy]).

A year earlier an embassy sent by Porsenna to Rome had met with the rejection of the minor as well as of the major demand (v.21). So he made war on the Romans and besieged their city. But, impressed by Mutius's attempt on his life, he again sent envoys to the Senate, this time instructed (v.31)

ut de Tarquiniis in regnum restituendis nulla verba facerent: sed postularent a Romanis ut bona illis restituerent, praecipue ea omnia quae Tarquinius Priscus heredibus suis reliquerat, et quae ipsi iuste parta possidebant: sin minus, ut saltem quantum fieri posset, integra rusticorum urbanorumque praediorum et pecoris et frugum, quas ex agris collegerant, pretia darent, utro modo eis magis conducere videretur, sive a possessoribus, qui iis fruebantur, conferri, sive ex aerario persolvi mallent.
(to say nothing about the return of the Tarquins, but to request the Romans to restore their property, in particular everything that Tarquinius Priscus had left to them and that they had legally inherited; otherwise they should pay as far as possible the value of the land, dwellings, livestock and produce, in whatever way seemed best, either from the people in possession who were enjoying its fruits or from the public treasury).

The hard-pressed Roman Senate accepted this condition along with others presented by Porsenna for his own benefit; but (v.32)

populus reliquas partes senatus consulti ratas fecit; sed bonorum restitutionem non tulit, quinimo contra scirit, ut neque ex aerario neque a privatis hominibus quicquam Tarquiniis restitueretur (the people ratified all the other parts of the Senatus consultum, but would not tolerate the restoration of their property; on the contrary, they decreed that no compensation should be paid to the Tarquins either by private individuals or from public funds).

However, the people asked Porsenna to arbitrate between Rome and the Tarquins. Then intervenes the story of Clelia's escape, with the other virgin hostages, from the Etruscan camp, of their being returned by the Romans to show their good faith and of Tarquin's traitorous attempt to ambush them on their way back to the Etruscan camp. Porsenna, indignant at this crime against the law of nations, renounced the Tarquins' friendship, and expelled them from his camp, thus putting an end to their hope (v.34) 'vel tyrannidem Etruscorum opera et auxilio recepturos, vel bona sua recupera- turos (either of recovering the kingship with Etruscan help and co-operation, or of regaining their property)', which is the last we hear of the begging for that property. Let us add, however, that later (v.53) as well as earlier (v.3) we hear of large bribes secretly distri- buted by Tarquin in order to recruit supporters to his cause; so that his pretended destitution appears as a despicable deception.

Our summary of Dionysius' narrative has proved, perhaps superabundantly, Tarquin's insistence upon the recovery of his property, an insistence implicitly considered as begging by those who had possessed themselves of it. But, returning to Shakespeare's lines, one may well ask: what of 'his queen'? She was, of course, the notorious Tullia, a female pattern of fiendish ambition beside whom Lady Macbeth might be considered mild and sentimental.

Well, Livy refers to her after Lucrece's suicide once only, to tell us that she fled from her house, the people cursing her (1.59.13): 'execrantibus, quacumque incedebat, innocantibusque parentum furias viris mulieribusque (pursued wherever she went by the curses of both men and women, who invoked the furies, avengers of her parents).' This is even more than Dionysius has to say about her; he simply ignores her after her criminal accession to the throne. So that we can only guess that Shakespeare mentioned her along with her husband in order to provide symmetry with the hardly less hellish Tamora, Saturnine's 'empress'.

The justification, if any, of this lengthy piece of research will be found in a brief yet twofold conclusion. First, that Shakespeare was acquainted with Dionysius of Halicarnassus remained a conjecture but we hope we have strengthened it somewhat. At the same time we feel – is it a delusion? – that we have witnessed the working of Shakespeare's mind. Some years ago a great historian of Rome, now dead, submitted to me a guess of his concerning the source of an incident related in one of the Roman plays; I in turn submitted the guess to Professor Kenneth Muir. Too courteous to answer that the resemblance was less than faint, he wrote that not impossibly 'Shakespeare's beautifully inaccurate memory' had there used apparently irrelevant material. By Professor Muir's kind permission I now use the phrase, with a little more confidence, to characterise Shakespeare's placing 'at the gates' Tarquin's 'begging' and thus fusing two reminiscences into one forceful line.

© Pierre Legouis 1975

'THE MERCHANT OF VENICE'
AND THE PATTERN OF ROMANTIC COMEDY

R. F. HILL

Nicholas Rowe doubted the propriety of considering *The Merchant of Venice* a comedy, going so far as to conjecture that it was 'design'd Tragically' by Shakespeare,[1] while two and a half centuries later W. H. Auden asserted that it should be classed among his 'Unpleasant Plays'.[2] Interpretations of the play, whether arguing for its romantic idealism or its disturbing realism, or for a compromise between these extremes, has necessarily grappled with the problem of the moral status of both Shylock and the Christians. Yet, despite the views of Rowe and Auden, and other stances of unease in response to that issue, *The Merchant of Venice* retains its place among the romantic comedies. The present undertaking is not to affirm or deny that placing, and certainly not to fish again in the troubled waters of the 'Shylock problem', for that occupation can divert attention from other equally significant features that make the play eccentric among the romantic comedies. The friendship of Antonio for Bassanio has attracted attention but the uniqueness of that portrayal has not been sufficiently stressed, or at least been given the right kind of stress. It is importantly related to another unique feature of the play which, given its major significance, can be said to have been neglected. If *Love's Labour's Lost* has a special place among the romantic comedies in that 'Jack hath not Jill' at the end of the play so also has *The Merchant of Venice* in that its marriages occur halfway through. These unique features are instrumental in giving a perspective on love which is peculiar to this comedy. But any attempt to define that perspective cannot rest with the elucidation of these alone. I am not the first to observe that *The Merchant of Venice* is not a particularly funny play, and this has its bearing too. As a comedy of love it is in certain respects singular by comparison with Shakespeare's other romantic comedies.

Characteristically the perspective on the experience of sexual love is ambivalent. The bliss envisioned in the union with the beloved is set against the pains endured and the follies committed on the path to that goal. The hymeneal riches and blessings formally celebrated at the end of *A Midsummer-Night's Dream* and *As You Like It* coexist in the world of the comedies with Valentine's catalogue of the woes of courtship:

> To be in love – where scorn is bought with groans,
> Coy looks with heart-sore sighs, one fading
>   moment's mirth
> With twenty watchful, weary, tedious nights;
> If haply won, perhaps a hapless gain;
> If lost, why then a grievous labour won;
> However, but a folly bought with wit,
> Or else a wit by folly vanquished.
>
> (*T.G.V.* I, i, 29–35)

And the nuptial bliss itself may not be un-alloyed – Oberon and Titania illustrate that – while badinage, or something more earnest, about cuckoldry and shrewish women is common:

> What! I love, I sue, I seek a wife –
> A woman, that is like a German clock,
> Still a-repairing, ever out of frame,

[1] 'Some Account of the Life etc. of Mr. William Shakespeare', *Works*, 6 vols. (1709), I, xix–xx.
[2] *The Dyer's Hand* (1963), p. 221.

And never going aright, being a watch,
But being watch'd that it may still go right!

(*L.L.L.*, III, i, 179–83)

Of course, the ambivalent attitude to sexual love has been a norm throughout the ages. When Troilus cries out, 'if love be good, from whennes cometh my woo?'[1] and Adonis observes, 'For I have heard it is a life in death',[2] they reiterate a view of love which can be traced back to the ancient identifying of love with death, and Sappho's 'bitter-sweet'.[3] Troubadour poetry agonised over the pains of love, inseparable from the joy proposed in fulfilment,[4] and the puzzlement was further complicated by medieval satire of women, Petrarchan idealisation, and sixteenth-century neo-Platonic fervours about the spiritual goal of the true lover. The latter intensified yet another element in the tradition, love as ennobling, the beloved being a source of inspiration to high thoughts and high deeds.[5] Such is the bundle of disparate ideas which informs the love literature of the sixteenth century. The ambivalent nature of the experience of sexual love, its pains and pleasures, its follies and inspirational force, finds sophisticated expression in Lyly's plays and *Euphues*, and in Sidney's *Arcadia*. And such debate, whether directly expressed or implicit in action, seems to be open-ended. Love is inescapable and also inescapably a mingling of sweet and sour; and because – as the Elizabethans never tired of repeating – irrational, a tame madness, beyond a rationalisation of its contradictions. Platonic theorising about the heavenliness of rational love was but an evasion of the reality as Sidney indicates in *Astrophil and Stella*, while so ardent a Platonist as Spenser shows us the agonies and frustrations of love in the stories of Amoret and Scudamour, Florimell and Marinell.

Shakespeare's romantic comedies are shot through with such ambivalence; the felicity in love finally achieved has sharp qualifiers in the preceding actions. They are love comedies in a double sense; because the lovers pass through difficulties to happy unions but also because love and lovers are frequently subjects of mirth. Furthermore, love is often presented as a painful and disturbing passion. The *locus classicus* for the comic and painful manifestations of love is *A Midsummer-Night's Dream*. Hermia and Lysander lament such trials as arise from social status, difference of age, enforced and love-less marriage (I, i, 132–40). If these crosses do not impugn love itself Helena gives a traditional characterisation; that love is blind, makes that which is worthless seem worthy, is precipitate and therefore often wrong in judgement, and is subject to inconstancy (I, i, 232–41). The play copiously illustrates such charges. The harmony and blessings which conclude the play cannot erase what it has postulated about love in the inconstancy of Demetrius, the jealous squabblings of Titania and Oberon, and the picture of the ethereal Titania enamoured of the ass-headed Bottom. The comedies generally, apart from the numerous direct strictures which add to the effect even if qualified by context, provide in their actions a perpetual commentary on the follies, errors, and trials incident to sexual love. Their dramatic life is largely the sum of the tensions and laughter precipitated by the vagaries of love. Love is flawed by inconstancy in *The Two Gentlemen of Verona*, by jealousy in *The Comedy of Errors*, by faithlessness in *Much Ado About Nothing*, by self-

[1] *Troilus and Criseyde* I, 402.

[2] *Venus and Adonis*, l. 413. The text used for all Shakespeare references and quotations is that of Peter Alexander, *The Complete Works* (London and Glasgow, 1951).

[3] Cf. Edgar Wind, *Pagan Mysteries in the Renaissance* (1967), pp. 106–3.

[4] Cf. Maurice Valency, *In Praise of Love: An Introduction to the Love-Poetry of the Renaissance* (New York, 1958), pp. 154–7.

[5] *Ibid.*, pp. 177–80; also Richard Barber, *The Knight & Chivalry* (1970), p. 60.

conceit in *As You Like It* and *Twelfth Night*. The thralls of love are frequently absurd in behaviour, and this is true not merely of those who are in other respects butts of mirth like Don Armado and Malvolio, or misguided in their courtship like the young men in *Love's Labour's Lost*. It may also be true of the romantic heroes and heroines who, it is implied in the joyous conclusions, have arrived at a felicity of love. In *The Two Gentlemen of Verona* Julia is laughable in the fluctuations of anger, feigned indifference, remorse, and sentimentality which mark her response to Proteus's letter – 'Fie, fie, how wayward is this foolish love' (I, ii, 57); and so is Valentine as with comic naïveté he falls into the Duke's trap, advising precisely the same means of reaching the beloved as he has planned for himself (III, i, 81ff.). The worth of Orlando and Rosalind is established beyond doubt, as is the fulness and depth of their love, yet, aside from the implicit commentary afforded by the behaviour of Silvius and by Rosalind's own erosion of conventional ideals of love, the behaviour of both at times places their love in a comic perspective. *Much Ado About Nothing* develops an aspect of the comedy of love earlier seen in *The Two Gentlemen of Verona* (II, iv, 124–34), the penance to be suffered for resisting love. The militance of the initial skirmishes of Beatrice and Benedick is comic because, whatever each thinks of his or her prowess in insult, we recognise it as a mechanism of defence to mask an underlying attraction. Subsequently, when Benedick starts shaving and Beatrice starts sighing the humour is double; Shakespeare is poking fun at the 'marks of love' in a general way, and at these two in particular for their *volte face* from derision to a state of love exhibiting its conventional marks. One hesitates to generalise about so subtle a play as *Twelfth Night* but this much in brief can be said. Love is presented less as giving rise to absurdities of behaviour than as a madness driving men and women on in the teeth of reason, even when (as with Antonio and Olivia) there is a realisation of irrational conduct.[1] What is disturbing in this play is the degree of pain and disillusionment (even if temporary) suffered as a result of the passion of love which is not commensurate with the deserts of the sufferers. Touchstone's remark rings true for the romantic comedies: 'We that are true lovers run into strange capers; but as all is mortal in nature, so is all nature in love mortal in folly.'

So much for the sour of love. What of the sweet? What demonstration have we that the frustrations and follies of courtship are well counterpoised? One answer comes pat – that the lovers reach their goal of marriage. But this does not prove that love is therefore good. Lovers in romantic comedy, as in real life, are impelled by an irresistible urge to union, and that union is envisaged as a bliss of physical, emotional, and moral fulfilment. Experience teaches that such bliss may or may not be achieved, may or may not be lasting. Romantic comedy, however, stops at the point of union, hence one reason why 'romantic' is appropriate. Of course, unless we are cynics, we allow ourselves to be carried by the final flood of joy as if the lovers were washed up on some beach of timeless felicity. Indeed, we should not ponder what lies in store for the lovers beyond the fall of the curtain, unless Shakespeare prompts us as he does, for example, at the end of *The Taming of the Shrew*. When he chooses to do more than hint at what may succeed the honeymoon, as in *The Comedy of Errors* and *The Merry Wives of Windsor*, he is not writing romantic comedy. Be that as it may, in the romantic comedies the good of love, the happiness of the lovers, is only fully realised at the end of the play; it is a postulate which the form asks us to accept.

[1] Clifford Leech, *Twelfth Night and Shakespearian Comedy* (Toronto, 1965), stresses the disturbing element in the play.

Yet can the good of love be dismissed so simply? Shakespeare does not reward his heroes and heroines with promised bliss for nothing. As well as being handsome and beautiful they must live by the right values of generosity, fidelity, chastity and so on. Lapses must be corrected before happiness is granted. The worth of the romantic lovers implies assurance of happiness in marriage. Moreover, the association of good people with the experience of being in love generates the feeling that love itself is good. This impression is strengthened when there exists a sharing of values between the lovers and those who are, as it were, on the side of love and are closely associated with the lovers – one thinks of Duke Senior and Don Pedro.

Yet such considerations are not enough. We might expect the experience of sexual love to demonstrate its goodness in actions. It is a commonplace of the romantic tradition that a man in love is spiritually uplifted and inspired to noble actions. Love ennobles. Spenser, in whom the chivalric and Platonic streams combined, is a fervent exponent of the idea. That does not mean we should expect to find it in Shakespeare's thinking. The idea has no place in the Sonnets, nor amidst all the raillery aimed at the folly of love in the romantic comedies do we find explicit praise of the fruits of love. His heroes and heroines are praised for their virtues but not love itself – certainly not in the sense of its ennobling, inspirational power; it is the fruitfulness of achieved union in marriage that is honoured by Hymen in *As You Like It*. There is one exception, Berowne's doctrinal exposition of the 'Promethean fire' of women's eyes in *Love's Labour's Lost*. Yet the exception may be more apparent than real since the doctrine is undercut by irony, being only advanced to justify the perjury of oaths.

When we look to the actions of the romantic comedies we find decisions and deeds to be admired but do they arise from the experiencing of sexual passion? Love in the wider sense of friendship and kin often demonstrates its virtue. Aegeon and Antipholus of Syracuse endanger their lives in the quest of lost relations; Celia's love for Rosalind takes her into voluntary exile while Orlando saves the life of his brother despite his ill-treatment at Oliver's hands; Beatrice champions the cause of her cousin Hero while Don Pedro assists Claudio in winning Hero; Antonio gives his purse to Sebastian and risks his life in following him to Orsino's court; Adam shows 'The constant service of the antique world' in devoting his person and means to his young master Orlando while the latter's gratitude is subsequently demonstrated.

By contrast, consideration of the effects in action of sexual love throws up a significant point; it is characterised by self-interest. Sexual love designs and suffers for its own ends. The very role of lovers in the pattern of romantic comedy defines them as self-interested; their goal is identical with the goal of the form, union in love, and the major effort of the lovers is actions, or acquiescence in actions, which will achieve that end. In their various ways the plots of *The Taming of the Shrew*, *The Two Gentlemen of Verona*, *Love's Labour's Lost*, *A Midsummer-Night's Dream*, *Much Ado About Nothing* and *Twelfth Night* illustrate the point. Even *As You Like It* is only a special variant; Orlando acquiesces in the fiction of 'Ganymede' being Rosalind in default of any other action to woo and win her, while she has devised the stratagem perhaps to try the quality of his love, and certainly to indulge a piquant pleasuring of her feelings for him. To be sure there are some exceptions to this broad characterising of self-interest. The textbook romance of *The Two Gentlemen of Verona* furnishes examples. Sir Eglamour's succouring of Silvia is part of the moral elevation which appears to derive from his love for his own deceased lady (IV, iii). Valentine is prepared to hand over his beloved Silvia to Proteus (if we take the obvious reading of his words), although the nobility of this act is less an effect of sexual passion than an exalted illustration of the dues of friendship. Julia self-sacrificingly acts on behalf of her beloved Proteus in his courtship of Silvia; yet even she avers, with engaging honesty, that she will woo for him but 'coldly' (IV, iv, 102), and follows Proteus to Mantua 'to cross [his] love' (v, ii, 55) for Silvia. It is in *Twelfth Night* that we find the clearest example of self-sacrificing love. Viola is faithful in the courtship of Olivia for Orsino, and this can only be qualified by observing that it enables her to remain close to him and to take a melancholy pleasure from the indulgence of her undisclosed passion.

Such qualified exceptions aside, we do not find lovers confronted with choices that demand the sacrifice of their own good, nor given important areas of action to demonstrate an ennobling effect of sexual passion, such as will overflow in concern for any but the beloved. That the women are sometimes the saviours of their men does not negate the point of ultimate self-interest. Shakespeare presents his romantic heroines as virtuous, and his romantic heroes as honourable, or retrieving lost honour, but their actions are in all important respects directed to their own happiness. In defining the ambivalent character of dominion by sexual passion the romantic comedies plentifully illustrate the ludicrous, the painful and the deplorable; on the other hand, despite the moral attributes of the heroes, and more particularly the heroines,[1] its ennobling power is more there by inference than by demonstration. *The Merchant of Venice*, however, eludes this generalisation. It seems designed to show love in an unusually comprehensive light and also as an unequivocal good. Ambivalence has been toned down almost to the point of disappearance.

For the lovers in this play trial and difficulty are surmounted with almost painless efficiency, and the ring-plot initiated at the end of the trial scene functions more as restoration of the comic mood than as admonition – more of this later. In the other romantic comedies the lovers suffer estrangements, misunderstandings, trials, often severe in character, and such problems bear directly on their happiness. But after the uniquely early union of the lovers in *The Merchant of Venice* a problem remains which has only indirect bearing on their happiness, and, most significantly, the extent of that bearing is for them to decide, the nature of that decision being a measure of the quality of their love. It would have made no material difference to Portia and Bassanio had they ignored the plight of Antonio. In fact the achievement of the marriage goal half-way through points to a radical difference between *The Merchant of Venice* and the other romantic comedies. In the latter sexual passion is self-interested, its sphere confined to that which directly concerns it. That sphere expands in *The Merchant of Venice*; precisely at the fulfilment of the love of Bassanio and Portia it becomes active in the salvation of Antonio. There was obligation for Bassanio but not for Portia, and there is no self-interest in the postponement of the nuptials beyond that perhaps hinted in 'For never shall you lie by Portia's side / With an unquiet soul' (III, ii, 307–8). Portia herself expresses the fulness and refinement of her idea of love, ending with a characteristic personal disclaimer:

> I never did repent for doing good,
> Nor shall not now; for in companions
> That do converse and waste the time together,
> Whose souls do bear an equal yoke of love,

[1] J. W. Lever, 'Shylock, Portia and the Values of Shakespearian Comedy', *Shakespeare Quarterly*, III (1952), 383–6, observes that the positive values of love find their chief expression in the maturer romantic comedies 'through the attributes and conduct of the heroine' (p. 383).

There must be needs a like proportion
Of lineaments, of manners, and of spirit,
Which makes me think that this Antonio,
Being the bosom lover of my lord,
Must needs be like my lord. If it be so,
How little is the cost I have bestowed
In purchasing the semblance of my soul
From out the state of hellish cruelty!
This comes too near the praising of myself.

(III, iv, 10–22)

Lorenzo has just praised Portia's exalted under-standing of love: 'You have a noble and a true conceit of godlike amity.' In an obvious sense her action on behalf of Antonio is altruistic, and undertaken at some personal sacrifice. Yet at the platonic level of her own reasoning it is not so, for Antonio and Bassanio share an identity of soul, and therefore in assisting Antonio she is assisting Bassanio and herself 'In purchasing the semblance of my soul / From out the state of hellish cruelty!'

And here we encounter that other distinctive feature of *The Merchant of Venice*, its unwith-holding portrayal of male friendship. This is not the place to give an account of medieval and renaissance friendship literature although in that context, so far as I am aware, the friendship in *The Merchant of Venice* combines several unusual characteristics. John Vyvyan points out that the superiority of love between friends to that between the sexes was a view widely held in the Middle Ages.[1] An opposition was set up between rational and sensual love, and the idea is implicit in many Elizabethan charac-terisations of love and friendship.[2] *The Mer-chant of Venice*, by contrast, shows the two kinds of love as of equal validity. Again some friendship stories examined the dilemma of two friends in love with the same woman as, for example, *Palamon and Arcite*, *Titus and Gisippus* and *The Two Gentlemen of Verona*. Shakespeare sets up no such triangular situation in *The Merchant of Venice*; or rather, the triangle is of a very different kind – a man and woman in love with the same man. And in

saying that one has implied something very unusual about the character of Antonio's friendship for Bassanio. It is not quite the love of David and Jonathan 'passing the love of women' for the play surely invites us to see the friendship – at least on Antonio's side – as emotionally equivalent to the love of woman. Of course, friendship is a form of love, and Spenser demonstrates the particularly elevated renaissance view of friendship by placing male lovers in close juxtaposition to heterosexual lovers in his Temple of Venus.[3] However, his phrasing shows the distinction he is making between two kinds of love, eros and agape, sexual passion and a concord of mind and spirit. Such a distinction normally prevails in Shakespeare's writing, male friendship being characterised by deep affection and camaraderie. The nearest we get to the relationship of Antonio and Bassanio is that of Antonio and Sebastian in *Twelfth Night*.[4] But although Antonio is grieved by the latter's apparent ingratitude Shakespeare does not suggest that his marriage is an emotional loss for Antonio.[5]

The love of Antonio for Bassanio is of another order. The description of the parting of the two (II, viii, 36–49) is eloquent of Antonio's misery, and Solanio rightly conjec-tures that 'he only loves the world for him'. In the trial scene Antonio seems to welcome death and in default of an expressed reason we

[1] *Shakespeare and the Rose of Love* (1960), p. 91.
[2] The irrational and sensual element in love needs no illustrating. True friendship is portrayed in Elyot's *The Governour* (Book II, chs. 11–12) and in *Damon and Pythias* as a bond of virtue. Lyly in *Endimion* (III, iv, 122–41) specifically sets the one above the other.
[3] *The Faerie Queene*, IV, x, 25–7.
[4] Even in the Sonnets, despite the intense feelings the Poet expresses for the Friend, he does not con-template the marriage of the Friend with sorrow because involving loss for him – indeed, the Friend is urged to marry.
[5] The 1974 Stratford production clearly implied that it was but the text does not support this reading.

may conjecture the relevance of Bassanio's marriage; he wants it only to be remembered 'Whether Bassanio had not once a love'. He oddly sees himself as fit for death because a 'tainted wether' and 'the weakest kind of fruit', yet there is nothing to substantiate such judgements. In the absence of evidence to the contrary we may suppose him young; he is surrounded by friends and prosperous, his recent losses notwithstanding. And why does Shakespeare make so much initially of his melancholy and then subsequently drop it from overt consideration? Surely to dismiss some obvious explanations to confront us immediately with the real, though implied, explanation. When the young men leave Antonio and Bassanio together it is Antonio, not Bassanio, who at once broaches the subject of their conversation:

> tell me now what lady is the same
> To whom you swore a secret pilgrimage,
> That you to-day promis'd to tell me of?

(I, i, 119–21)

This is the source of his inward trouble. He contemplates the loss of a friend, not one who can be replaced but one without whom existence is meaningless – 'I think he only loves the world for him'. Shakespeare is delicately inferring the same emotional experience in a male relationship as in a male–female relationship. Moreover, the relationships are not set in conflict. Of course, Antonio feels deeply the expected loss, or weakening, of his emotional tie with Bassanio but such pain is an inevitable datum of the situation and is not allowed to develop into a jealous opposition of Bassanio's suit to Portia. The sense of loss, muted but unmistakable, functions in another purpose, to establish that this is not usual male friendship but friendship as love.

The Merchant of Venice presents a more comprehensive picture of love than we find elsewhere in the romantic comedies in depicting a male as well as a heterosexual love relation-

ship; more than this it subjects both to strains which they triumphantly survive. Antonio's love is such as to make double sacrifice of himself for the happiness of Bassanio; it is the sacrifice of the deepest need of his being as well as the sacrifice of his life if need be. He is totally selfless in his response to Bassanio's remark that he will return swiftly from Belmont:

> Slubber not the business for my sake, Bassanio,
> But stay the very riping of the time;
> And for the Jew's bond which he hath of me,
> Let it not enter in your mind of love;
> Be merry, and employ your chiefest thoughts
> To courtship.

(II, viii, 39–44)

Upon the forfeit of his bond to Shylock even his one request that Bassanio be present at his death is put not as a moral obligation but as deferring to Bassanio's feelings: 'if your love do not persuade you to come, let not my letter' (III, ii, 24–5).[1] Antonio has given all, demanded nothing, in the furtherance of a venture whose success appears to involve a profound curtailment of his own needs in love.

Portia's answering to the strain placed upon her barely won union with Bassanio is so total in its generosity that the presence of strain is our conceiving rather than an actual experience of the drama. Considerations that might have given pause – that Bassanio had engaged his friend to an enemy to provide for his own love venture, that the untimely news might defer her own pleasure – are submerged in the tide of concern for a stranger. It is an unreflecting generosity of feeling, not a measured answering of obligation. The emphasis is upon her concern for such a 'dear friend', one 'of this description' (III, ii, 293, 303), and upon Bassanio's distress. The selfless urgency is imperious: 'O love, dispatch all business and

---

1 'Your love' could be ambiguous, as referring also to Portia. If so, Antonio need not have doubted that Portia's persuasion would be as strong as his letter.

be gone' (l. 324). Antonio is present to her mind not as a problem to be solved but as a person to be brought with Bassanio within the embrace of her love: 'When it [the debt] is paid, bring your true friend along' (l. 310).

The suffering experienced by lovers in *The Merchant of Venice* is of a distinct order. It has nothing to do with the customary crosses of love – parental objection, love unreciprocated, unfortunate estrangements, jealousy, inconstancy, female wantonness, pride and shrewishness. External obstacles are quickly surmounted and there are none internal to the love relationships which are presented as unflawed. The pain associated with love is, paradoxically, good, sacrifices willingly not unavoidably undertaken, and the measure of love's plenitude. Does Cupid then exact no tributes in this play? The answer is not quite an unequivocal negative; the contention is that the tragically threatening and comic manifestations of love are but very lightly touched on by comparison with the other romantic comedies. Evidence for the opposition may be thought to be present in the Lorenzo–Jessica story and in the ring plot. But first a brief word should be said about the casket choice and Portia's suitors. Her fun at the expense of the suitors enumerated by Nerissa does not impugn love; if the portraits are just the mere folly of their characters and manners deserves the ridicule. As for Morocco and Arragon, they are not ridiculous – that would have cheapened Bassanio's success – and if we do smile at them it is not for any absurdity they are driven to by love. Their reasonings are not contemptuous but limited, and tainted by self-regard, proving them unworthy of the kind of wealth for which Portia stands. The casket choice itself is a variant of that parental authority, common in romance, that impedes the course of true love, and Portia laments that 'the will of a living daughter [is] curb'd by the will of a dead father' (I, ii, 20–1). However, the case is special

since her father has not chosen, or objected to, a particular man, but devised a test to find the right man. Nerissa invests it with religiosity – 'Your father was ever virtuous, and holy men at their death have good inspirations' – and is therefore assured that the right casket will never be chosen except by one whom Portia will love. Portia's lament is but momentary, and the filial piety that answers to her father's good inspiration – 'If I live to be as old as Sibylla, I will die as chaste as Diana, unless I be obtained by the manner of my father's will' (I, ii, 95–7) – assures us that Nerissa's faith will not prove misplaced.

The Jessica–Lorenzo action may be thought to strike some false notes in the harmony of love. Jessica is heartless towards her father while Lorenzo is a spendthrift young Venetian who pays and risks nothing for what he gains. Opinion will divide here largely depending upon one's response to Shylock's treatment by the Christians. My own view is that the Jessica–Lorenzo action is not so portrayed as to invite close moral or psychological scrutiny. Its justification lies in its broad consonance with the play's ethical pattern. Morally and spiritually Jessica is no kin of her father and to find love she must escape the bonds of hate – 'Our house is hell.' Her squandering with Lorenzo of her father's wealth is a reiteration of what Portia and Antonio demonstrate of love's wealth,[1] a free outgoing of that which was not given us to hoard. So Lorenzo is an 'unthrift love'.

The exchange of Jessica and Lorenzo at the beginning of Act v certainly glances at love's tragic potential, yet we should beware of heavy-handed dealing with a passage so delicately poised. Alexander Leggatt sensitively observes that the very patterning of the exchange makes the tragic tales seem remote, and goes so far as to say that the passage is 'a

[1] See J. R. Brown, *Shakespeare and his Comedies* (1957), p. 70.

comic exorcism of the tragic side of love'.[1] Secure in the happiness of their own love they indulge a sweet vein of melancholy, recollecting tales of less happy loves. Lorenzo identifies with Troilus sighing his soul towards the Grecian tents, but the faithlessness of Cressida slides away unremarked. Jessica does not take up any implication of slight upon her sex by countering with the story of Dido's abandonment by Aeneas – that is given to Lorenzo. Instead she enjoys the frisson of identifying with Thisbe running in terror from the lion, a story, incidentally, of faithful love. Jessica's recollection of Medea is too generalised to signify anything material. The speeches are not so arranged as to suggest a veiled exchange of recriminations against the opposite sex. It is a lyric duet, stimulated by, and providing outlet for, their high pitch of feeling. Eventually Lorenzo descends from sentiment to banter and Jessica returns in kind. It is, as Lorenzo observes, slander, such as achieved love delights in, secure in the knowledge of its falseness.

What finally of the ring plot in which Bassanio and Gratiano are pained by divided obligations, break pledges, and become subjects of mirth? As for laughter the point to be made in the context of my argument is that it is not occasioned by culpable love antics. We laugh with them, not at them, in the happy savouring of a jest set up in a spirit of pure fun:

> We shall have old swearing
> That they did give the rings away to men;
> But we'll outface them, and outswear them too.
>
> (IV, ii, 15–17)

We can confidently enjoy the ladies' accusations and threats in the last act, secure in the knowledge as they themselves are that their husbands are innocent.

Consideration of the serious implications of the ring plot should begin with that short sequence in the trial scene which involves related issues:

Bassanio.
> Antonio, I am married to a wife
> Which is as dear to me as life itself;
> But life itself, my wife, and all the world,
> Are not with me esteem'd above thy life;
> I would lose all, ay, sacrifice them all
> Here to this devil, to deliver you.

Portia.
> Your wife would give you little thanks for that,
> If she were by to hear you make the offer.

Gratiano.
> I have a wife who I protest I love;
> I would she were in heaven, so she could
> Entreat some power to change this currish Jew.

Nerissa.
> 'Tis well you offer it behind her back;
> The wish would make else an unquiet house.

Shylock.
> [Aside] These be the Christian husbands!
>
> (IV, i, 277–90)

Superficially the protestations of Bassanio and Gratiano appear to be a betrayal of their wives yet they are not felt to be so. The death of Antonio seems imminent, and his immediately preceding lines of resignation and patent love drive Bassanio to an ecstasy of emotion. His response is unreflecting, unreasoning, the impulse being somehow to answer the fulness of Antonio's love, sacrifice with sacrifice. Moreover, Portia is only part of the sacrifice; nor, though 'sacrifice' carries that implication, is Bassanio preferring the death of his wife to that of Antonio. He would give her up, with all the happiness her love means to him, just as he would give up his own life and the riches of the world. So also with Gratiano what is involved is the loss of his own happiness in love, and he wishes his wife to heaven (no bad place to be) where she may solicit for the defeat of Shylock. The context of high feeling mitigates their apparent easy disposal of their wives; further, what is central in both cases is the sacrifice of their own happiness. Portia had earlier referred to Antonio as the 'semblance'

[1] *Shakespeare's Comedy of Love* (1974), p. 143.

of Bassanio in the sense of the identity of souls of 'bosom lover[s]'. Bassanio now confirms this with a sacrificial love equal to Antonio's. Shylock's taunt only assures us of the rightness of their feelings even though the comedy cannot accommodate a proving of these large assertions. It is enough that they have been made, and the sincerity of the feelings of Bassanio and Gratiano are to be tried in the light-hearted, yet importantly symbolic, business of the rings.

The ring sequence itself is not initiated by Portia and Nerissa, as it might have been, as a somewhat shrewish chastisement of their husbands. However we judge the tone of their lines[1] –

> Your wife would give you little thanks for that,
> If she were by to hear you make the offer.
>
> 'Tis well you offer it behind her back;
> The wish would make else an unquiet house

– does not alter the fact that neither makes further reference to the matter. In her conversation with the Duke, Antonio, and Bassanio at the end of the trial Portia is anxious to leave and it is only upon Bassanio's insistence that she take something as a 'remembrance' that she is prompted to ask for the 'remembrance' represented by the ring. Insofar as it is a test of Bassanio's fidelity to his 'bond' he survives it, refusing to give the ring despite his sense of the 'Doctor's' deserving and the pain of Portia's tongue-in-cheek taunts. Her parting shot, the apparently ironic 'well, peace be with you!', may well indicate her real satisfaction with his conduct. Bassanio has adhered to the law, his bond with his wife; his legalism parodies that of Shylock, but whereas Shylock's legalism, motivated by hate, is wrong, that of Bassanio, motivated by love, is both right and wrong. His bond with Portia cannot be absolute for that would be an impoverishment of the generosity of love. In love, as in justice, claims may arise which must involve an appeal

to equity. Portia herself makes the point against legalism here (as she had done in the trial):

> An if your wife be not a mad woman,
> And know how well I have deserv'd this ring,
> She would not hold out enemy for ever
> For giving it to me.
>
> (IV, i, 440–3)

These lines are immediately succeeded by the entreaty of Antonio and only then does Bassanio relent:

> My Lord Bassanio, let him have the ring.
> Let his deservings, and my love withal,
> Be valued 'gainst your wife's commandment.

Despite appearances this is not an opposition of the claims of love and friendship for Bassanio is equally bound in love to Portia and Antonio. The single soul which, in effect, Portia had argued the three shared means that neither Antonio's entreaty nor Bassanio's submission can be contrary to what she herself would wish, even though she is used by Shakespeare to exploit the situation's comic potential. Love acts rightly, for Bassanio, in satisfying the plea of one love, gives the ring back to his other love. The three are held together in a bond of reciprocal love.

What is to be said about the second act of the ring plot is implicit in the foregoing reading of the first. If part of Portia's intention in demanding the ring was to test Bassanio he triumphs in the sequel, and well may Portia be gay. He answers her feigned anger with dignity and truth; he will not 'add a lie unto a fault' (v, i, 186). His defence is telling. Did she know the claims of both love and honour that enforced his action she would 'abate the strength of [her] displeasure' (l. 198). Even

[1] I agree with Murray Biggs, 'A Neurotic Portia', *Shakespeare Survey* 25 (1972), 153–9, that Portia 'takes a good-humoured view of Bassanio's nobly impulsive gesture' (p. 155). A number of points in my discussion of the ring sequence have been anticipated in this article.

more, had she been present she 'would have begg'd / The ring of me to give the worthy doctor' (ll. 221–2). Bassanio's judgement of her putative responses must be right in the light of her statements about mercy and the soul-bond uniting her with both Antonio and Bassanio. Given that relationship none could act in a way which another would deem wrong. With respect to the rightness of Bassanio's conduct, Portia's awareness of this and consequent wholly jesting attack, it is worth noting that part of her argument is false and she knows it:

What man is there so much unreasonable,
If you had pleas'd to have defended it
With any terms of zeal, wanted the modesty
To urge the thing held as a ceremony?

(v, i, 203–6)

He did defend the ring with zeal and she did lack modesty in the face of the ceremonious argument: 'That 'scuse serves many men to save their gifts' (IV, i, 439).

In the ring plot we encounter aspects of the pains of love – divided loyalties and infidelity – but their treatment is not such as to erode the dominant assertion of the benignity of love. The conflicts are precipitated in jest. In the plenitude of love sacrifice answers to sacrifice throughout the play. Bassanio sacrifices his oath to his wife at the entreaty of a friend and she accepts that sacrifice despite her delight in teasing her husband. The teasing ends with a restatement of soul kinship:

Antonio.
I once did lend my body for his wealth,
Which, but for him that had your husband's ring,
Had quite miscarried; I dare be bound again,
My soul upon the forfeit, that your lord
Will never more break faith advisedly.
Portia.
Then you shall be his surety.

Portia does not need such assurance since she knows that the breaking of faith was merely technical, being, paradoxically, a confirmation of an identity of soul in arbitrating the claims of love. But the surety is given as a climactic act in the play's ethic of sacrificial love.

Just as the tragic possibilities of love are made remote in the lyric duet of Jessica and Lorenzo so in the ring plot they are sealed off from the reality of the love of Portia and Bassanio (and at a lower level that of Nerissa and Gratiano) because enclosed within an elaborate joke. It cannot be denied that we are reminded, as are Bassanio and Gratiano, that love has its unideal side, that male infidelity will be answered by female wantonness. But it is dramatic sleight of hand. The very act of the jest, lightly insinuating the manipulative role and sharp tongue of woman, together with what is smuggled in under its guise, keeps the portrayal of love on the windy side of the impossibly ideal. Nonetheless, the ennoblement of love is demonstrated as nowhere else in the romantic comedies.

In writing of the reciprocal love uniting Portia, Antonio, and Bassanio I am not unaware of the view that Antonio does not belong in the love world of Belmont. The point has been most strongly urged by Graham Midgley who sees the play as a study in loneliness, Shylock and Antonio being both outsiders, the latter because he is an unconscious homosexual.[1] In the modern climate of opinion about race and sexuality this view does not surprise, nor does it convince. In the discussion of Antonio's love for Bassanio the word homosexual was avoided because it is likely to project on to the play ideas about deviation and social isolation which are foreign to its purposes. In portraying the love of Antonio for Bassanio as the emotional equivalent of love for woman, as I think was Shakespeare's intention, he is moving into territory where one fumbles for the defining

[1] '*The Merchant of Venice*: A Reconsideration', *Essays in Criticism*, X (1960), 119–33.

word. Let the word go, then, and accept the experience as Shakespeare offers it. And it is surely not offered as something which finally has no place in Belmont. That Antonio is an isolated figure there the action of the play seems designed to deny; significantly he is not forgotten as Ansaldo was by Giannetto in Shakespeare's source. It is untrue to say, as Midgley does, that Antonio is forgotten after Portia's formal words of welcome. Nor is his visualisation of the scene, with the happy lovers going off in pairs leaving Antonio to walk off alone, any more than a staging of his interpretation. Portia simply says, 'Let us go in', and the text ends with a general exeunt. That going in could be quite differently staged. Antonio is melancholy in anticipating the loss of Bassanio but it is, arguably, a point of the play that he learns differently; moreover, he has gained the love of Portia. In one way the play makes distinctions between different kinds of love irrelevant. If Belmont is regarded as an inclusive symbol of the Temple of Love the love of Antonio belongs there because sharing in its values. The play as a whole enforces this and if there is a feeling of awkwardness in the conclusion this is because such a statement about love cannot easily be accommodated in the romantic form where the ultimate emphasis necessarily falls upon the happiness of lovers united in marriage.

This discussion of *The Merchant of Venice* has surprisingly got so far with only the barest reference to Shylock. In fact he is of first importance in determining its unusual love perspective. Whereas the other romantic comedies may be said to 'debate' conflicting ideas about love, the conflict in *The Merchant of Venice* is of a different kind. Love, as nowhere else in the romantic comedies in the like degree, takes its stand against an enemy outside its own walls and Shakespeare can therefore allow no place to treachery within. He excludes, or by dramatic sleight lessens, those tributes so often exacted by blind Cupid. Conversely, he enacts a plenitude of love unique in the romantic comedies. The story of romantic love is so organised as to modify the customary focus on sexual love, setting it within the larger concept of charity. Love, rising above its own immediate satisfactions to answer the demands of charity, defines its own perfection.

Shylock determines this perspective, for as the disruptive element in the comedy he is the enemy of charity. The disruptive elements in the other romantic comedies, whether flaws in the lovers themselves, adverse circumstances, opposition of parents or enemies, stand in the way of the union of the lovers, but this is not the function of Shylock. He is placed in opposition to the principles by which Portia and Antonio live and they may be subsumed under charity. The terms of that opposition, defined in attitudes towards usury and justice, have been canvassed by others.[1] Whether Shylock is too simply dismissed as standing for hate, given his treatment by Venetian society, and whether the mercy he receives quite accords with Christian charity, are questions beyond the scope of this essay. Like other 'romantic idealists' I can only affirm the presence of opposed principles even if their human agents elude simple black-and-white categorisation.[2] Such considerations may place a question-mark against the play's success in enacting what its ethical pattern would enforce. But I am here concerned with the pattern itself, the way in which the opposition of love and hate significantly modifies the ambivalent portrayal

[1] E.g. E. C. Pettet, 'The Merchant of Venice and the Problem of Usury', *Essays and Studies*, XXXI (1945), 19–33. Nevill Coghill, 'The Governing Idea. Essays in Stage-Interpretation of Shakespeare. 1. *The Merchant of Venice*', *Shakespeare Quarterly* (Austria), I (Summer, 1948), 9–17.

[2] M. C. Bradbrook, in *Shakespeare and Elizabethan Poetry* (1965), says of *The Merchant of Venice* that 'the characters are at the same time fully human, and symbolic or larger than human' (p. 172).

of love in the romantic comedies. The concerns of *The Merchant of Venice*, the romantic framework and tone notwithstanding, point to a kinship with *Measure for Measure*, another play in which the comic dimension of love has little place, and love is seen in the larger context of charity and justice. That is another story.

© R. F. HILL 1975

THE INTEGRITY OF
'MEASURE FOR MEASURE'

ARTHUR C. KIRSCH

Measure for Measure has an exceptionally vexing critical history. It has disturbed or antagonized critics from the time of Dr Johnson, and almost every aspect of it is a subject of controversy in modern criticism. It has had adherents, but the usual reaction has been ambivalent, if not unfavorable, and the consensus of its most recent critics is that it must be judged at least a partial failure.[1] The following verdict, by Harriett Hawkins, is typical of what is rapidly becoming the modern orthodoxy:

And if, say, the ending of *Measure for Measure* has disturbed and disappointed the overwhelming majority of commentators, of all types and schools – including Dr Johnson and Coleridge, A. C. Bradley and L. C. Knights, E. M. W. Tillyard and Mary Lascelles – in the eighteenth, nineteenth and twentieth centuries alike, the odds are pretty good that it disturbed and disappointed some of its Elizabethan spectators as well. Even if not, even if the ghost of King James himself came back to announce publicly that the original audience viewed *Measure for Measure* 'from beginning to end', as 'pure comedy, based on absurdity, like *The Mikado*, full of topical allusions to a current best seller, and every situation exaggerated into patent theatricality', the recorded evidence of the more complicated response of the critical audience since then would still outweigh this statement because the original audience is dead as earth, but the audience provided by literary criticism survives.[2]

This is indeed a formidable audience, but I would like to argue that it could be wrong, and wrong precisely because it has been unable or unwilling to place itself in the position of the play's first audience. *Measure for Measure*, it seems to me, has suffered more than any other of Shakespeare's plays, with the possible

exception of *The Merchant of Venice*, from the passage of time and the development of attitudes which even his art could not anticipate. The result has been that both the intellectual and formal structures of the play have been consistently misunderstood, and problems have been created where they were not intended and need not exist.

It is astonishing, to begin with, how many critics are unwilling to take the play's Christian ideas seriously.[3] Alone among Shakespeare's plays, the very title is drawn from the Scriptures – and not from its dark corners, but from the Sermon on the Mount and a passage in Luke which was regularly read in the liturgy of the fourth Sunday after Trinity. The action is dominated by religious images – for most of the play the Duke appears in the habit of a friar, and Isabella appears throughout in the habit of a novice – and the language is suffused

[1] For critical histories of the play, see Jonathan R. Price, '*Measure for Measure* and the Critics: Towards a New Approach', *Shakespeare Quarterly*, XX (1969), 179–204; and Michael Jamieson, 'The Problem Plays, 1920–1970: A Retrospect', *Shakespeare Survey 25* (Cambridge, 1972), 4–7.

[2] *Likenesses of Truth in Elizabethan and Restoration Drama* (Oxford, 1972), pp. 23–4. The critic whom Harriett Hawkins quotes is Josephine Waters Bennett, *Measure for Measure as Royal Entertainment* (New York, 1966), p. 158. The model which Miss Hawkins herself suggests, at least for the first part of *Measure for Measure*, is *Antigone* – so dialectically extreme are the disagreements elicited by this play.

[3] The most notable exceptions, of course, are G. Wilson Knight, '*Measure for Measure* and the Gospels', in *The Wheel of Fire* (1930); and R. W. Chambers, 'The Jacobean Shakespeare and *Measure for Measure*', a British Academy lecture reprinted in *Man's Unconquerable Mind* (1939).

liturgy, the Gospel reading for the twenty-second Sunday after Trinity.

What is apparent about all these texts, even to the modern reader, is that they apply – literally chapter and verse – to the behavior of Angelo, a hypocrite who casts out a mote in his brother Claudio's eye while he has a beam in his, who will not and cannot forgive a small debt even when he comes to know the enormity of his own. What is perhaps less apparent is the implicit stress upon the hypocritical condition of all men who do not perceive their inherent corruption and the infinite mercy of Christ's Redemption. For the obvious hypocrite, like Angelo, is merely a parabolic instance of the hypocritical condition of all Adam's descendants. We are all Angelos, all born with a beam in our eye, with an infected will, with an immeasurable debt of sin from which we can be ransomed only through grace.

Elizabethan commentaries on these Gospels make exactly these points, and in ways which are particularly suggestive for *Measure for Measure*. In his commentary on Luke vi, 36–42, for example, Thomas Becon writes:

For with the same measure, saith he, shall other measure to you, as you have measured with. And we can not deny but GOD hath given us good measure. For if he would have given us after our desertes, he mighte have plagued us with wrathe, plague, pestilence, and all evill, and put us to death, assone as we were borne. I will not rehearse how manifolde waies we have offended hym, through all our life with sinnes. This might worthely be given to us as measure, even death and hell. But what doth GOD: He putteth awaie that that we have deserved, that is to saie, wrathe, indignation, judgement, death, hell. &c. and bringeth to us, heaven, grace, libertie, and a quiete mynde, from the condemnation of the lawe, and of an evill conscience...This is truely a large and plentifull measure, but whereas thou deniest other the same measure after that, thinke not, but like measure shalbe given to thee from GOD, as thou givest other.[1]

Another commentator, Antonius Corvinus, linking the passage from Luke to the Lord's Prayer ('And forgive us our dettes, as we also forgive our detters'), remarks: 'Yea if Christe wold handle us according to our wickednes which we have committed against him, and according as we have deserved, when shulde we come unto salvation?'[2] The same commentator connects the parable of the unmerciful servant in Matthew xviii with the Lord's Prayer and concludes:

The summe of this gospell is, that by grace our sins are forgiven us, wherefore we likewise ar bound, to forgive our neighbour their offences done unto us... There is no man under heaven, but is bounde to observe the lawe, and yet nevertheles is a transgressour thereof, in especiall if God would contende with us in judgement...Wherefore we must needs say, that we all are this kinges detters, that is, we be al sinners. For els how can my sinnes be forgiven me, without I felt them and knowledged them.[3]

Finally, William Perkins, in his exposition of Matthew vii, 1–5, writes:

A man must turne the eye of his mind inward, and cast his cogitations towards his owne life and conscience, that so he may see and know the principall sinnes of his owne heart and life. To this purpose serveth the morall law, which is as a glasse to let us see our maine and principall sinnes, which be the *beames* in our eyes here meant. And for direction herein I will note out some speciall maine sinnes, which be in all men naturally; and which every one must well consider of, that will cast this beame out of his owne eye.[4]

The first of the sins Perkins notes out is 'a guiltinesse in Adams first offence...the sinne of mans nature', and he proceeds to the 'natural disposition and pronenesse to every thing that is evill', which is 'the second head of originall sinne'; idolatry; hypocrisy, 'which

[1] *A New Postil... upon all the Sonday Gospelles*, II (1566), sig. [Ddviii].
[2] *A Postill... upon every gospell through the yeare* (1550), sig. Piiiiv.
[3] *Ibid.*, sigs. Xiiii–Xiiiiv.
[4] *A Godly and Learned Exposition of Christs Sermon in the Mount* (Cambridge, 1608), sig. [Dd5].

naturally raigneth in all men, till grace expell it'; pride; and finally particular sin or sins.[1]

Shakespeare occasionally gave such religious sentiments explicit voice, as in Isabella's plea; in Portia's comment that 'in the course of justice, none of us / Should see salvation';[2] in Hamlet's remark, less expressly theological but of similar import, that if we 'use every man after his deserts, who should 'scape whipping'; and in Prospero's final words to the audience: 'As you from crimes would pardoned be, / Let your indulgence set me free'. It seems to me that Shakespeare himself shared such beliefs and their implications, but in any event there in no question that in *Measure for Measure* he was interested in dramatizing them. The ultimate burden of the Gospels to which the play refers, as the commentaries universally make clear, is an apprehension, at once theological and moral, both of the possibilities of grace in human life and of the need for it, and it is just this apprehension that it is the Duke's aim to make his subjects learn and Shakespeare's goal to make us experience.

Measure for Measure begins with an ostensive emphasis upon politics and civil justice. The Duke's opening words allude to the 'properties of government', and we shortly learn from his conversation with the friar that at least one of his reasons for leaving Vienna is to make use of Angelo to remedy the injustices his own clemency has created:

Duke.
> We have strict statutes and most biting laws,
> The needful bits and curbs to headstrong jades,
> Which for this fourteen years we have let slip;
> Even like an o'ergrown lion in a cave
> That goes not out to prey. Now, as fond fathers,
> Having bound up the threatening twigs of birch,
> Only to stick it in their children's sight
> For terror, not to use, in time the rod
> Becomes more mock'd than fear'd: so our decrees,
> Dead to infliction, to themselves are dead,
> And Liberty plucks Justice by the nose,
> The baby beats the nurse, and quite athwart

> Goes all decorum.
Friar. It rested in your Grace
> To unloose this tied-up justice when you pleas'd;
> And it in you more dreadful would have seem'd
> Than in Lord Angelo.
Duke. I do fear, too dreadful.
> Sith 'twas my fault to give the people scope,
> 'Twould be my tyranny to strike and gall them
> For what I bid them do: for we bid this be done,
> When evil deeds have their permissive pass,
> And not the punishment. Therefore indeed, my father,
> I have on Angelo impos'd the office;
> Who may in th'ambush of my name strike home,
> And yet my nature never in the fight
> To do in slander.

(I, iii, 19–43)

The immediate inspiration of these lines is almost certainly James I's discussion in *Basilicon Doron* of his own 'over-deare bought experience' in 'being gracious at the beginning' of his reign,[3] a fact which should alone suggest that Shakespeare did not intend them to cast doubt on the Duke's character or motives. It could be argued, indeed, that regarded as a revelation of character, these speeches would help confirm the Duke's wisdom and essential graciousness. But the intrinsic purpose of the speeches is neither psychological nor topical. Their function is to establish the particular situation with which Angelo must cope and at the same time to suggest a more general moral condition.

Initially, what the Duke says anticipates the arguments Angelo employs when he himself comes to judge and even predisposes us towards them, for the Duke stresses the common

[1] *Ibid.*, sigs. [Dd5]–Dd5*v*.

[2] Portia continues with a direct reference to the Lord's Prayer: 'we do pray for mercy; / And that same prayer doth teach us all to render / The deeds of mercy' (IV, i, 195–8).

[3] (Edinburgh, 1603), sig. [D8]. For a full discussion of the analogies between James I and the Duke, see David L. Stevenson, *The Achievement of Shakespeare's 'Measure for Measure'* (Ithaca, N.Y., 1966), pp. 134–66.

Elizabethan dissociation of justice and mercy in the practice of civil law. All the homilies on Matthew vii and Luke vi, as well as the glosses in the Geneva and Genevan-Tomson Bibles, make a sharp and virtually unbridgeable distinction between the charity which must govern our souls and the justice by which we must be governed to be effective rulers and magistrates and parents. The 'indecorum' of leniency with children is the cap-stone of all the homiletic arguments.[1] The Duke's use of these arguments, however, is disingenuous, because he voices them eventually to disarm them. His speeches are not unlike the laments of the shepherds at the beginning of *The Second Shepherds' Play* – they disclose real political and social abuses, but their ultimate purpose is to describe an unregenerate moral condition which must be redeemed rather than solved. The 'mess' which modern critics enjoy saying the Duke has created and which he leaves Angelo to 'clean up' is, in practical terms of course, never remedied – neither are the injustices in *The Second Shepherds' Play*. The birth of Christ does not permanently prevent landlords from exploiting tenants or wives from dominating husbands; no more does the return of the Duke forever rid Vienna of its stews and brothels. The focus of both plays is not upon political or social institutions themselves, but upon the spiritual limitations and resources, the spiritual condition, of the human beings who compose them.

This focus is immediately apparent in the subplot of *Measure for Measure*. Before the Duke even mentions the corruption of law in Vienna to the friar, we are introduced to it in the persons of Mistress Overdone, Pompey and Lucio – a madam, a pimp, and their libertine associate, if not client. They are set strikingly before our eyes in the second scene, and the play (unlike many of its critics) never thereafter allows us to forget them. They are not merely part of its atmosphere, they constitute the very ground of its moral texture. It is through them that we learn of Claudio's predicament, it is against them that the law seems most impotent, and it is their trade of sex that we are constantly required to hold in mind as we watch the more introspective drama of sexuality played out by Angelo and Isabella. In the immediate and most important source of *Measure for Measure*, Whetstone's *Promos and Cassandra*, an underplot involving a prostitute and pimp figures very prominently in the action and is made the basis for direct homilies on man's sinful condition. Shakespeare's handling of his subplot is less explicitly homiletic and more complex, but its eventual effect upon us is similar. Mistress Overdone and Pompey are a projection of man's irreducible instincts, the flesh which any governor must contend with and understand, not only in his subjects, but in himself. They cannot be exorcised unless, as Pompey observes, you 'geld and splay all the youth of the city' (II, i, 227–8).

This is a reality of which both Angelo and Isabella are essentially ignorant and which a large measure of the Duke's plot is designed to make them experience. Significantly, at different points in the play, both of them parody the words of Paul's Epistle to the Romans vii, 14–15: 'For we knowe that the Lawe is spiritual, but I am carnal, solde under sinne. For I alowe not that which I do: for what I wolde, that do I not: but what I hate, that do I.' Isabella probably parodies the Epistle deliberately when she first tries to excuse her brother's vice, 'For which I would not plead, but that I must; / For which I must not plead, but that I am / At war, 'twixt will and will not' (II, ii, 31–3). Angelo's evocation of the verses is perhaps less conscious and occurs at the end of his unsuccessful effort to

[1] See Elizabeth M. Pope, 'The Renaissance Background of *Measure for Measure*', *Shakespeare Survey* 2 (Cambridge, 1949), 66–9.

convince himself that Claudio had to be killed: 'Would yet he had lived. / Alack, when once our grace we have forgot, / Nothing goes right; we would, and we would not' (IV, iv, 30–2). For both characters, however, and for Claudio as well, the Pauline words have a literal application which each of them must come to learn.

Angelo's schooling is calculated, transparent and dramatic. The Duke deliberately tests him, leaving the city in his hands specifically to put him on trial, as he explains to the friar:

> Moe reasons for this action
> At our more lesiure shall I render you;
> Only this one: Lord Angelo is precise;
> Stands at a guard with Envy; scarce confesses
> That his blood flows; or that his appetite
> Is more to bread than stone. Hence shall we see
> If power change purpose, what our seemers be.
>
> (I, iii, 48–54)

As this speech, with its Scriptural reference, suggests, Angelo's is a case not only of Pharisaical self-righteousness, but of severe human perversion.[1] He boasts in condemning Claudio:

> When I that censure him do so offend,
> Let mine own judgement pattern out my death,
> And nothing come in partial.
>
> (II, i, 29–31)

He does, of course, 'so offend', and in a way which compels us as well as him to see his fall not simply as a particular judgement, but as an instance of general and natural human weakness. In her concluding plea for her brother's life, Isabella tells him,

> Go to your bosom,
> Knock there, and ask your heart what it doth know
> That's like my brother's fault. If it confess
> A natural guiltiness, such as is his,
> Let it not sound a thought upon your tongue
> Against my brother's life.
>
> (II, ii, 137–42)

It is exactly at this point that Angelo, in an aside, first lets us know of his own lust, and with a pun which is to acquire considerable significance later in the play. 'She speaks, and 'tis such sense / That my sense breeds with it' (II, ii, 142–3). His fall thereafter is rapid. In a soliloquy he probes his own corruption and turns his own earlier words ironically upon himself:

> O, let her brother live!
> Thieves for their robbery have authority,
> When judges steal themselves.
>
> (II, ii, 175–7)

By the time he meets Isabella again, however, the sense of his argument has become entirely carnal – 'Nay, but hear me; / Your sense pursues not mine' (II, iv, 73–4) – and he both solicits her and later condemns her brother without mercy. He remains a creature of his passion until the moment when he stands totally exposed before the Duke and his community, and then his change is once again swift. For the first time, his awareness of his own sin becomes partially redeeming.

> O my dread lord,
> I should be guiltier than my guiltiness
> To think I can be undiscernible,
> When I perceive your Grace, like power divine,
> Hath looked upon my passes. Then, good prince,
> No longer session hold upon my shame,
> But let my trial be mine own confession.
> Immediate sentence, then, and sequent death
> Is all the grace I beg.
>
> (V, i, 364–72)

His final words in the play, spoken after Isabella pleads for his life and before Claudio is revealed

---

[1] Matthew vii, 9: 'For what man is there among you, which if his sonne aske him bread, wolde give him a stone?' Lucio subsequently amplifies this theme, on a lower key, when he remarks that Angelo is 'a man whose blood / Is very snow-broth' (I, iv, 57–8) and that 'Some report, a sea-maid spawned him. Some, that he was begot between two stockfishes. But it is certain that when he makes water, his urine is congealed ice: that I know to be true. And he is a motion ungenerative; that's infallible' (III, ii, 104–8).

alive, are those of a genuinely penitent man. Escalus laments that he should have slipped 'so grossly, both in the heat of blood / And lack of temper'd judgement afterward', and Angelo answers:

> I am sorry that such sorrow I procure,
> And so deep sticks it in my penitent heart
> That I crave death more willingly than mercy;
> 'Tis my deserving, and I do entreat it.
>
> (v, i, 470–5)

The beam in Angelo's eye is large and its meaning obvious. The beam in Isabella's eye is smaller, and its perception, both by her and by us, more subtle. She is certainly fully committed to the religious ideals she argues before Angelo, but her idealism, not unlike his, is inexperienced and based on an ignorance of her own human composition. It is significant that we first see her immediately following the Duke's speech declaring that Angelo 'scarce confesses / That his blood flows', and that she is shown to us not only about to enter a nunnery, but 'wishing a more strict restraint' (I, iv, 4) in its rules. Her argument with Angelo is probably meant to be problematic. An Elizabethan audience would hardly have regarded chastity as a technicality, and Angelo's assault, in addition, amounts to a rape. On the other hand, there is truth to the assertion, even though Angelo makes it, that 'our compell'd sins / Stand more for number than for accompt' (II, iv, 57–8), and there is, as Angelo also points out, a cruelty equal to the law's in her refusal to save her brother's life. Shakespeare seems deliberately to have complicated his sources to make their debate as equivocal as possible. What is clearly not equivocal, however, is Isabella's subsequent behavior with Claudio. When she visits him in prison and explains Angelo's proposal, he wavers and cries out to her:

> Sweet sister, let me live.
> What sin you do to save a brother's life,

> Nature dispenses with the deed so far
> That it becomes a virtue
>
> (III, i, 132–5)

An argument not entirely unlike Angelo's, but this time from her brother, who is on the verge of death and afraid, and to this appeal her only response is hysteria. She shows no understanding of his feelings, no sympathy for his fear, no compassion. She has argued movingly of Christ's example of the need for mercy, but at this moment of trial, in her own heart, for her own brother, she finds none.

> Take my defiance,
> Die, perish! Might but my bending down
> Reprieve thee from thy fate, it should proceed.
> I'll pray a thousand prayers for thy death;
> No word to save thee.
>
> (III, i, 142–6)

There can be extenuation, but no excuse for such words. Just as surely as Angelo, Isabella betrays the ideals by which she wishes to live, and she does so, like Angelo, because she cannot accept the realities of human instinct. As a number of critics have noticed, there is a strong erotic undercurrent in her characterization. Angelo's lust for her seems to him, and perhaps at first to us, simply perverse and diabolic, but I think we are eventually meant to understand that she herself offers unconscious sexual provocation. There is a hint in Claudio's description of why she might succeed with Angelo:

> For in her youth
> There is a prone and speechless dialect
> Such as move men; beside, she hath prosperous art
> When she will play with reason and discourse,
> And well she can persuade.
>
> (I, ii, 172–6)

But if the equivocation of 'prone', 'move' and 'play' are only suggestive, the erotic drift of at least one of her own speeches is unmistakable. When Angelo asks her, hypothetically, if she

would not sacrifice her virginity to save
Claudio, she answers:

> As much for my poor brother as myself;
> That is, were I under the terms of death,
> Th' impression of keen whips I'd wear as rubies,
> And strip myself to death as to a bed
> That longing have been sick for, ere I'd yield
> My body up to shame.
>
> (II, iv, 99–104)

What this speech conveys, and her subsequent
abuse of her brother (including its hysterical
image of incest) confirms, is that Isabella is
afraid not only of Angelo's desires, but of her
own.

It is in this context that her behavior in the
final acts of the play must be understood. After
witnessing the scene between her and Claudio
in prison, the Duke praises her: 'The hand that
hath made you fair hath made you good'
(III, i, 179–80); but he proceeds at the same
time to place her in a situation which will
enlarge her understanding both of herself and
others. He keeps her ignorant that Claudio is
alive, but even more important, he involves her
intimately with Mariana, a woman whose
sexual desires are at once open and legitimate.
Nothing is clearer in a stage production than
that Mariana wants her man, and far from
being a scandal, it is an education for Isabella
to help her get him. For when at the end of the
play Mariana kneels to ask her to plead for
Angelo, and when the Duke, invoking the
ghost of Claudio, says 'Against all sense you
do importune her', it is precisely with a
dilated understanding of sense that she is able
to respond. She kneels to the Duke, and says,

> Most bounteous sir:
> Look, if it please you, on this man condemn'd
> As if my brother liv'd. I partly think
> A due sincerity govern'd his deeds
> Till he did look on me. Since it is so,
> Let him not die. My brother had but justice,
> In that he did the thing for which he died:
> For Angelo,
> His act did not o'ertake his bad intent,

And must be buried but as an intent
That perish'd by the way. Thoughts are no subjects;
Intents, but merely thoughts.

> (V, i, 441–52)

That Isabella should thus argue her case in
terms of law, not Christ, and particularly that
she should refer to her own effect upon Angelo,
is not a betrayal of religious faith, but an
exemplification of it. However legally tenuous
it may be, her plea – in behalf of the man who
she thinks executed her brother – is surely an
extraordinary enactment of the kind of mercy
for which she had argued only in theory
before; and it is made possible precisely
because her recognition of herself as a woman
has taught her the human need for mercy. Her
sexual awareness is not vanity, it is humility.

The deepest education in humility, however,
is reserved for Claudio, the third of the characters of whom the Duke deliberately makes
trial, and with Claudio the recognition of the
limitations of human nature is extended beyond
sexuality to the whole Pauline realm of the
flesh, including mortality itself. In his disguise
as a friar, the Duke counsels Claudio to 'Be
absolute for death: either death or life / Shall
thereby be the sweeter', and he rehearses for
him a litany of man's frailties: 'A breath thou
art...thou art Death's fool...Thou art not
noble...Thou'rt by no means valiant...Thou
art not thyself...Happy thou art not...Thou
art not certain...If thou art rich, thou'rt
poor...Friend hast thou none'; and he
concludes,

> Thou hast nor youth, nor age,
> But as it were an after-dinner's sleep
> Dreaming on both; for all thy blessed youth
> Becomes as aged, and doth beg the alms
> Of palsied age: when thou art old and rich,
> Thou hast neither heat, affection, limb, nor beauty
> To make thy riches pleasant. What's yet in this
> That bears the name of life? Yet in this life
> Lie hid moe thousand deaths; yet death we fear
> That makes these odds all even.
>
> (III, i, 32–41)

There is not a word in this well-known speech of Christ or salvation, but there does not need to be. The friar is the Duke, and he has no intention of administering the last sacrament because he has no intention of letting Claudio die. Even more important, however, his whole purpose with Claudio, as with Angelo and Isabella, is not to set down what is in heaven, but the things in earth which inspire belief in heaven. The *contemptus mundi* attitudes which he articulates – many of them paraphrased from the Book of Job[1] – were the conventional premises of Christian faith. In an essay entitled, 'That to philosophie, is to learne to die', upon which Shakespeare may well have drawn for the Duke's speech, Montaigne observes that 'Our religion hath no surer humane foundation, then the contempt of life'.[2] It is this human foundation that the Duke intends, and unlike many critics of the play, Claudio at least does not misunderstand him. He says to the Duke,

> I humbly thank you.
> To sue to live, I find I seek to die,
> And seeking death, find life.
>
> (III, i, 41–3)

In the Gospel according to St Matthew (xvi, 25), these lines read: 'For whosoever wil save his life, shal lose it: and whosoever shal lose his life for my sake, shal finde it.' That Claudio should subsequently falter and desperately cling for a moment to life is not an argument against this faith but a proof of its urgency.

There is another, and crucial, point to be made about the Duke's speech and Claudio's answer to it, and that is that the contempt of the world, properly understood, is redemptive in purely human terms as well, because it leads finally not to a denial of human life, but to an affirmation and enrichment of it, literally to its inspiration. This is the paradox which clearly interested Montaigne, and it is also, I think, the ultimate burden of *Measure for*

Measure. But to appreciate this fully, we must first perceive yet another Scriptural source in the play, a parable which informs the action at a profound level, the parable of the talents (Matthew xxv, 14–30 and Luke xix, 12–27).

The parable describes a lord, about to depart on a long journey, who summons his servants to him.

> And unto one he gave five talents, and to another two, & to another one, to everie man after his owne habilitie, & straight way went from home.
> Then he that had received the five talents, went and occupied with them, and gained other five talents.
> Likewise also, he that *received* two, he also gained other two.
> But he that received that one, went & digged it in ye earth, & hid his masters money.
>
> (Matthew xxv, 15–18)

When the lord returns he praises the faithfulness of the first two servants, but condemns the wickedness of the last:

> Thou evil servant, & slouthful, thou knewest that I reap where I sowed not, and gather where I strawed not.
> Thou oghtest therefore to have put my money to the exchangers, and then at my comming shulde I have received mine owne with vantage.
>
> (Matthew xxv, 26–7

The parable had a rich exegetical history in the Middle Ages, but its essential force remained undiminished in the Elizabethan period as well: that we must make a spiritual investment and a spiritual profit of our own lives. As the Geneva gloss (1560) put it: 'This similitude teacheth how we oght to continue in the knowledge of God, and do good with graces yᵗ God hathe given us.'

The parable clearly preoccupied Shakespeare in the Sonnets and elsewhere, and he may have been specifically led to it in *Measure for*

---

[1] See Richmond Noble, *Shakespeare's Biblical Knowledge* (1935), p. 226.
[2] *The Essayes . . . of Michaell de Montaigne*, trans. John Florio (1603), sig. E.

Measure by a process of association with the talents mentioned in the parable of the unmerciful servant in Matthew xviii. In any event, like the lord in the parable of the talents, the Duke leaves on an indefinite journey, summoning his servants and committing his powers to them. His departing speech is particularly suggestive. Before Angelo appears he asks Escalus, 'What figure of us, think you, he will bear?' and to Angelo himself he says,

> Angelo:
> There is a kind of character in thy life
> That to th' observer doth thy history
> Fully unfold. Thyself and thy belongings
> Are not thine own so proper as to waste
> Thyself upon thy virtues, they on thee.
> Heaven doth with us as we with torches do,
> Not light them for themselves; for if our virtues
> Did not go forth of us, 'twere all alike
> As if we had them not. Spirits are not finely touch'd
> But to fine issues; nor nature never lends
> The smallest scruple of excellence
> But, like a thrifty goddess, she determines
> Herself the glory of a creditor,
> Both thanks and use.
>
> (I, i, 16, 27–40)

This speech is a clear injunction to Angelo to use his credit with vantage, and the financial imagery, with its traditional spiritual connotations, is unmistakable and insistent. Angelo intensifies its import by picking up and playing upon the figure of coining:

> Now, good my lord,
> Let there be some more test made of my metal,
> Before so noble and so great a figure
> Be stamp'd upon it.
>
> (I, i, 47–50)

The play upon the word 'metal', whose spelling was at that time interchangeable with 'mettle', is almost an exact analogue of the metaphorical extension of the word 'talent' in the parable.

Images of investment and coining persist in the remainder of the play and are turned, with remarkable literalness, to the central issue of the action: human coinage and usury, sexual intercourse and procreation. 'It were as good', Angelo lectures Isabella at the start of their second interview,

> To pardon him that hath from nature stolen
> A man already made, as to remit
> Their saucy sweetness that do coin heaven's image
> In stamps that are forbid. 'Tis all as easy
> Falsely to take away a life true made,
> As to put mettle in restrained means
> To make a false one.
>
> (II, iv, 42–9)

Moments later, he asks her if she would not, if necessary, procure 'credit' with her brother's judge by laying down 'the treasures' of her body, and she replies that to yield to such shame would be an ignominious 'ransom', that her brother's death would be 'the cheaper way', and that she does something 'excuse the thing I hate / For his advantage that I dearly love' (II, iv, 92, 96, 111, 105, 119–20). Angelo then remarks, 'We are all frail... Nay, women are frail too', and Isabella rejoins,

> Women? – Help, heaven! Men their creation mar
> In profiting by them. Nay, call us ten times frail;
> For we are soft as our complexions are,
> And credulous to false prints.
>
> (II, iv, 121, 123, 126–9)

The same sentiment and imagery is echoed in the subplot shortly afterwards, when Elbow castigates Pompey for his trade:

Elbow. Nay, if there be no remedy for it, but that you will needs buy and sell women like beasts, we shall have all the world drink brown and white bastard.
Duke. O heavens, what stuff is here!
Pompey. 'Twas never merry world since, of two usuries, the merriest was put down, and the worser allowed by order of law.

> (III, ii, 1–8)

The deep relationship between the two usuries is expressed in the two senses of 'angel' in

Angelo's very name, as the Duke suggests when he laments for him:

> O, what may man within him hide,
> Though angel on the outward side.
>
> (III, ii, 264–5)

The Scriptural implications of these images of coining and profit sustain themselves, but they are in addition deepened by their frequent collocation with another train of images, elicited (again with conspicuous literalness) by the play's title and primary Scriptural source, images of measuring, weighing, scaling, grading, testing. Angelo, at the very start, questions the Duke's 'test' both of his metal and mettle. At the end of their second meeting, after Isabella protests that she will denounce him, Angelo asserts, 'Say what you can: my false o'erweighs your true' (II, iv, 169); Claudio wishes his sister to 'assay' Angelo (I, ii, 171); Lucio bids her to 'assay the power' she has (I, iv, 76); and the Duke tells Claudio that Angelo's proposal to her had been designed only to make 'an assay of her virtue' (III, i, 161–2). Then, as now, the word 'assay' meant equally to measure the nature and quality of a person or the composition and purity of a metal.

The cumulative result of these configurations of images and action in *Measure for Measure* is to compel us to understand man's instincts, and particularly sexuality, as simultaneously a manifestation of sin and a form of spiritual capital which must be invested to realize the deeper purposes of human life. The Duke makes his subjects recognize that the corruption which boils and bubbles in Vienna is within themselves, a moral condition, a beam in their own eyes. In the words of the homilist, he makes them turn the eyes of their minds inwards so that they may recognize the principal sins of their own lives and hearts. He also, however, and this is the ultimate purpose of his deceptions and contrivances, enables them to find a redeeming expression of their humanity by bringing them to marriage. Marriage always in Shakespeare has sacramental value, and never more than in *Measure for Measure*, where it is seen as a sanctification of impulses which could otherwise damn us, as the means through procreation by which we can make true coin of the currency of our lives, by which we can – literally – remake ourselves in the image of our Creator. It is thus the most perverse combination of Victorian prudery and modern cynicism to regard the bed-trick as unseemly or to imagine, as one recent director has, that Isabella should recoil from the Duke's proposal at the end of the play. The bed-trick miraculously transforms Angelo's libidinousness, turning it to the consummation of a betrothal he had betrayed, and the Duke's proposal offers the promise that in marriage Isabella can fully express her newborn awareness of herself as a woman. The one action moderates scope, the other restraint – the two poles of sexuality in the play – and both are at once gracious and creative.

Objections to the bed-trick and Isabella's marriage with the Duke are only symptoms, of course, of a larger category of modern discomfort with *Measure for Measure*, and that is the dissatisfaction with its form. There are various, though related, arguments against the form of the play: that the Duke is incoherent as a character, a manipulative *deus ex machina* represented in incompatible naturalistic and allegorical modes; that Shakespeare depicts Claudio, if not Isabella, in essentially ambivalent ways; and above all, that the play arouses an appetite for tragedy that it cannot fulfil and indeed wilfully denies. 'The first half of the play shows us what is in fact the case; the second half is escapist fiction.'[1] Though

[1] Hawkins, *Likenesses of Truth*, p. 76. Essentially the same objections are raised, though more subtly, by A. P. Rossiter in *Angel With Horns*, and even by Mary Lascelles at the end of her book, *Shakespeare's Measure for Measure* (1953).

ostensively formal, such objections rest to a considerable extent upon a fundamental mis-apprehension of the play's ideas. As I hope I have made clear, the grace offered and achieved at the end of *Measure for Measure*, rather than contradicting the experiences of the beginning, is their consequence and is inherent within them. It is an understanding of 'what is in fact the case' about human behavior that makes possible its charitable expression in forgiveness and creativity; and the Duke, in bringing his subjects to such an understanding, combines his political and spiritual roles by reconstituting both their souls and the soul of his society. Elizabethans would have appreciated, even if we do not, that

All temtation or tryal is not evell, For God tempteth his servantes: one freend is tempted of another: the childe is tryed by the Father, the Wyfe by her Husbande, the Servaunt by his Master, not that they might be hurt by triall, but rather that they might thereby be profited.[1]

So, surely, are the characters who are tempted and tried in *Measure for Measure*.

If, however, the failure to understand these ideas is the final cause of critical anxiety about the play's form, the efficient cause, and one that is endemic in Shakespeare criticism, is the failure to appreciate its dramaturgy, the way it is designed to affect an audience, on stage, in performance; and it is with this subject that we must finally deal. To begin with, one would hardly guess in reading the pages of many of its critics that the play is often funny. The most insistent comedy, of course, occurs in the sub-plot, which is as important to the tonal texture of the play as to its intellectual substance, since just as the sexuality of Vienna's underworld subsumes the more serious drama enacted in the main plot, so does its bawdy humor. Before the main action develops, we are introduced to a judgement scene (II, i), the play's first, which is dominated by a melange of Elbow's mala-propisms and Pompey's puns, and a similar

mood, broad and usually bawdy, is sustained whenever the low-life characters appear. The prison itself, a central image as well as location of the play's action, is transformed by them. Pompey remains as 'well acquainted' there as he was in his own 'house of profession' (IV, iii, 1–2) – and as witty – and even Master Barnardine, 'insensible of mortality, and desperately mortal' (IV, ii, 142–3), 'unfit to live or die' (IV, iii, 63), stays undaunted and resolutely comic.

Equally resolute, and even more insistent on stage than the subplot, is the complex comedy of Lucio. His role is particularly apparent in performance, where his ubiquitousness is matched only by the Duke's. He pops up everywhere, moving freely through both plots, acting pervasively as a sardonic commentator. He has jokes for everyone and for all occasions – for Claudio, for Isabella, for Pompey, and for the Duke, especially for the Duke. Early in the play he shows some affection for Claudio and possibly admiration for Isabella, to whom he delivers the one speech in the play which explicitly and richly describes the fruitfulness of human generation (I, iv, 40–4), but as the play proceeds, his libertine wit becomes progressively more irreverent and sterile until finally, with the Duke, it ends in outright slander. For us, given the theatrical situation, the slanders are comic, but the Duke himself is conspicuously not amused. His irritation is itself funny, but it should not be construed, as it has been by many modern critics, as vindictive or petty, for Lucio, who becomes the Duke's comic shadow, is also his most serious antagonist. His slanderousness, for Elizabethans, would have marked him as a kin of the Blatant Beast, an enemy both of social and

[1] Augustine Marlorate, *A Catholike and Ecclesiastical exposition of the holy Gospell after S. John* (1575), sig. [Bb4]. Marlorate's discussion of temptation occurs in his exposition of the parable of the woman taken in adultery, a parable which is itself relevant to *Measure for Measure*.

moral order, and would have related him quite directly to the underlying ideas of the play. William Perkins considered slander to be the essential subject of Matthew vii, 1–5. The verse, 'Judge not, that ye be not judged', he read as a reference to 'rash judgment' and as specifically an injunction against slanderers:

He that gives rash judgment of another, is worse than a theefe that steales away a mans goods: for he robbes him of his *good name*, which (as Salomon saith) *is to be chosen above great riches*, Prov. 22. 1. Againe, riches may be restored, so can not a mans good name beeing once blemished in the hearts of many. Againe, a man may defend himselfe from a theefe, but no man can shunne an other mans evill minde, or his badde tongue: nay, the backbiter is worse then a murtherer, for he killeth three at once; first, his *owne soule* in thus sinning: secondly, his *neighbour* whose name he hurteth: and thirdly, the hearer who receiveth this rash and injust report: and for this cause the *slaunderer* is numbered among those that shall not inherit the kingdome of God, Psal. 15. 3 I Cor. 6. 10. and the Apostle chargeth Christians to account of such raylers as of persons excommunicate. I Cor. 5. 11.[1]

Lucio is such a soul as Perkins describes. His licentiousness has the excuse neither of trade, like Pompey's, nor passion, like Angelo's, and his condition is even more desperate than the drunken Barnardine's, because it is consciously faithless. Simply the thing he is shall make him live. Like Mak in *The Second Shepherds' Play*, as well as Parolles in *All's Well That Ends Well*, he constitutes a moral condition, the basic antithesis of the processes by which man becomes new made. Like them also, he is forgiven, though less as a promise of his own regeneration than as a signification of the power of charity. In Lucio's case forgiveness is grudging, but consistent with the mode in which he is represented throughout, it is also amusing. We know what is in store for him during most of the play, and the moment when he unhoods the Duke is a rich fulfilment of comic expectation and pleasure. 'This may prove worse than hanging' (v, i,

368), he says immediately, and in his terms it does. The Duke significantly leaves his sentence for the very last, and Lucio remains on stage for the whole of the final scene, modulating its seriousness with his own farcical discomfiture. When his turn comes, the Duke first says that he 'cannot pardon' him, but the Duke's tone, if not his language, is clearly playful:

> You, sirrah, that knew me for a fool, a coward,
> One all of luxury, an ass, a madman:
> Wherein have I so deserv'd of you
> That you extol me thus?

Lucio. Faith, my lord, I spoke it but according to the trick: if you will hang me for it, you may: but I had rather it would please you I might be whipped.

Duke.
> Whipped first, sir, and hang'd after.
> Proclaim it, Provost, round about the city,
> If any woman wrong'd by this lewd fellow,
> – As I have heard him swear himself there's one
> Whom he begot with child – let her appear,
> And he shall marry her. The nuptial finish'd,
> Let him be whipp'd and hang'd.

Lucio. I beseech your Highness, do not marry me to a whore. Your Highness said even now, I made you a duke; good my lord, do not recompense me in making me a cuckold.

Duke.
> Upon mine honour, thou shalt marry her.
> The other slanders I forgive, and therewithal
> Remit thy other forfeits. – Take him to prison,
> And see our pleasure herein executed.

Lucio.
> Marrying a punk, my lord, is pressing to death,
> Whipping, and hanging.

Duke.   Slandering a prince deserves it.
>   (v, i, 498–521)

The entire sequence is a consummate blend of comedy and seriousness, and Lucio leaves the stage, as he entered it, a perfect instrument of the play's peculiar tragicomic pitch.

Measure for Measure maintains this pitch, I think, in all its scenes, even those which are most serious. The three big scenes of the early

---

[1] *Exposition of Christs Sermon in the Mount*, sigs. Cc6v–[Cc7].

acts, for example – the two between Angelo and Isabella and the one between her and Claudio – are all intrinsically calculated on stage to contain the tragic possibilities they portray. The first meeting between Angelo and Isabella, witnessed by both Lucio and the Provost, is cast essentially as a debate in which we must respond to the emerging feelings of the participants not only, or even primarily, as naturalistic expressions of character, but as complex exemplifications of two arguments, theirs and Shakespeare's; and lest we be tempted to become too preoccupied with the feelings themselves, Lucio's role in the scene as Isabella's sardonic prompter acts as a further restraint. The second scene between Isabella and Angelo has no witnesses and is partly for that reason the most unsettling, but it too calls attention to itself as a debate and in addition, for all its brutality, verges upon comedy, since until virtually the end Isabella remains unviolated even by Angelo's words. She simply cannot understand him; and on stage at least, this is as funny as it is serious. There is, finally, a similar humor in the scene between her and Claudio which the Duke observes, a scene in which the gravity of Claudio's feelings is at once intensified and tempered by the adolescent transparency of hers. Again, in the theater, our partial amusement at Isabella's behavior is unmistakable, and even for a director bent on dark thoughts, difficult to suppress.

Beyond such subtle controls, however, beyond the comedy of Lucio and the subplot, beyond all else in the play, it is the Duke who is most responsible for setting the tone and determining the nature of our response. We learn at the outset of the drama, in the third scene, that he is remaining in Vienna to observe and control a situation he has deliberately contrived as a trial, and we are subsequently never allowed to forget either his presence or his power. He is kept before our eyes in a brief scene (II, iii), otherwise unnecessary for the

plot, which is interposed between the two meetings of Angelo and Isabella, and he is actually on stage observing the entire scene between Isabella and Claudio in prison. We therefore wonder not if he will intervene, but when and how. We expect his intervention, and this expectation alone suggests that the modern notion of the play's division between incompatible modes of fact and fiction is a falsification.[1] In the theater, our pervasive anticipation of the Duke's intervention, combined with the nature of his overt stage management later in the play, creates a unified, if highly sophisticated, effect. It necessarily disengages us to some extent from the action, even in the early scenes, and modulates our response to potentially tragic situations. We watch Isabella and Claudio and Angelo not only with the Duke, but in large measure through his eyes, and no matter how much they may suffer, we are always conscious that

---

[1] The alleged split in *Measure for Measure*, a shibboleth of modern criticism, is also a prime instance of the failure to understand the play as a theatrical text, for even a director who is dissatisfied with the play has no difficulty with the Duke's intervention in Act III. Despite a pronounced lack of sympathy with the play's conclusion, for example, John Barton has testified that 'One thing, however, did seem to emerge in rehearsal and performance. It has often been pointed out how, on reading the play, one finds it splitting down the middle. At the point Isabella leaves Claudio after her interview with him in prison, and is left alone with the Duke, the level of writing changes. The Duke for the first time goes into prose, and into plotting the bed-trick; and the play, which has in the first half been poetically intense and psychologically subtle, is then worked out on a lower, almost fairy tale, level. The change is obvious enough in the study; but in the theatre, I think the difference disappears. This is because the actors, if they have brought their characters to life in exploring the first half, can carry through that life into the play's more superficial resolution. I felt, in fact, that what seemed a problem in the study largely melted away in the theatre, when those characters were embodied by living actors.' ['Directing Problem Plays: John Barton talks to Gareth Lloyd Evans', *Shakespeare Survey* 25 (Cambridge, 1972), 65.]

they are actors in a drama he has contrived for their ultimate benefit. At the same time, because his active intervention is delayed, and by no means omnipotent when it comes, our feelings are deliberately involved in the action. Both Shakespeare and the Duke give Isabella, Claudio and Angelo the scope to develop their emotions with an intensity which moves us as well as them. The result, as Walter Pater wrote, is that the play 'remains a comedy, as is congruous with the bland, half-humourous equity which informs the whole composition ... yet it is hardly less full of what is really tragic in man's existence than if Claudio had indeed "stooped to death"'.[1]

The form which such a conjunction of responses describes is in fact tragicomedy, and in *Measure for Measure*, perhaps more than in any other of his plays, Shakespeare gives that form its most radical expression. Guarini had written that

He who composes tragicomedy takes from tragedy its great persons but not its great action, its verisimilar plot but not its true one, its movement of the feelings but not its disturbance of them, its pleasure but not its sadness, its danger but not its death; from comedy it takes laughter that is not excessive, modest amusement, feigned difficulty, happy reversal, and above all the comic order.[2]

Measure for Measure conforms to this definition fairly closely and shares with Shakespeare's other tragicomedies a number of distinctive developments of the pattern it describes.[3] It is exceptionally self-conscious, calling constant attention to its theatricality, not only late in the play but at the start, and it is deliberately designed to translate our awareness of theatrical artifice into a consciousness of Providence itself. The Duke truly moves through the play simultaneously 'like power divine' and like a stage director, an analogy which does not require us to see him as an allegorical representation of Christ, but which does encourage us to associate the workings of Providence with

the dynamics of the play itself. In this respect the patent theatricality of the ending is less an evasion of the play's serious ideas than a fulfilment of them. We have watched the play throughout both from the wings and the stalls, and in a paradox which is familiar in many of Shakespeare's plays but especially germane to this one, we are made to understand that what seems illusory is finally most real: that the 'after-dinner's sleep' and the 'seeming' are part of the earlier experiences of Angelo, Isabella and Claudio, and that the deeper and spiritual truth of their lives is the Duke's fiction.[4]

Measure for Measure also, like Shakespeare's other tragicomedies, has a generically appropriate overall effect. There is no sense, of course, of the epiphanies of the last plays, and perhaps not even of the wonder that characterizes *All's Well That Ends Well*. *Measure for Measure* has no miraculous cures, and the distance between Helena's vulnerable passion and the Duke's general equanimity is considerable. But the play is nevertheless not without marvelousness, and its own miracles are not less great because we are so aware of how they have been contrived. It remains a marvel, both theatrically and ideologically, that the punishment not only fits but transforms the crime, that mercy can eventually be consistent with justice, and that each of the characters in the play can

---

[1] *Appreciations* (1889), p. 171.

[2] *Compendium* to *The Pastor Fido*, translated by Allan H. Gilbert, *Literary Criticism: Plato to Dryden* (New York, 1940), p. 171.

[3] For a more extensive discussion of these developments, see Arthur C. Kirsch, *Jacobean Dramatic Perspectives* (Charlottesville, 1972), pp. 7–15, 52–74; and 'Cymbeline and Coterie Dramaturgy', *ELH* XXIV (1967), 285–306, reprinted in *Shakespeare's Later Comedies*, ed. D. J. Palmer (Penguin Shakespeare Library, 1971), pp. 264–87.

[4] The theatrical self-consciousness of this play has been much discussed, but see especially Francis Fergusson, *The Human Image in Dramatic Literature* (New York, 1957), pp. 148–53.

be meted a measure as good as it is exact. Moreover, both the language and action repeatedly reveal the wonder of regenerated life, not only literally, as character after character is reprieved from death, but more profoundly, as the desire for life is progressively illuminated by the kind of charitable understanding which culminates in Isabella's remarkable plea for the life of Angelo.

This understanding and these paradoxes, of course, are those of Christian experience itself, and in *Measure for Measure*, as in his other tragicomedies, Shakespeare identifies the form of the play with the shape of the life it represents. The Duke speaks explicitly of making 'heavenly comforts of despair' (IV, iii, 109), and the idea of *felix culpa* clearly lies at the heart of the play.[1] The action describes an arc which moves dialectically from tragic to comic possibilities: literally from the fear of death to the joy of anticipated marriage, from prison to freedom, from sin to grace. In no other play in the canon is the pattern of *felix culpa* more encompassing or more deep. Tragic experience is not merely the prelude to comic salvation in *Measure for Measure* but the means by which such salvation can be understood and achieved: 'For els how can my sinnes be forgiven me, without I felt them and knowledged them.'

The distinction of *Measure for Measure* among Shakespeare's other tragicomedies, I think, is that these antinomies and paradoxes are extraordinarily acute, and their resolution difficult, not only for the characters, but for us as well. The Duke is no Prospero, though he may resemble him, and the play is not entirely his, though he sets it in motion and eventually

sets it right. The human nature that is at once the subject and material of his drama is fallen and sometimes intractable. Because he delays his intervention, his actors overplay their roles, beyond even his expectation, and create painful problems, and when he does actively intervene, they still will not stick to his script. He must exert himself, and so must we.[2] To an extent that is thus unusual in tragicomedy, we ourselves are not only drawn into the action, but implicated in it: the degree to which we are entangled by Isabella, Claudio and Angelo is a measure of our own necessarily mortal condition, and our hope for their comic deliverance is an extension of the capacity for hope and forgiveness in our own lives. We experience, we do not merely observe, the process by which they are brought to self-knowledge and regeneration: what the Duke's play is for them, Shakespeare's is for us. Thus, to paraphrase Pater, 'the action of the play, like the action of life itself for the keener observer', develops in us not only the conception of charity, but the 'yearning to realise it'.[3]

---

[1] It is also an idea to which much recent criticism seems especially hostile. Philip Edwards, *Shakespeare and the Confines of Art* (1968), p. 118, says of the Duke's reasoning: 'God works in mysterious ways, but this beats all – willingly to cause despair in order to show the beauty of divine consolation.' It is odd, though symptomatic, that Edwards should at the same time declare that 'Modern criticism has established beyond disproof' that there is in *Measure for Measure* 'a Christian or near-Christian pattern of providence and redemption', 'a religious rhythm', a plot whose movement 'can certainly be an emblem of achieving grace' (p. 109).

[2] For an excellent discussion of this point, see Michael Goldman, *Shakespeare and the Energies of Drama* (Princeton, 1972), pp. 164–74.

[3] *Appreciations*, p. 183.

'TO SAY ONE': AN ESSAY ON 'HAMLET'

RALPH BERRY

The beginning of act v, scene ii finds Hamlet in a trough between action, released for once from the immediate stimuli of events. He is merely discussing his affairs with Horatio. It is a still moment, not with the felt danger of the moment that follows the acceptance of Laertes' challenge, but freer, less constrained. Horatio reminds him gently that the English authorities must shortly report on the death of Rosencrantz and Guildenstern. And Hamlet responds with these words:

> It will be short,
> The *interim's* mine, and a mans life's no more
> Then to say one.

That is what we have, and I reproduce it exactly in the terms that the Folio, our sole authority for this passage, supplies. 'A man's life's no more than to say one.' What does it mean? The editors – with, I think, a single major exception – pass the line by, its meaning being so obvious as to warrant no commentary. But I find that to explain the line, if I can, requires me to explain the play.

An editor can look the other way, but a translator cannot. We can usefully glance at two distinguished translations. Schlegel appears to stonewall successfully with 'Ein Menschenleben ist als zählt mans eins': in fact he has given the phrase a decisive inclination, for 'zählen' is to count, not utter. André Gide makes this rendering even clearer:

Et la vie d'un homme ne laisse même pas compter jusqu'à deux.

Since the tendency of French is always to be reductive of meanings, and of Shakespeare to expand possibilities, we can start with Gide's –

single – meaning. He takes Hamlet to be saying that man's life is brief, and that one must be ready for action. That is a legitimate meaning. John Dover Wilson suggests, in his New Cambridge edition, that 'one' is the fencer's word, the exclamation that one utters at the climax of the lunge: 'a single pass, then, will finish Claudius off'.[1] I think he must be right, but here too the single meaning pauperizes the riches of Shakespeare's wordplay here. 'One' is of all numbers the most resonant. It bears the implications of unity and self-hood, and it has moreover a significant past in *Hamlet*. Is not Hamlet saying that man's life is a quest for unity, for a profound accord between self and situation? But let us explore some of the ways in which the final scene permits Hamlet to say 'one'.

Hamlet is not a play that admits of ready, or final, description. I find L. C. Knight's term 'the Hamlet consciousness'[2] helpful, and I prefer to think of the play as a prolonged description of a single consciousness. At the beginning, that consciousness is aligned against its situation. It rejects external events, it lacks a stable base of self-hood: it is profoundly disturbed. At the end of the play, the consciousness is fully aligned with its situation. It is sufficiently self-aware, it has a base for judgment and action. Hamlet is, so to speak, *comfortable*. That, in broadest outline, is what happens in *Hamlet*.

[1] John Dover Wilson, *What Happens in Hamlet* (Cambridge, 1935), p. 272. References are to *The Complete Works*, ed. Hardin Craig (1951).

[2] L. C. Knights, *Some Shakespearean Themes and An Approach to Hamlet* (Stanford, 1966), pp. 191 ff.

(i) Certain elements predominate in the Hamlet consciousness, and can be identified here. We might, I think, begin by discarding a misleading term that figures in the commentaries, 'intellectual'. Hamlet is not an intellectual, in the sense that he is given to rational analysis of a problem. The formulation of categories and issues is not his forte. He has a superb, intuitive intelligence, but that is something quite different. This type of mind is especially good at perceiving meanings reflected back from the environment. A flair for symbolism is central to a poet, dangerous (if still vital) to a thinker. I instance the Danish drinking practices, the player's emotions, Fortinbras' march to Poland: events supply their meaning for Hamlet. But they have meaning only to the receiving mind, and to find 'sermons in stones' has always a certain intellectual naiveté. There is no such thing as a symbol *per se*. The crucial sampling of Hamlet's powers as intellectual is the 'To be or not to be' soliloquy. It is unreasonable to treat it as a philosophical disquisition – it is an associative meditation, the mind reviewing a diorama of concepts and images. But it is fair to point out that it suggests, in outline, a logical structure. Harry Levin, indeed, has stressed that Hamlet is using 'the method preferred by Renaissance logicians...the dichotomy, which chopped its subjects down by dividing them in half, and subdividing the resultant divisions into halves again'.[1] Nevertheless, there are so many questions left hanging in the air that the soliloquy appears to me quite unlogical in essence, if not in form. I instance a few: 'To be, or not to be: that is the question' surely implies another question. This is true whether (a) one accents 'that', implying the rejection of a preceding question, (b) one accents 'is', re-affirming the proposition after a previous doubt, (c) renders 'that is' as a spondee, thus more subtly re-affirming the question after a doubt. Then, is 'in the

mind' a tautology ('nobler' is a mental quality) or a meaningful choice, 'suffering' to occur to the body or the mind? Does 'And by opposing end them' mean that the forces of outrageous Fortune can be physically defeated, or that the act of opposition in itself is a means of dispersing them, or that the act of opposition must mean death, with its own resolution of the problem? Again, 'puzzles the will': this I take to be a fusion of 'puzzles the mind' and 'inhibits the will'. Is Hamlet aware of this fusion, or confusion? Presumably not, since he arrives at 'Thus conscience does make cowards of us all; / And thus...' as though a logical terminus of argument had been arrived at. He is, like his twin Brutus, a poor reasoner – just as Brutus *begins* with his conclusion ('It must be by his death') and then goes on to discover reasons, Hamlet begins with the reasoning, and then – more subtly – ends with what looks like a conclusion but is in fact the unacknowledged premise of the meditation. A good argument may be circular, as may a bad: the line of Hamlet's argument is not known to geometry. Whatever else Hamlet is, he is not an intellectual.[2]

The foundation of the play is precisely this separation between premise and conclusion, between action and awareness. This remains true even though the acknowledged premises – belief in ghosts, questions of damnation, conscience, and so on – may be, objectively, perfectly sound. The play is not concerned to identify the sources of this disjunction: it states the fact. And it presents a final situation in which the disjunction has either ceased to exist, or ceased to be important. Until then, Hamlet

---

[1] Harry Levin, *The Question of Hamlet* (New York, 1961), p. 69.

[2] The complement to Hamlet here is, as so often, Claudius. We have only one opportunity to observe his mind at close quarters, but he uses it to think hard – and accurately – about the issues. 'May one be pardoned and retain the offence?' (III, iii, 56) is a brutally precise way of defining the problem.

has at times appeared uncommonly reminiscent of Nietzsche's idealist: 'The creature who has reasons for remaining in the dark about himself, and is clever enough to remain in the dark about these reasons.'

(ii) The Hamlet consciousness is strongly egocentric, with an impulse to self-protection that takes several forms. A vein of self-vindication, which is a part of self-affirmation, runs throughout the play. The occasions on which Hamlet blames himself are obvious enough. Not so well understood are the passages in which Hamlet is providing a kind of alibi for himself. His opening words (after a muttered aside) negative the King, placing Claudius in the wrong: and his first speech of any length is a sustained justification of his appearance and conduct to the Queen, and Court:

> Seems, madam! nay, it is: I know not 'seems'.
> ...these indeed seem,
> For they are actions that a man might play:
> But I have that within which passeth show;
> These but the trappings and the suits of woe.
>
> (I, ii, 76–86)

There is here not only a defence, but an implicit appeal to the verdict of the Court. Then, in his discourse to Horatio and Marcellus on the sentry-platform, comes:

> So, oft it chances in particular men,
> That for some vicious mole of nature in them,
> As, in their birth – *wherein they are not guilty,*
> *Since nature cannot choose his origin –*

A man is guiltless of his genetic heritage: but note the conclusion:

> Shall in the *general censure* take corruption
> From that particular fault
>
> (I, iv, 23–36)

A curious word, 'censure', and a curious conclusion. Hamlet does not say that mankind is, of its origins, condemned to err or sin. He says that *public opinion* will regard the man as stained by the single fault. And that consider-

ation troubles him. (The final word in the speech, 'scandal', drives home the point.) 'Censure', moreover, is a word that reaches out, for Hamlet uses it later of an audience ('the censure of the which one must in your allowance o'erweigh a whole theatre of others' (III, ii, 31–3)). Is there not a strong hint here of what is plain elsewhere, that a part of Hamlet's self is derived from the opinion of others, that is to say, his audience, and that he is aware of this?

The existence of this audience is vital to the elucidation of 'That would be scann'd' (III, iii, 75). There is a problem here, and the editors have closed their ranks around it. All modern editions which I have consulted punctuate this passage with a colon or period after 'scann'd' and the universal gloss is that 'would be' here means 'requires to be'. 'Scann'd' is given as 'scrutinized', and the statement is thus rendered 'That needs to be scrutinized/considered carefully'. I propose an entirely different reading here. 'Scan', in sense 4 listed by the *O.E.D.*, means 'to interpret, assign a meaning to'. If we accept this, 'would be' takes on its normal modern conditional meaning. The reading looks stronger if we refer back to the pointing of the Second Quarto and the Folio, so often superior to modern punctuation. The Second Quarto gives no punctuation at all after 'scann'd':

> Now might I doe it, but now a is a praying,
> And now Ile doo't, and so a goes to heaven,
> And so am I revendge, that would be scand
> A villaine kills my father, and for that,
> I his sole sonne, doe this same villaine send
> To heaven.

The Folio gives a comma, thus:

> Now might I do it pat, now he is praying,
> And now Ile doo't, and so he goes to Heaven,
> And so am I reveng'd: that would be scann'd,
> A Villaine killes my Father, and for that
> I his soule Sonne, do this same Villaine send
> To heaven.

This rapid, fluent pointing makes the syntax and meaning perfectly clear. 'A Villaine killes my Father' is now a noun clause subordinate to 'scann'd', and not an autonomous unit of thought. I claim no originality for this reading: the *O.E.D.* actually cites the above passage in support of its sense 4. (It cites other contemporary passages for this sense.) But we have to conduct this exercise to jettison a useless (and, in my view, erroneous) meaning that has established itself over the years. For 'that would be scann'd' now means: 'that is how public opinion would interpret the matter', and the centre of the play shifts slightly but unmistakably. Hamlet's conscience increasingly takes on the aspect of the approval conferred on the self by others.

Allied to this consideration are Hamlet's uses of the 'antic disposition'. He exploits it with a certain elemental calculation. He indeed, with a premonitory awareness of the possibilities of madness, introduces the subject to his immediate audience:

> As I perchance hereafter *shall think meet*
> To put an antic disposition on
>
> (I, v, 171–2)

And this disguise has notable defensive qualities, throughout the manoeuvring of Acts II and III. At the same time, it takes on a therapeutic function. 'In personating a mad Hamlet, Hamlet is in fact personating a chaos of his inner self. It both is and is not Hamlet.'[1] But Hamlet is perfectly capable of distancing himself from his madness, when it suits him. 'Lay not that flattering unction to your soul, / That not your trespass, but my madness speaks' he tells Gertrude (III, iv, 144–5). To Laertes, before the Court, he proclaims:

> This presence knows,
> And you must needs have heard, how I am punish'd
> With sore distraction. What I have done,
> That might your nature, honour and exception
> Roughly awake, I here proclaim was madness.
> Was't Hamlet wrong'd Laertes? Never Hamlet:

> If Hamlet from himself be ta'en away,
> And when he's not himself does wrong Laertes,
> Then Hamlet does it not, Hamlet denies it.
> Who does it, then? His madness
>
> (v, ii, 239–48)

This speech is normally taken as a handsome, indeed noble, offer of amends. On the contrary, I regard it as an adroit and (largely successful) attempt to win over public opinion, and to place the responsibility for his actions on to his 'distraction'. It is disingenuous to plead the 'antic disposition' which he himself chose. The speech is an *apologia pro vita sua*, disguised as an apology. If this reading seems too harsh, I ask for an explanation of 'I'll be your foil, Laertes: in mine ignorance / Your skill shall, like a star i' the darkest night, / Stick fiery off indeed' (v, ii, 266–8). Hamlet knows perfectly well, and has told Horatio earlier, that he is in excellent training and will win at the odds. He in, in fact, exhibiting a widely-encountered trait, that of the player who cries down his skill either to lull his opponent or to magnify his achievement. We should today call it gamesmanship: we should certainly not sentimentalize Hamlet's conduct. Hamlet – and here we move to the existential truth of the situation – is presenting himself to the Court as the flower of Renaissance chivalry, an illustration stepped forth from the pages of Castiglione, the fencer whose success comes always as a surprise to himself. Besides, the Queen has let him know, through a messenger, that some kind of graceful gesture ('some gentle entertainment to Laertes') would be in order. And he now divests himself of his responsibility for outrageous conduct. He is, then, starring in the drama about to be played. And the drama ends, for Hamlet, with his concern for his 'wounded name', i.e. his reputation.

I am suggesting, then, that Hamlet's consciousness exhibits a profound concern for

[1] David Horowitz, *Shakespeare: An Existential View* (1965), p. 39.

himself, for his *self*. This is far more than a simple concern to protect his body, though it includes that consideration. It is rather a consistent desire to present his actions in the most favourable light, an awareness that the 'censure of the judicious' is what matters. Horatio is several things for Hamlet: a friend and aide, a sounding-board, an instrument for communication with the world, a participant in the self-dialogue. It is to himself, as well as to Horatio, that Hamlet says 'is't not perfect conscience, / To quit him with this arm?' (v, ii, 67–8). Hamlet needs the approval of himself and of others. He does not get it in the passage I have just cited, for Horatio turns the subject instead of answering directly. But it is with others that the final appeal lies, and to others that the consciousness of this supreme egotist is directed.

(iii) And this is contained within the final element in Hamlet's consciousness that I wish to touch on, his awareness of self as that of the actor. Maynard Mack is, I am sure, right in taking '"Act"...to be the play's radical metaphor...What, this play asks again and again, is an act? What is its relation to the inner act, the intent?'[1] Michael Goldman has also written well of the play as a search for the significance of action.[2] I want here, however, merely to stress the psychological implications of 'actor' for Hamlet.

An actor, as Mr Goldman observes, is a man who wants to play Hamlet.[3] Hamlet, I would continue, is an actor profoundly dissatisfied with his part, now that he has got it. His opening scene (I, ii) is consistent with this view. It is one of the classical paradoxes of theatre: '*Flourish. Enter Claudius King of Denmark, Gertrude, the Queen; Council, as Polonius, and his son, Laertes, Hamlet and others.*' An impressive entrance: but no audience has ever looked at Claudius, or ever will. It is looking at the still, aloof figure who alone of the Court has not abandoned mourning, and

is effortlessly accomplishing that most exquisite of actor's satisfactions, wordlessly upstaging a whole cast. In context, indeed, he is destroying the production, Claudius' first speech from the Throne. But that is not how it appears to Hamlet. *He* is upstaged by Claudius. We must remember how Hamlet reacts to bad acting – the directive to the players, the explosion at Ophelia's funeral, 'Nay, an thou'lt mouth/ I'll rant as well as thou' (v, i, 306–7) followed by the later admission 'But, sure, the bravery of his grief did put me / Into a towering passion' (v, ii, 79–80). And in his opening scene Claudius is *bad*, as he never is again. His speech is a series of contorted subordinate clauses, collapsing into main clauses that themselves crumple into further subordinates. Claudius is, of course, nervous – the jumpy, slightly illogical transitions give him away. ('now follows ...So much for him. / Now for ourself...' Claudius has earlier talked of himself; in fact he goes on to talk of further action in the Fortinbras affair, a matter he has just seemed to dismiss.) Claudius gives the impression of continually backing into meaning, a process which continues until 'But now, my cousin Hamlet, and my son' (I, ii, 64). I labour the point, which is made vastly more subtly in the text, that Claudius is not doing too well in I, ii. And this is the man who has dispossessed Hamlet. May we not add, to the ferment of emotions expressed in the first soliloquy, an inchoate rage that this far from well-graced figure has annexed *his* role?

We may, of course, reject the possibility, on the grounds that the first soliloquy can only express what is there. In this most devious of all plays, that is scarcely an adequate position; for we have then to explain away Hamlet's

[1] Maynard Mack, 'The World of *Hamlet*', *Yale Review*, XLI (June, 1952), 513.
[2] Michael Goldman, *Shakespeare and the Energies of Drama* (Princeton, 1972), pp. 74–93.
[3] *Ibid.*, p. 74.

later, and perfectly unequivocal, statement to Horatio, that Claudius 'Popp'd in between the election and my hopes' (v, ii, 65). There are really only two ways of taking this reference, which is presumably a crystallization of the earlier 'Excitements of my reason and my blood' (iv, iv, 58). Either Hamlet is providing a pseudo-motive, a rounding-out of the indictment against Claudius to make it respectable to Horatio and himself: or a genuine motive, slowly rising from the depths of his mind, has now broken surface and can be formulated and uttered. I take the second possibility to be the right one. Hamlet, then, is enmeshed in a central paradox. His role requires him to 'act' – to feign, put on an antic disposition, to produce and introduce a play, to assume different styles of speech, to plot and deceive – and moreover to *act*, to resolve the whole Claudius problem: yet the role is the wrong one for him. And what, then, is the right role? It is the function of the play to answer that question.

The features of the Hamlet consciousness, then, I take to be these: an intuitive though not wholly rational intelligence, an egocentricity that is especially concerned with the protection of his self as it appears to others, and an actor's capacity to appreciate that self in its manoeuvrings. The course of the play demonstrates, I suggest, the truth of what that 'strange fellow' whom Ulysses has been reading has to say:

> Who, in his circumstance, expressly proves
> That no man is the lord of anything,
> Though in and of him there be much consisting,
> Till he communicate his parts to others;
> Nor doth he of himself know them for aught
> Till he behold them form'd in the applause
> Where they're extended.
>
> (*Troilus and Cressida*, III, iii, 114–20)

'Applause': that is a part of the resolution of the *Hamlet* issues. Now: my central contention is that Hamlet is a man moving towards the final awareness and affirmation of self. We

must, therefore, regard the death of Hamlet as his final statement, and while it is tedious to work backwards from it – progressive chronology has too many uses to be lightly discarded – I think we ought to take note of the quality of that final position. Hamlet's death is curiously gratuitous, actorish. All the other deaths (of the protagonists) in Shakespeare's major tragedies have an elemental, obvious necessariness. A continued living (*pace* Johnson) is unthinkable for Lear, as for Othello, Macbeth, Coriolanus, and Antony. There is, simply, nothing to add to their lives. But Hamlet has, as it seems, much to live for. He is young, greatly gifted, likely to have proved most royal. His death is unfortunate and premature. It certainly appears to be of a different order from the other major tragic figures. But is it? I prefer to advance the hypothesis of the necessary death, that is, the completed life-statement. I regard the final position as the consummation (Hamlet's own word) of his life, one that combines the notions of significant and expressive action, duties accomplished, and the assurance that the 'mutes or audience' will be given the full information necessary for the understanding and appreciation of the spectacle they have just witnessed. This latter is the only point that seems to concern Hamlet at the last. He raises the matter, and elaborates it after Horatio's impulsive gesture of suicide. The Court/audience must applaud, and approve. The death scene of Hamlet is, then, satisfying in a double sense. Hamlet the actor, and the actor playing Hamlet, fuse in the climax of the drama.

That is the situation at the moment of Hamlet's death. We can now read more closely the movement leading up to it, that is to say the final scene (v, ii). Since Hamlet's drive towards significant action takes the mode of the duellist and fighter, we can note that the metaphor of fighting virtually opens the scene. There is much imagery of war throughout the play, now much better understood than it used to be;[1] the point of Hamlet's metaphor here is that it reflects a change of mental orientation:

> Sir, in my heart there was a kind of fighting,
> That would not let me sleep.
>
> (v, ii, 4–5)

'Sleep': the threat to sleep, in the 'To be or not to be' soliloquy, and the admission to Rosencrantz and Guildenstern (II, ii, 262), is bad dreams. Now it is 'a kind of fighting'. That is action, and aggressive action. Hamlet goes on to tell the story. He tells it well, with a relish of its dramatic possibilities and his own role:

> Being thus be-netted round with villanies, –
> Ere I could make a prologue to my brains,
> They had begun the play.
>
> (v, ii, 29–31)

This is an obvious and characteristic concept of the self as hero. Less obvious is the import of his action: he imitates Claudius, he becomes Claudius in his pastiche of the King's tumid rhetoric:

> As England was his faithful tributary,
> As love between them like the palm might flourish,
> As peace should still her wheaten garland wear
> And stand a comma 'tween their amities,
> And many such-like 'As'es of great charge
>
> (v, ii, 39–43)

(The style of this missive is assimilated into his later note to Claudius, details of which we have already been given (IV, vii, 43–8). It is florid, politic, dangerous. Hamlet is taking on the persona, or the assumptions, of Claudius.) And, in a moment of exquisite symbolism, he ratifies his action with his father's seal:

> I had my father's signet in my purse,
> Which was the model of that Danish seal.
>
> (v, ii, 49–50)

Hamlet now becomes Hamlet senior. Is it possible that Hamlet, with his flair for sym-bolic interpretation, has no inkling of what he is doing? The central fact is clear: Hamlet is now moving towards the mode of his father, as politician, fighter, and – the encounter with Fortinbras comes to mind – as duellist. This is the vital metaphor, the self-conceptualization that Hamlet projects:

> Why, man, they did make love to this employment;
> They are not near my conscience; their defeat
> Does by their own insinuation grow:
> 'Tis dangerous when the baser nature comes
> Between the pass and fell incensèd points
> Of mighty opposites.
>
> (v, ii, 57–62)

In the immediate context, this is a further piece of self-justification: the point is that it is dangerous to come between two duellists, and thus Hamlet acquits himself of any guilt in the deaths of Rosencrantz and Guildenstern. But the justification pushes Hamlet a little more firmly in the direction in which he is moving anyway. To be guiltless, he must be a duellist. Horatio's exclamation, 'Why, what a king is this!', leads Hamlet to his vindication of his future conduct:

> Does it not, thinks't thee, stand me now upon –
> He that hath kill'd my king and whored my mother,
> Popp'd in between the election and my hopes,
> Thrown out his angle for my proper life,
> And with such cozenage – is't not perfect conscience,
> To quit him with this arm? and is't not to be damn'd,
> To let this canker of our nature come
> In further evil?
>
> (v, ii, 63–70)

That is the bill of indictment against Claudius, and it is the basis of the appeal to Horatio's sense of 'conscience', as to Hamlet's own. It is, even its final image, a call to action, for whether 'canker' means 'ulcer' or 'maggot' it implies a positive course of remedial action. The question

[1] See especially Maurice Charney, *Style in Hamlet* (Princeton, 1969), pp. 6–30: and Nigel Alexander, *Poison, Play, and Duel* (London and Lincoln, Nebraska, 1971).

is not one for Horatio to comment directly on, and he reminds Hamlet that the time for effective action is limited:

Horatio.
  It must be shortly known to him from England
  What is the issue of the business there.
Hamlet.
  It will be short: the interim is mine;
  And a man's life's no more than to say 'One'.

(v, ii, 71-4)

'Man's life's no more than to say "One"': in the brevity of life, one can at least achieve a moment of significant, aggressive action. The affirmation of self is the end of life: and 'one' denotes, among other things, the unity of self. The word harks back to the meditation on the sentry-platform, and its recognition of the 'one defect' which may 'Soil our addition; and indeed it takes / From our achievements, though perform'd at height, / The pith and marrow of our attribute' (I, iv, 20-2). M. M. Mahood's commentary is especially valuable here: 'Addition, besides being our applied title, is the sum total of our natures, what we add up to in ourselves. Attribute, according to the N.E.D., can mean not only a quality ascribed or assigned but an inherent or characteristic quality'.[1] The final implications of these terms, then, are that the 'one' of self must include the 'one defect', together with the sum of our inherent and attributed parts. Clearly, this 'one' cannot be adequately stated with the mere vulgar striking of a blow. Nor can it be expressed through the arts of the stage, though Hamlet had once, in a moment of devastating self-revelation, indicated that these would express him:

Hamlet. Would not this, sir, and a forest of feathers –
  if the rest of my fortunes turn Turk with me – with
  two Provincial roses on my razed shoes, get me a
  fellowship in a cry of players, sir?
Horatio. Half a share.
Hamlet. A whole one, I.

(III, ii, 286-91)

Identity can only be an experimental truth. It is confirmed in the moment of equipoise between self and situation, which must include the will to action and the public awareness of the act. The problem, then, is to encounter the moment that offers the opportunity of significant action. And this moment will present itself in the essential form of a challenge.

The challenge takes on the actuality of the King's wager. It is a formal, and symbolic, solution to Hamlet's predicament. Hamlet has previously indicated no plan, but a determination to use the time at his disposal: and his 'I am constant to my purposes, they follow the King's pleasure' is no less than the truth. He will react to the situation that 'special providence' supplies. He must have a dark awareness that in fencing with Laertes he is opposing the 'pass and fell incensèd point' of his adversary, the King. The challenge, then, gives Hamlet this: it is an opportunity for the duel, a symbolic yet real combat; it provides an audience, before which he can both vindicate and dramatize himself; and it is the imitation of a great act once performed by his father. The 'union' which is the central pun of the final scene is that of Hamlet himself, as – in death – with Laertes, with Claudius, with his father and mother, the 'one flesh' to which he had once referred (IV, iii, 54). The sword-play itself proceeds through the phases of symbolic contest, genuine fighting, and the ultimate act of killing the King. We should note that Hamlet does not kill Claudius until Laertes has gasped out the truth. The Court, therefore, knows it too – and apart from cries of 'Treason!' it does nothing to impede Hamlet in his regicide. He acts, then, upon the implied state of public knowledge and sanction – to which his last words enjoin Horatio. In the final minutes of

[1] M. M. Mahood, Shakespeare's Wordplay (1957), pp. 116-17.

his life, Hamlet has become King: and tragic hero. 'Il est devenu ce qu'il était.'

And perhaps this, the final position in Hamlet's life, is the answer to the kingly summons of the first scene, 'The bell then beating *one*...' Or perhaps we reflect back the soldierly rites of the conclusion into the prime meaning of Hamlet's 'one'. For Hamlet does say it. After the courtesies that precede the duel, Hamlet willing as ever to react rather than act invites Laertes to the first attack, 'Come on sir', and Laertes returns the invitation, 'Come my lord'. The rapiers touch then, and we may conceive of Hamlet, after that, launching the first attack. The dialogue of the foils, with its staccato interrogations and metallic elisions, is Hamlet's final scanning of his universe. Sooner or later he will pose Laertes a question to which the stock answer will come a fiftieth of a second too late. And then the counter-thrust slides inside its parry, and travels through free space home to its target, *one*.

© RALPH BERRY 1975

'THE TEMPEST' AND KING JAMES'S 'DAEMONOLOGIE'

JACQUELINE E. M. LATHAM

The Tempest offers a twentieth-century audience more problems for a full understanding than most of Shakespeare's plays, and these problems are the more insidious because action, language and characters seem transparently clear. Yet the play is highly intellectual and despite the work of scholars who have explored many of the ideas raised by the varied but scant sources there remain elements that still seem to fit uneasily, and one character, Caliban, who eludes even the simplest definition. This essay seeks to develop two aspects of contemporary thought by means of which Caliban can be seen not more clearly but in even greater complexity, and it proposes King James's *Daemonologie* as a possible source for these ideas. Contemporary beliefs about devils could, of course, be found elsewhere, but James's relationship to Shakespeare as patron of the King's Men, the clarity and dialectical skill of his *Daemonologie* as well as its content make the King's famous work a likely source for some of the ideas of Shakespeare's strange play.

The problem of Caliban's birth, while receiving little attention on its own account, crops up from time to time in more general discussions of *The Tempest*. Unfortunately, though many critics agree that Caliban is the touchstone by which the civilised world is judged, his actual status – human, sub-human or demi-devil – is rarely subjected to close examination, and critics tend to take the view which suits their particular interpretation of the play. To cite an obvious example, Professor Kermode, in his brilliant Arden Introduction,

places the 'salvage and deformed slave' within the tradition of the European savage man, and in a note added when this edition was in proof, draws attention to *Wild Men in the Middle Ages* by R. Bernheimer, whose views, incidentally, are far more complex than Kermode's brief summary allows.[1] In the same way, Caliban can be seen in the context of the exploration of the New World, corrupted by a supposed civilisation or corrupting the civilised. These are two important dimensions within which Caliban can fruitfully be viewed, but there are others, like the problem of his birth.

For Kermode, 'Caliban's birth, as Prospero insists, was inhuman; he was "a born devil", "got by the devil himself upon thy wicked dam". He was the product of sexual union between a witch and an incubus, and this would account for his deformity, whether the devil-lover was Setebos (all pagan gods were classified as devils) or, as W. C. Curry infers, some aquatic demon.'[2] Yet, even in this simple account of Caliban's origin there lurk ambiguities, as I intend to show.

In what would appear to be a key study, 'The Magic of Prospero', C. J. Sisson merely remarks in passing that 'the powers of Sycorax derived from evil communion with the devil, the father of her son Caliban',[3] thus distinguishing the source of her powers from those

[1] *The Tempest*, ed. F. Kermode (1958), Introduction, pp. xxxix, lxii–lxiii. All quotations from *The Tempest* are from this, the sixth, edition. References to passages in other Shakespeare plays are from the single-volume Oxford edition of W. J. Craig.
[2] *The Tempest*, Introduction, p. xl.
[3] *Shakespeare Survey 11* (Cambridge, 1958), 75.

of Prospero. More recently, Robert Egan in his interesting article 'This Rough Magic: Perspectives of Art and Morality in *The Tempest*' comments, 'Caliban is not a devil – thoroughly evil and unredeemable – but a type of humanity' and in a footnote on the same page adds that Caliban, who makes frequent references to his mother and her god, never mentions an infernal father,[1] apparently missing the point that Setebos is probably his father, in the tradition that false gods are to be identified with devils. Yet Egan is surely correct in his insistence that Caliban's 'qualities as a character are clearly not satanic but human'. There is, then, an apparent contradiction: the text proclaims (and critics sometimes accept) the demonic origin of Caliban: 'A devil, a born devil', cries Prospero (IV, i, 188); yet if we wish to see Caliban as the touchstone of the civilised (or semi-civilised) world, we need to see him in relation to the world of nature or in some definable sense outside it – not, of course, in the world of art but, perhaps, as a symbolic figure, as Bernheimer's book would suggest, representing social, psychological and sexual aspects of man. Alternatively he can be seen as an intermediate link in the chain of being, below man but higher than the animals.

An examination of sixteenth-century views about the incubus may enable certain aspects of *The Tempest* to be seen more clearly. Although it is important to bear in mind R. H. West's wise warning in the first chapter of his study, *The Invisible World*, that 'the literature of pneumatology was rarely so cool and judicial as the ideal required', we can, I think, agree with him that there can be little doubt 'that, within degrees proper to works of art, and each in its own way, these plays [*Doctor Faustus*, *Macbeth* and *The Tempest*] and others accommodate it'.[2]

Traditions of witchcraft in England and on the Continent were very different. This is stressed by Barbara Rosen in her perceptive

introduction to the collection of English texts entitled *Witchcraft* and by Keith Thomas in his widely acclaimed *Religion and the Decline of Magic*. In England trials were chiefly concerned with *maleficium*, harm to others, either their person or possessions; the familiar in the form of a domestic creature like cat, toad or fly was also a typically English manifestation. On the other hand, continental witchcraft was frequently concerned with the diabolic nature of the witches' compact and the sexual orgy of the witches' sabbath. As Barbara Rosen says, 'The English witch was frequently unchaste, but in the usual prosaic fashion.'[3] The incubus is, therefore, late in appearing in native accounts of witch trials and Keith Thomas claims that 'the more blatantly sexual aspects of witchcraft were a very uncommon feature of the trials, save perhaps in the Hopkins period', the mid-seventeenth century.[4] We have, then, an odd situation when we look at *The Tempest*. Shakespeare's island world, for all its concern with magic, is far from the witch hunts and trials of his own country. And yet, untypical as Sycorax and Caliban are of the English tradition of witchcraft, there were notorious continental studies of witchcraft (some translated into English) and other ways in which the idea of diabolic intercourse could have become familiar to an educated Elizabethan.

If we accept the likelihood that Shakespeare kept one eye on his royal master while writing *Macbeth* and *The Tempest*, then King James's *Daemonologie*, first published in Edinburgh in 1597 but reprinted in London on James's accession to the English throne, provides a helpful gloss on this aspect of *The Tempest*; it has, moreover, further aspects which suggest that Shakespeare may well have read it closely.[5]

[1] *Shakespeare Quarterly*, 23 (1972), 179.
[2] *The Invisible World* (Athens, Georgia, 1939), p. 4.
[3] *Witchcraft* (1969), p. 338 footnote.
[4] *Religion and the Decline of Magic* (1971), p. 568.
[5] I have used the Bodley Head Quarto of the *Daemonologie* edited by G. B. Harrison (1924).

King James was writing in a particular and personal context. *Newes from Scotland declaring the damnable life and death of Doctor Fian, a notable Sorcerer* had been published anonymously in Scotland and London in 1591. The story of the tempest, supposedly raised by witchcraft, which sank one boat-load of jewels and provided a contrary wind for King James, though not for his accompanying vessels, is well known. But more significant is that the account of the trial of Dr Fian and the witches included torture, the devil's mark, a witches' sabbath, and obscene kiss,[1] a christened cat bound to the 'cheefest partes' (p. 16) of a dead man, and intercourse with the devil. James followed the trial closely, and when he came to write his *Daemonologie* he explicitly directed it against two sceptics: John Weyer, the German physician, whose *De Praestigiis Daemonum* (1563) remains untranslated, and Reginald Scot, the Kentish author of *The Discoverie of Witchcraft* (1584) which it is thought Shakespeare read. Scot's immensely long and overtly sceptical work serves as an advertisement of the continental views that he is refuting. His sources include Jean Bodin's untranslated *De la Démonomanie des Sorciers* (1580), Cornelius Agrippa and the notorious *Malleus Maleficarum* (1486?), and though his refutation of the continental writers is based on common sense and a skilful use of *reductio ad absurdum*, he betrays an almost prurient enjoyment of some of the more scabrous tales, including a detailed account, which takes up most of Book IV, of the problems of sexual relations with an incubus, whetting his readers' appetite at the end of Book III by urging those whose 'chaste eares cannot well endure to heare of such abhominable lecheries' to skip the next pages with their 'bawdie stuffe'. His major discussion in Book IV leans heavily upon J. Sprenger and H. Institor's *Malleus Maleficarum*.[2] It seems then likely that the Elizabethan and Jacobean public could derive a fairly full account of continental witchcraft practices from *Newes from Scotland* and from *The Discoverie of Witchcraft*, but even, for example, Samuel Harsnett's *A Declaration of egregious Popish Impostures*, which Shakespeare knew well, ascribes to Bodin the belief that devils may 'transforme themselves into any shape of beasts, or similitude of men, and may [...] have the act of generation with women, as they please'.[3]

King James's *Daemonologie* has a remarkably balanced tone. This derives in part from its dialogue form, in which the good tunes are distributed fairly equally between the credulous Epistemon and the more sceptical Philomathes. The argument is close, clear and free from the tedious capping of scriptural quotations which makes Henry Holland's *A Treatise against Witchcraft* (Cambridge, 1590) such unrewarding reading for us. In chapter 3 of the Third Book Epistemon explains that the devil has two means of effecting the union between himself and a woman – the male authors of works on demonology are strangely reluctant to discuss the mechanics of the succubus. He can steal sperm from a man, dead or alive, and inseminate the witch, or by inhabiting a dead body he can have visible intercourse with her. In both cases the sperm is cold; hence the fact that witches so often report the coldness of union with the devil. Spirits, having no sex,

All quotations from the work are followed by parenthetical page references which are identical with the 1597 edition. *Newes from Scotland* is usefully included in the same volume, but since the original is unpaginated the page reference refers only to the reprint.

[1] English innocence is demonstrated by Peele's *The Old Wives' Tale* where Madge telling the burlesque romance to her sleepy listeners threatens them, 'Hear my tale, or kiss my tail.'

[2] This remained unavailable in English until Montague Summers edited and translated it in 1928.

[3] *A Declaration of egregious Popish Impostures* (1603), p. 133. It should be noted that Shakespeare echoes Harsnett in *The Tempest*. See II, ii, 10–11 and Kermode's note.

can have no seed of their own; in this James is following the traditional Christian view. A child born of the union of witch and incubus is therefore human. But even the credulous Epistemon is doubtful whether this union can actually take place; this kind of devil, he says, 'was called of old' (p. 67) an incubus or succubus, and his account of the intercourse is hedged with the proviso 'might possibly be performed' (p. 67). So when the inquirer Philomathes asks 'How is it then that they say sundrie monsters have bene gotten by that way' (p. 68), Epistemon can dismiss the notion with 'These tales are nothing but *Aniles fabulae*' and go on to explain that if it were possible '(which were all utterly against all the rules of nature) it would bread no monster but onely such a naturall of-spring, as would have cummed betuixt that man or woman and that other abused person'. The devil's part is merely carrying 'And so it coulde not participate with no qualitie of the same' (p. 68).

James is surprisingly cavalier in dismissing monstrous births as old wives' tales; Shakespeare was obviously more interested in them. There had, after all, been a very long tradition of extraordinary offspring of unusual parentage: Romulus and Remus and Augustus Caesar were, presumably, a tribute to their unusual fathers. In *Mandeville's Travels* the 'fendes of Helle camen many tymes and leyen with the wommen of his generacoun and engendred on hem dyverse folk, as monstres and folk disfigured, summe withouten hedes, summe with grete eres, summe with on eye...'.[1] Here we are nearer to the 'mooncalf' of *The Tempest*. But Britain, too, had its monstrous births. Geoffrey of Monmouth's *Historia Regum Britanniae*, incorporating Merlin's prophecies, was popular Tudor propaganda, and gives an account of Merlin's mother being visited in a convent by an incubus in the form of a handsome young man. Nearer home for James is Hector Boece's *Scotorum Historiae*

translated by John Bellenden in 1531. In Book VIII chapter 14 he follows an account of Merlin's birth with recent examples of intercourse with the devil, in the last of which the woman is delivered of 'ane monstir of mair terribill visage' than had ever been seen before. From this digression Boece returns quietly to his 'dedis of nobill men'.[2] Shakespeare possibly read Holinshed's close paraphrase of Boece's narrative, which inserted, as Boece had done, the fifteenth-century events immediately after reference to Merlin: 'It is foolishlie supposed that this Merline was got by a spirit of that kind which are called *Incubi*.'[3] Holinshed's scepticism contrasts with Boece's credulity.

Shakespeare emphasises not merely Caliban's demonic paternity but his monstrous birth; he is described as a 'deformed slave' in the list of characters, and in II, ii Stephano calls him a mooncalf and is followed by Trinculo with 'monster', repeated thirteen times in that scene and becoming the name by which Stephano and Trinculo usually address Caliban. Shakespeare is prepared to accept – or exploit – the tradition having before him many of the same examples as James, as well as *The Mirror for Magistrates*, the 1578 edition of which added the tragedies of Eleanor, Duchess of Gloucester, and her ill-fated husband Humphrey Plantagenet, whose story Shakespeare had told in *2 Henry VI*. In *The Mirror* the Duke says that King Henry II reported:

> that his Auncient Grandame
> Though seeminge in Shape, a Woman naturall,

[1] *Mandeville's Travels*, ed. M. C. Seymour (Oxford, 1967), p. 160. I owe this example to R. R. Cawley's pioneering study, 'Shakspere's use of the Voyagers', *PMLA*, XLI (1926), 722.

[2] *The Chronicles of Scotland*, trans. J. Bellenden, ed. R. W. Chambers and E. C. Batho, The Scottish Text Society, 3rd ser. (Edinburgh and London, 1938), I, 348.

[3] *Holinshed's Chronicles of England, Scotland and Ireland, Scotland* (London, 1808), v, 146. In the same volume Holinshed refers to Alphonse, King of Naples, and his son, Ferdinand, p. 454.

Was a Feende of the Kinde that (*Succubae*) some call.[1]

Caliban is not, however, Shakespeare's only 'salvage and deformed slave'. As early as *3 Henry VI* the birth of Richard, Duke of Gloucester, is described in unmistakable terms. After the owl had shrieked, his mother brought forth:

> To wit an indigest deformed lump,
> Not like the fruit of such a goodly tree.
>
> (v, vi, 51–2)

The most interesting of the references to Richard as monster, however, comes in *Richard III* when Queen Margaret cries:

> Thou elvish-mark'd, abortive, rooting hog!
> Thou that was seal'd in thy nativity
> The slave of nature and the son of hell!
>
> (I, iii, 228–30)

Here Richard, like Caliban, is a monster whose outer form indicates a moral depravity which itself has explicit demonic overtones. As Barbara Rosen points out, 'Imperfection was one of the traditional marks of anything created by the Devil in imitation of God'.[2] (Hence the search for the devil's mark in Continental and Scottish witch-hunts.)

Moreover, the Broadside ballads of the sixteenth century reflect a grossly morbid interest in deformed births where the crudity of description is made more offensive by the moralising tone.[3] Such births were accounted for not by intercourse with Satan but by the more homely sins of vanity, pride or fornication. The Reverend Stephen Batman, too, in *The Doome Warning all men to Judgement* (1581) gives a hideous collection of monsters illustrated by woodcuts as a warning to blasphemers and adulterous women. Although continental writers are concerned with demonic intercourse, they give similar horrific descriptions of monstrous births, while some take a more naturalistic – though still moralistic – view. N. Remy in Book 1 chapter 6 of *Daemonolatreiae Libri Tres* (1595) describes the birth of a shapeless mass like a palpitating sponge, arguing that it is the impression of the demon on the mother's imagination that has produced the monstrosity; physically the child is wholly human. Bodin has an account of a hideous monster without head or feet, with a liver-coloured mouth in the left shoulder, and Boguet in *Discours des Sorciers* (1590) believes, like the English writers, that monstrous births may be God's punishment for men's sins. A much more scientific view is given in *Des Monstres et Prodiges* (1573) by the surgeon Ambroise Paré, though his illustrations are quite as extreme as those of Stephen Batman. Anyone who has seen Peter Hall's 1974 production of *The Tempest* for the National Theatre has only to recall the 'living drollery' (III, iii, 21) of 'monstrous shape' (III, iii, 31) bringing in the banquet to have an unforgettable image of these sixteenth-century monsters. Even Stephano's discovery of Caliban and Trinculo under the gaberdine with four legs, two at either end, can be paralleled from contemporary illustrations of headless monsters. Therefore, if King James's reference to monsters is tersely dismissive, it appears to assume both mythical and, more important, popular information; on the other hand, Shakespeare makes his interest manifest, and his monster's relevance to the concerns and images of the age is very close indeed.

King James was clearly more aware of the continental tradition of witchcraft than were most Englishmen, and the chief value for our understanding of *The Tempest* in James's discussion of the incubus is that biologically

[1] *The Mirror for Magistrates*, ed. L. B. Campbell (New York, 1960), p. 447.

[2] *Witchcraft*, p. 18.

[3] See J. H. Pafford's Arden edition of *The Winter's Tale* (1963) for his footnote list of references on p. 105.

even Epistemon, the credulous expositor of demonology, would consider Caliban human, as indeed would Reginald Scot and most continental writers. If, then, Shakespeare and his audience like their King were sceptical of the possibility of demonic paternity, then Caliban's essential humanity must be emphasised and his character qualified only by those human factors of nature and nurture so persuasively discussed by Professor Kermode in his Introduction.

At this point the evidence seems decisive, the interpretation of Caliban simply as natural man acceptable and we can return with confidence to accounts of natives in the New World or wild men in the old, forgetting demonology – as most critics have – but perhaps with the image of the monster more clearly fixed in our minds. Yet *The Tempest* is more elusive and interpretation more difficult than is allowed by the argument so far put forward. If Shakespeare had read King James's *Daemonologie*, why did he make Prospero so insistent upon Caliban's demonic nature? After all, though the incubus was not a protagonist in English witch trials, the audience would be likely to accept Prospero's repeated statements with the same kind of willing suspension of disbelief with which in a romance it accepted Ariel and the spirits presenting the Masque.

It seems probable that, as so often, Shakespeare seized upon ambiguities in order to exploit them; Caliban perhaps has more facets than have previously been recognised: as a native of the New World, wild man, demi-devil and monster. As a new-found primitive man he serves as touchstone of the civilisation which has, in one sense, usurped his island as Prospero's throne has been usurped; he seems in this context superior to Trinculo and Stephano though inferior to Ferdinand. As a wild man, he may symbolise the untamed within us, but like Spenser's Sir Satyrane offer hope of

ultimate self-discipline. As a man – whether primitive or wild – despite the attempted rape of Miranda and his glorying in the physical details of the proposed murder of Prospero, he may be capable of redemption. However, if we see him as a 'demi-devil' his state is lost; his last intention, to 'seek for grace' (v, i, 295) is, then, a tactical move born of cunning. Moreover, the associations of 'monster' in neo-Platonic, demonic and popular thought emphasise the distortion of human nature by evil; for the twentieth century 'monster' has become trivialised, so that we need to recall its power in the sixteenth century. The reiteration of the word in *King Lear* indicates that Shakespeare felt its force adequate for the most terrible of the tragedies; and the word surely retains some of its strength even in the new context of *The Tempest*. Caliban is literally a malformed creature, a mooncalf; he may, too, take on something of the word's further sense as a creature part brute part human ('a man or a fish?' II, ii, 25); finally, there is the new sixteenth-century sense, exploited in *Lear*, of moral depravity. The connotations, therefore, of 'monster' serve to emphasise Caliban's evil. Moreover, the moralising interpretation of monsters in contemporary popular writing may also give some support to the view of Caliban as externalising Prospero's own propensity to evil, since for Prospero, as for the audience, Caliban's monstrous form must, as I have shown, have had a religious and moral message lost to us. Prospero's concession, 'this thing of darkness I / Acknowledge mine' (v, i, 275–6), now takes on a new resonance.

King James's *Daemonologie*, however, has further relevance to *The Tempest*. His Preface includes a reference to the power of magicians who can 'suddenly cause be brought unto them, all kindes of daintie disshes, by their familiar spirit'. This point is developed more fully in Book I chapter 6. Here Epistemon repeats the traditional view (only to reject it) that at the fall of Lucifer some spirits fell into the elements of air, fire, water and land, the spirits of air and fire being 'truer' (p. 20) than those of water and land. However, he grants a spirit the ability to carry news 'from anie parte of the worlde' (p. 21) and refers to the 'faire banquets and daintie dishes, carryed in short space fra the farthest part of the worlde' (p. 22). In this the devil deceives through his agility, as he does when he produces 'impressiones in the aire' of 'castles and fortes' (p. 22). The similarity of this to *The Tempest* is obvious; even the 'insubstantial pageant' (IV, i, 155) of Prospero's great speech is prefigured.

There remains some slight additional evidence that Shakespeare had read the *Daemonologie*.[1] James, as one would expect, refers to magicians making circles, as Prospero does to charm the court party in Act V. More interesting, however, in chapter 2 of Book I James gives the three ways the devil 'allures' (p. 7) persons by the 'three passiones that are within our selves' (p. 8). These are curiosity, thirst of revenge and 'greedie appetite of geare' (p. 8). Although James goes on to relate the allurement of curiosity to magicians or necromancers, and the last two to sorcerers and witches, they remain oddly relevant to three important temptations in *The Tempest* as a whole. First, it is the curiosity of Prospero that has led to his secret studies and to his downfall as Duke of Milan. Second, though Antonio was dry for sway Prospero overcomes his thirst for revenge saying 'the rarer action is / In virtue than in vengeance' (V, i, 27–8). Finally the greedy appetites of the three men of sin could be tempted by the illusory banquet, and Trinculo and Stephano, too, are far from controlling their unrestrained passions when confronted by the 'geare' that Prospero displays to distract them.

[1] H. N. Paul, *The Royal Play of Macbeth* (1950), pp. 255ff. and K. Muir, *Shakespeare's Sources*, I (1957), p. 178, provide some of the evidence.

© JACQUELINE E. M. LATHAM 1975

SIGHT-LINES IN A CONJECTURAL RECONSTRUCTION OF AN ELIZABETHAN PLAYHOUSE

D. A. LATTER

This article arises from work carried out on the construction of a model of an Elizabethan Playhouse, with some thoughts which have occurred to me subsequently. It is not suggested that the description which follows corresponds to any actual playhouse; rather an attempt is made to develop an 'ideal' Elizabethan stage, using such evidence, both direct and inferential, as we have. I hope, in so doing, to demonstrate that certain of the facts that are known can be made to fit into a structure much more rationally than has hitherto appeared.

Nevertheless, it should be stressed that this reconstruction deals in possibilities, not provable facts. Much of it is based on the use of sight-lines, and there is no evidence that Elizabethan theatre builders were much concerned with them. Hotson has said that the attention paid to sight-lines is of recent date. On the other hand, there is no evidence that any part of the audience could *not* see the stage: we are not precluded from making suggestions which would allow everyone to do so. By using the dimensions given or implied in various documents, and by placing them within the parameters set by the sight-lines, a structure can be developed which does fit together remarkably well. It is at any rate possible that some of the dimensions we have represent the result of a certain amount of trial and error, and were not arbitrary. Aspects of the structure developed on the basis of sight-lines, and using these measurements, may then be worthy of consideration. In short, although

the theatre I am about to describe may never have existed, it may none the less represent something that could have been built.

The basis of my approach was summed up by Dr Johnson: 'No man but a blockhead ever wrote, except for money.' The Elizabethan theatre was built to make money – and did. It is therefore reasonable to arrange this reconstruction so as to hold the maximum number of people, especially in the more expensive seats. I intend, as I have said, to use the dimensions that we have: that is, those from the Fortune and Hope contracts, and to follow almost every reconstructor by using a polygonal ground plan. But two fundamental details must be inferred: the number of sides in the polygon and the diameter. I have taken twelve sides, and a diameter of 90 ft (27·4 m – all metric equivalents are approximate), for the following reasons. As can be seen from fig. 1, the back of the stage is formed by taking a chord across three of the segments, starting from the *inner* face of the lowest gallery. A stage extended from this line to a point half-way across the area enclosed produces a stage very much of the proportions given in the Fortune contract,[1] and leaves the

---

[1] (The spelling of quotations is modernised, since their purpose is simply to call to mind the passages to which reference is made.)

Part of the contract for the building of the Fortune Theatre, 1599. 'The frame of the said house to be set square and to contain fourscore foot of lawful assize every way square with one foot of assize at the least above the ground – to contain three stories in height,

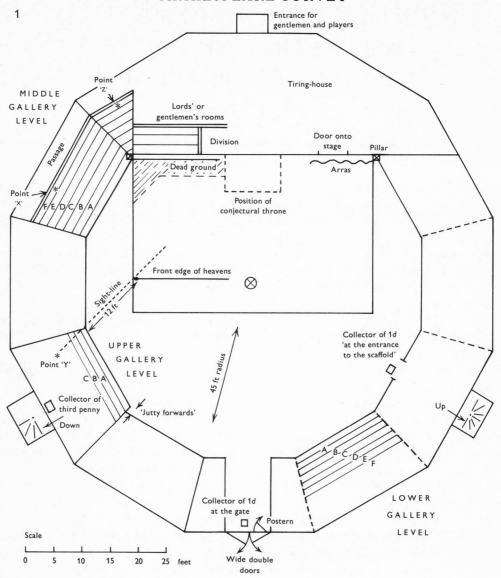

1

Entrance for
gentlemen and players

Point
'Z'

MIDDLE
GALLERY
LEVEL

Tiring-house

Lords' or
gentlemen's rooms

Passage

Division

Door onto
stage

Pillar

Point
'X'

F/E/D/C/B/A

Dead ground

Arras

Position of
conjectural throne

Front edge of heavens

Sight-line
12 ft

Collector of 1d
'at the entrance
to the scaffold'

Point 'Y'

UPPER
GALLERY
LEVEL

C B A

45 ft radius

Collector of
third penny

'Jutty forwards'

Up

Down

A B C D E F

Collector of 1d
at the gate

LOWER
GALLERY
LEVEL

Scale

0 5 10 15 20 25 feet

Postern

Wide double
doors

Fig. 1

rather narrow wedges at the side also in accordance with the evidence of that contract, and of such drawings as we have. Within a sixteen-sided polygon (which some have put forward)

the first to contain 12 foot of lawful assize in height, the second eleven and the third or upper storey nine: all of which stories shall contain twelve foot and a half

of lawful assize in breadth throughout, besides a jutty forwards in either of the said two upper stories of 10 inches . . . The stage and tiring house to be made erected and set up within the said frame, which stage shall contain in length forty and three foot of lawful assize and in breadth to the middle of the yard . . . and to be in all other proportions contrived and fashioned like unto the stage of the said playhouse called the Globe.'

Gallery ...	Lower	Middle	Upper	
Row A	10	10	10	⎞
B	10	10	10	⎟
C	11	11	10	⎟ Capacity of each
D	12	12	—	⎬ row, according to
E	13	13	—	⎟ the letters on
F	14	14	—	⎟ Fig. 1
Standing			15	⎠
Total	70	70	45 = 185	

the relative measurements come out disproportionately. We know that the Fortune stage measured 43 ft × 27 ft 6 in (13 m × 8·4 m); if we take a twelve-sided polygon, inscribed with a 90 ft (27·4 m) circle, with the lowest gallery 12 ft 6 in (3·8 m) deep (as in the Fortune), we get a stage very close to that of the Fortune in size. In fact, if we set the rear of the stage back 18 in (0·5 m) from the line of the chord (for reasons to appear later), and extend it to the 'mid-point of the yard' rather than to the centre of the circle, we get a depth of 27 ft 6 in (8·4 m). Further, if we place a substantial pillar at the front end of the gallery, as marked, and put the stage inside it, then we get a width of 43 ft (13 m). This arrangement makes much better sense in terms of actual building, than just drawing a line straight out from the point of intersection of the inner face of the segment, and the chord. (Too often, to my mind, conjectural reconstructions have dealt in terms of lines on paper, rather than considering actual beams, pillars and solid walls.)

There is no reason to suppose that all Elizabethan stages were exactly alike, but it is not unreasonable to feel that most stages were likely to be of roughly the same size – for if a stage were bigger than average, there would be less space for spectators, and a reduced 'gate'; whereas if it were smaller, the actors would have complained! Therefore, to take a shape and dimensions which produces a stage almost exactly of the size of that at the Fortune, is better than plucking numbers out of the air. However, I am not sure whether the phrase in the Fortune contract, 'to be in all other proportions contrived and fashioned like unto the stage of...the Globe' means that the plan dimensions are somewhat different, but the others are the same, or that, just as the plan dimensions are similar, so are all the others. Who can tell?

A polygon 90 ft (27·4 m) across also, as it happens, allows for just about 3,000 people to be crammed inside, which matches the number mentioned by de Witt. Anyone who has been to a football match will be aware of the remarkable number of *standing* people that can be crammed into a given space. Here we have a yard of about 1,800 square ft (167 m²) and I think that 1,200 or more could have packed their way in. Then, supposing that each person occupied a width when seated on the benches, of 18 in (0·5 m) (not much, but enough), each segment could contain 185. There are 9 segments in which spectators could sit. Add on (to anticipate a later paragraph) some people behind and on the stage, and we have a total of something like 2,900. It is interesting that until recently many commentators regarded de Witt's figure as an exaggeration, or else made the circular playhouses much bigger than the Fortune, and had to face, or ignore, the problem about the relative size and proportions of stage and yard. Neither expedient is necessary.

What is required, however, is to get as many people in the galleries as possible – which, considering they paid twice and three times that paid by the groundlings, is sound commercial sense. I shall also try to arrange for adequate sight-lines – as a kind of speculative hypothesis – and see how things fit together, when this requirement is borne in mind. Let us assume that the foundations and the frame were built up 1 ft (0·3 m), as at the Hope,[1] and that the beams at the front of the first gallery raise the feet of the spectators another 9 in (0·27 m). A reasonable height for a seat is 1 ft 4 in (0·4 m), and for an average person, the eyes are about 2 ft 6 in (0·8 m) above the seat. So the line of sight of the front row would, as shown on fig. 2, just clear the heads of the groundlings (they being, I suppose, shortish on the whole). For the 'going' of the benches, I have taken 1 ft 6 in (0·5 m); people on the next row up would sit with their feet digging into the haunches of those on the tier below. In this way, and taking the Fortune depth of 12 ft 6 in (3·8 m), six rows would bring the backs of the people in the last row up to 2 ft 6 in (0·8 m) from the back wall; just room for others to pass along behind them, as they moved round the segments looking for a seat – a necessary space. (In passing, it may be noted that there appear to be six rows in the 'Swan' drawing.)[2]

And now we find something rather interesting: the eyes of someone on this last row will be just about 11 ft 3 in (3·4 m) from the bottom of the frame, that is, 9 in (0·27 m) below the bottom edge of the next gallery, if we take the Fortune measurement of 12 ft (3·7 m) for the height of the first storey. His sight-line, therefore, slopes up. The stage was probably 5 ft 6 in (1·7 m) high, so that the groundlings crammed up against it could just about see, and those further back had the best possible sight-line (since for a crowd standing on the flat, unraked yard, the higher the stage, the better the view). Above the stage was a gallery, and whatever is thought about putting spectators there, at any rate it is clear that sometimes it was used for action 'above'. I have placed this gallery as low as possible, for reasons which appear when we move over to that side of the stage: say 5 ft 6 in (1·7 m) up to the underside of the floor. So the heads of the people in the gallery would be about 15 ft (4·6 m) from the ground. We then find that the line of sight of a spectator on the top step of the bottom gallery rises just sufficiently to give a view of these people. Moreover, it reaches this height at a horizontal distance of 35 ft (10·7 m) from his eyes. This represents the view from the worst position, in the segment sideways onto the stage, up to the centre of the gallery 'above'.

This arrangement for the bottom storey appears to fit together very well: but there is an immediate objection that the ceiling would be only 3 ft 3 in (1 m) above the top row, and above the space along which I have supposed spectators walking. To solve this problem, I have supposed that the underside of the

[1] Part of the contract for the building of the Hope Theatre, 1613. 'And shall also build two staircases without and adjoining to the said playhouse . . . the inner principal posts of the first storey to be twelve foot in height and ten inches square; the inner principal posts of the middle storey to be eight inches square; the innermost posts in the upper storey to be seven inches square. The prick posts in the first storey to be eight inches square'. The prick posts for the middle and upper storeys were to be 7 in (0·18 m) and 6 in (0·15 m) square respectively, and the brestsummers and binding joists were to be, in the three storeys, 9 in × 7 in (0·18 m), 8 in × 6 in, and 7 in × 5 in. These are pretty substantial timbers.

[2] Since the drawing by Arend van Buchell is a copy of what might have been a very rough sketch, it is easy to dismiss as an error any feature which does not agree with one's speculations; nevertheless, it is the only drawing we have of the interior of an Elizabethan theatre, and I have tried, in my conjectures, to produce something that accords with the drawing as closely as possible.

2

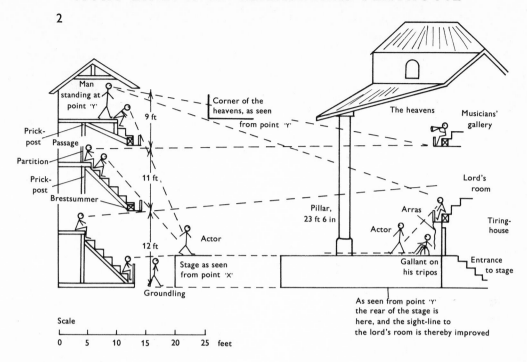

Fig. 2

second storey, forming the ceiling to the first, sloped up until it reached the back row, and then turned through an angle, to form the flat passage behind the seats. This would provide the height required, it would be a cheaper construction, using less timber, and finally, it would give a meaning to the 'prick-posts'. These 'intermediate posts', as they have been defined, would be the upright posts set to support the angle where the sloping and flat beams (the binding joists) met. They would in fact be the mysterious posts noted in the Swan drawing, which seem to stop some way up on the steps inside the first storey. (Dr Southern indeed surmised that this is where they must be: I am suggesting a purpose for them, and an explanation for their being where they are.)

The alternative to the sloping ceiling would be to make the rise of the steps much less, say 1 ft (0·3 m), and have five rows only. But this would provide far fewer spectators, and would mean that some of the space would be wasted at the back, because it would perforce have been broader than required.

For the second storey, I propose an arrangement similar to the first, with six rows each of 1 ft 4 in (0·4 m) rise, and 1 ft 6 in (0·5 m) going. However, the rows are set forward relative to those of the lower storey, by the amount of the 'jutty forwards' given in the Fortune contract, that is, 10 in (0·25 m) (fig. 2). It has been pointed out that one effect of the jutty forwards is to make the sight-lines slope steeper to view the nearer part of the stage from the oblique segments – those nearest the stage. But the difficulty is apparent, not real. Fairly substantial beams are required in the sort of structure we are considering, and we know from the Hope contract how large they might have been.[1] The brestsummers at

[1] See footnote 1 on p. 128.

the Hope (which were probably the beams across the inner face of each segment) were 9 in × 7 in (0·23 × 0·18 m) for the bottom storey, and 8 in × 6 in (0·2 m × 0·15 m) for the middle storey. By having an overhang, these large beams could be placed under the seats of the front row, instead of having to go under the feet of those in this row. Since no-one would actually walk on the overhang, the floorboards could be quite thin, and supported between the brestsummer and the front panel. Thus the effective height of the middle and upper storeys can be lowered by some 8 in and 15 in (0·2 m × 0·4 m) respectively, which compensates for their being set further forward (it should be remembered that the measurements were not given 'in the clear' but, as Dr Southern has convincingly argued, were given to *include* the depth of floors). This explanation of the reason for the jutty forwards gains added support, to my mind, from the fact that 10 in (0·25 m) would be just about the length of a typical Elizabethan's foot.

As to the sight-lines from the middle storey, we find that in fact, to take the worst position from the oblique segments (point x in fig. 1), an actor standing on the edge of the stage would be seen down to his waist; this is surely acceptable, for I suppose the actors knew very well that any lying down had to take place a few feet in from the edge. Thus the lower sight-line is adequate. The upper sight-line would be from the eye of a spectator on the back and highest step. His eye would be nearly 11 ft (3·4 m) from the bottom of the storey. If we assume a height of 11 ft for the storey itself, as at the Fortune, then the spectator's line of sight would be pretty well horizontal. This, of course, presents no problem, since he is sitting higher than anyone in the gallery over the stage.

One effect of the overhang is to bring all six rows of seats forward, so that the space behind the backs of the rearmost people

becomes 3 ft 6 in (1·1 m). There is thus room for a passage-way, and I am sure Dr Southern is right in thinking that there was a wall behind the sixth tier, and that the windows visible in the Hollar long view lit the corridor so formed. This corridor is necessary. People intending to sit in the lowest storey could, once they had passed the men collecting their penny at one of the two entrances from the yard (fig. 1 shows that on the right hand side; there would be another in the corresponding segment of the lower gallery, on the left hand side), spread out along the segments, and only late-comers would have to shuffle round the back. But those who climbed the staircase leading to the middle gallery, all emerged at one of two points, and the corridor gave them a space free of spectators, to move round to the door leading to the segment they fancied.

But perhaps an even more important purpose of the corridor was to control egress. Amid the general mirth at the story of the man whose britches caught alight, when the Globe burned down in 1613, it has not been sufficiently remarked that everyone did in fact manage to leave the (fiercely burning) building unharmed.[1] How was it done? Firstly, I am going to assume that the main entrance to the yard was much larger than has usually been supposed – much more like the doors to the inn yards from which, in one sense, the theatre developed. A postern would control admission; for exit, the doors would be flung wide. So the yard could empty quickly, and those in the lowest gallery could, in haste, leap over the spikes on the palings. But there would be a grave danger of a scrum on the staircase, if everyone tried to descend together. The fact that those in each segment of the middle storey had to leave through a doorway, and could not all at once gain access to the peripheral corridor and

[1] Sir Henry Wootton says that the fire consumed 'within less than an hour the whole house to the ground'. It was a fierce fire.

thence to the stairs, would give a measure of crowd control. (If there were a wide main gate, then the 'two narrow doors' mentioned by Wootton could, reasonably enough, be those at the bottom of the staircases.)

It is true that those in the top gallery *could* all rush for the staircase, but there would be fewer up there, for reasons which will appear as we now consider this part of the structure. The first question is whether there were any benches at all, for de Witt called this gallery a 'porticus' – a place for perambulation. I think there were seats, with a promenade behind. Only a very limited number could have stood on a flat promenade, and seen the stage, whereas two or three rows of benches in front of those standing would increase the total number with a view. And although some no doubt paid their third penny to the collector at the head of the stairs, in order to have a quiet standing for purposes quite other than watching a play, most people up there wanted to see something.[1] In fact, they could have seen pretty well everything, although the problems of providing adequate sight-lines are undoubtedly greatest in respect of this gallery. I have assumed that the front face was vertically above that of the middle gallery, with the same arrangement of a footwell 10 in (0·25 m) wide, and the main beam under the first bench. In other words, I am taking it that the words of the Fortune contract ('a jutty forwards in either of the said two upper stories') mean that each upper gallery jutted forwards relative to the bottom one, by the same amount. Thus we have the main downwards thrust from the front of the galleries (and from the roof) carried on a vertical line.

Figure 2 shows three rows of seats, with a rise of 1 ft 8 in (0·5 m) to give those behind a steeper sight-line down to the nearest point of the stage. Those sitting on the top step, or standing just behind them, could, by leaning over, get a sight, even in the 'worst possible position' before mentioned, down to an actors' head and shoulders. The three steps bring the promenade up to the height necessary to give head room in the corridor below (another strong argument for the steps' existence), and it will be noted that the 9 ft (2·7 m) for the upper storey mentioned in the Fortune contract would bring the roof down as low as it can be. The kingpost design shown in the diagram was entirely possible at the time, and means that those standing had just sufficient height; there would be a kind of gable to provide headroom in the way out to the staircase. The roof would descend over the benches, and the upper sight-line, limited by this roof, of people standing, would slope downwards, but would still (just) give a view of those over the stage.

I hope that the reader will by now be sharing something of the interest – and indeed excitement – which I felt when I realized how accurately the measurements all fit together in this conjectural reconstruction of the galleries. I have taken the 'Fortune' dimensions and applied them within what seems to be a very possible size and shape of theatre; and the result is the same as if I had calculated, almost to an inch, those that would allow adequate sight-lines. I should again repeat that this does not *prove* that sight-lines were calculated by the builders of any Elizabethan playhouse, but when what we know fits so organically, so purposefully, into what is conjectural, one feels that the plan as a whole

[1] In Lambard's Perambulation of Kent, we find that spectators paid 1*d* at the gate, another at the entry to the scaffold, and a third 'for a quiet standing'. I have therefore placed one collector at the main gate, others at the two entrances from the yard to the galleries, and two more at the head of the stairs, where they give on to the upper storey. Surely Dr Southern is right in suggesting that although the staircases were built outside the frame, access to them was obtained from the lowest gallery.

makes sense. At the least, it gives a possible explanation for the precise dimensions given in the Fortune and Hope contracts.

We turn now to the stage side of the play-house, and the first thing is to work out the height of the heavens. Again, it is helpful to take the 'worst possible position'; this is for a man standing in the upper gallery, at a point on a line projected from the back centre of the stage, through one of the front corners of the heavens (i.e. at point Y in fig. 1). Along this line, the distance from the front corner of the heavens, to the front face of the upper gallery, would be 12 ft (3·7 m), and I have shown the corner at this position, in fig. 2. The height at which it is drawn is such that a view of the stage is just possible to a person standing at point Y. In fact, the upper gallery would seldom have been crowded, and a man standing here could improve his view either by stepping *back*, or *sideways*. Nevertheless, it is reasonable to take this sight-line as setting the height for the corner – and, therefore, for the front edge of the heavens. But if this height is continued along the horizontal *sides*, then they will increasingly block the sight-line of those in the oblique segments. However, there is no need for the heavens to have horizontal sides, and I am suggesting that they had a pent-house roof. By this means, as a man walked round towards the stage, he would find the side of the heavens rising just sufficiently to clear his line of sight over to the far side of the stage: a very neat piece of design!

If the heavens extended to within 2 or 3 ft (0·6 m or 0·9 m) of the front edge of the stage, then the slope up to the level of the gallery roof would not, as it stands, be sufficiently steep for thatch. However, if the roof sloped up both from the front *and* from the sides, towards the hut, the slope would be steeper. I find support for this conjecture in the Swan drawing, which shows both the front and side of the hut. Obviously something went wrong

with the sketch here, but one can more readily perceive how the arrangement I have supposed, could be badly drawn to produce what we see in the sketch, than could an arrangement with horizontal sides. The pillars in my drawing come out with a height of 23 ft 6 in (7·2 m). Most reconstructions have to make them longer; Mr Hodges terms 20 ft (6·1 m) a 'comfortable' size, but settles for 24 ft 6 in (7·5 m). So 23 ft 6 in is, one may feel, reasonable – and indeed I cannot see any way to make it less. In the second Globe we know that the heavens were much more massive, and were extended out to the gallery roof on either side. It may well be that the construction with the pent-house roof supported entirely on pillars had been found unsatisfactory.

At the back of the stage I have shown two galleries, the top one for musicians, and the lower one for the gentlemen's rooms.[1] So far I have avoided declaring myself on this vexed question, but now I must do so. We know there was a gallery over the stage, and I cannot imagine such a prime position not being used to make money. If anyone sat there at all, it must surely have been the gentlemen, paying 12*d* to do so.[2]

Action 'above' would then take place actually in the gentlemen's rooms. This is one reason for bringing the gallery as low as possible – with its bottom edge 5 ft 6 in (1·7 m) or 6 ft (1·8 m) above the stage; so that Romeo could jump up, and Arthur fall down. A low gallery also helps the sight-lines, firstly because those in the galleries opposite could then see

[1] The terms 'gentlemen's rooms', and 'lord's room', seem to have been used indifferently for the best seats; but I wonder whether there was a tendency for the latter expression to have been more frequent in the early period. If so, the increasing use of 'gentlemen's room' might relate to the development from a throne to a room set back, discussed in the final paragraphs.

[2] Almost all the drawings we have do in fact show some people sitting in a gallery placed behind the stage.

the action 'above' the stage, and secondly because, being then no higher than the middle gallery of the frame, those in the oblique segments of that gallery, and next to the stage, could have a sight-line down onto the stage over the heads of the gentry (from point z in fig. 1). The galleries 'over the stage' for gentlemen and musicians come out at much the same height as the middle and upper galleries in the frame; but the general impression remains that the frame and its galleries were considered as one unit, *within* which a stage and tiring house, with gentlemen's rooms and musicians' gallery incorporated, was placed, as a separate entity, and this is the sense given in the contracts.

I have supposed that the gallery for the gentlemen's rooms had an overhang and was built similarly to those of the frame, but with rather more room for the feet. The actual stage would then extend under the front edge of the gallery, perhaps by the 18 in (0·5 m) mentioned earlier. If the divisions, and front pillars (if any), between the rooms stopped at the brest-summers, the footwell would form a kind of small open gallery. This would make much easier the playing of such scenes as the court-ship between Wittipol and Mistress Fitzdottrel in *The Devil is an Ass*. I follow Mr Hosley in placing a curtain or arras hanging from the front edge of this gallery, covering the doors on each side[1] and leaving a space behind, in the centre, where for example Polonius could hide (and be killed immediately below the gentlemen, no doubt to their great satisfaction). If the gentlemen's rooms *were* over the stage, there could have been no inner stage, and the discovery scenes must either have been con-trived with temporary structures, or, as Mr Hosley suggests, have taken place within the wide doors shown on either side in the Swan drawing. Neither solution is satisfactory, but perhaps discoveries *were* rather awkwardly handled on the public stage, and this may be

why, as Mr Hosley points out, they were not very frequent.

The economic logic of the structure compels me to place the gentlemen over the stage: a further reason is the difficulty of placing them anywhere else. The only other possibility is the oblique segments, which would give a very poor view indeed. Nor can placing them there be reconciled with the remark in the Induction to *The Magnetick Lady*: 'The faeces or grounds of your people, that sit in the oblique caves or wedges of your house.[2]' Surely Dr Hotson must be right in supposing a kind of transverse action rather than action in the round, with the main part of the audience, except when the theatre was crammed, placed to one long side of the stage, and with the gentlemen on the other. Incidentally, Florio defines *scena* as 'the fore part of the theatre, where actors make them ready', which suggests that the front of the stage was, for the actors, the side facing the most important spectators. There is one argument in favour of gentle-men's rooms at the side; this would give a purpose to the lower windows shown by Hollar (to light a passage leading to them). But I think that what happened was that the

---

[1] 'Tarleton, when his face was only seen,
  The tire house door and tapestry between'
  Thalia's Banquet

The tapestry, although continuing right across the back of the stage, would have a gap in front of each door; Tarleton made his entrance by first poking his head through the gap, and pulling faces at the groundlings. In some plays the exact moment when an actor enters is at times not clear; perhaps he stood behind the arras, visible but not 'on stage', in order for example to overhear something, and then advanced on to the stage proper.

[2] I am indebted to Sir David Hunt, of the Foreign and Commonwealth Office, for the suggestion that the original reading should be 'oblique cunes and wedges'. Cunes, from the Latin for a wedge, makes better sense, and accords with Jonson's latinity. Jonson goes on to describe the people in these oblique wedges as 'sixpenny mechanicals'. I take this to refer to their wages, not to the price of their tickets.

space under the seats in the lowest gallery, otherwise wasted, was used for storage. The windows would give light into the most useful part of this space, next to the tiring house.

Finally, let us consider the gallants on the stage. Most reconstructions show them at the side, but I don't think their fine cloaks would have lasted long unsmirched, if groundlings were standing just behind them. The natural place for them to sit would be with their backs to the arras, just below the gentlemen's rooms. This is, as it happens, the *only* part of the stage which is dead ground to part of the audience, and could not be used for acting. If the gallants were there, then much better sense can be made of the passage from the *Gull's Hornbook* which speaks of their being planted 'under the state of Cambyses himself' (i.e. under the Lords' room), 'beating down the mews and hisses of the oppos'd rascality'.[1] If the groundlings were opposed, the gallants must have been facing them. The gentlemen, and more especially the gallants, went to the theatre as much to be seen themselves, as to see the play. As the *Gull's Hornbook* describes, they competed with the actors for the attention of the audience; what is the point of a gallant's going to the theatre, if he isn't noticed! A further point emerges from the *Gull's Hornbook*. Dekker writes, 'Let our gallant presently advance himself up to the throne of the stage. I mean not into the Lords' room (which is now but the stage's suburbs).' Surely this must imply that the 'Lords' room' was at one time a kind of throne, or else he would not have explained that that was what he did not mean. (In that case, the Lords' room certainly could not have been in 'the oblique wedges'.) Dekker goes on, 'No, those boxes, by the iniquity of custome, conspiracy of waiting women and gentlemen ushers, that there sweat together, and the covetousness of sharers, are contemptibly thrust into the rear'. I wonder whether, in early playhouses, there was an

actual throne for the Lords attending the play, built like those made for pageants and triumphs, though not with 'two and twenty degrees to the top'.[2] Perhaps the frontispiece to 'The Wits' shows a recollection of this arrangement. Walter Hodges indeed suggested, most convincingly, just such a 'throne' for Cleopatra's monument, but as a temporary structure. In early theatres it may have been permanent. Then, in course of time, it was realised that more money could be made by removing the throne sticking out into the stage, and by having the Lords' or gentlemen's rooms running right across: hence, 'the covetousness of sharers'; while the space at the back of these rooms, being then much more out of sight, would provide more scope for the gentlemen ushers. (A temporary throne could still have

[1] *The Gull's Hornbook*, the satire by Thomas Dekker, was published in 1609. The relevant passage reads: 'Let our gallant presently advance himself up to the throne of the stage. I mean not into the Lords' room (which is now but the stage's suburbs). No, those boxes, by the iniquity of custom, conspiracy of waiting women and gentlemen ushers, that there sweat together, and the covetousness of sharers, are contemptibly thrust into the rear, and much new satin is there damned by being smothered to death in darkness. But on the very rushes where the comedy is to dance, yea and under the state of Cambyses himself, must our feathered ostrich, like a piece of ordnance be planted valiantly (because impudently) beating down the mews and hisses of the opposed rascality.'

[2] *The English Wagner Book* (1594) speaks of a 'high throne, wherein the king should sit . . . proudly placed with two and twenty degrees to the top'. I am suggesting that the spirit which led to the pageants and triumphs so popular at the time, produced also a throne on the stage for the chief spectators to present themselves. This would be in essence a platform about 6 ft (1·8 m) square, suitably decorated, projecting from the centre of the back of the stage. The lords would make their entry on to it from the rear; it must have been rather like the entry of the Queen today at a Command performance at the opera. Is it possible that when the Shrew was acted at the Globe, there was some such throne to which Sly was taken up? It would certainly have been dramatically effective!

been put up when needed.) This passage, then, gives support to the placing of the gentlemen's rooms over the stage, with the gallants sitting below them, this being a development from an earlier pattern with a permanent throne jutting out from the tiring house frame.

In this essay I have, in passing, suggested a function for the prick-posts, and have put forward arguments for a pent-house roof to the heavens, and for a wide door to the yard. I have shown that 3,000 could have been accommodated, and have argued against the inner stage. But my main purpose has been to show how, by insisting on the provision of sight-lines, and on the requirement that the theatre should make as much money as possible, a structure can be developed which fits together remarkably well, with nothing in it arbitrary or there by chance. Of course I am not suggesting that any one playhouse was exactly like this. But I hope that these suggestions, stemming from this particular approach, could form the basis for the reconstruction of an 'ideal' Elizabethan Playhouse.

© D. A. LATTER 1975

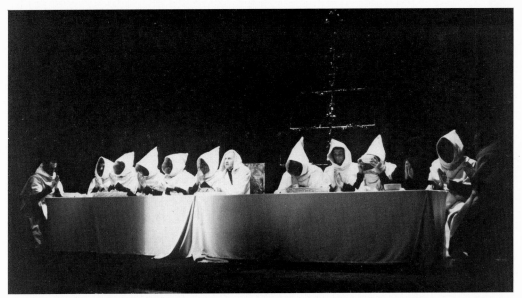

I *King John*, Royal Shakespeare Theatre, 1974. Directed by John Barton with Barry Kyle, designed by John Napier with Martyn Bainbridge. Emrys James (centre) as King John.

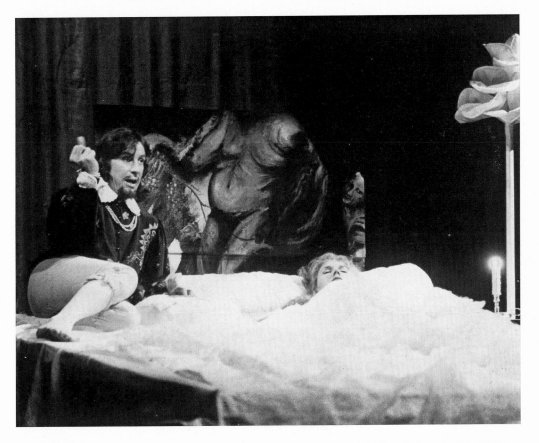

II *Cymbeline*, Royal Shakespeare Theatre, 1974. Directed by John Barton with Barry Kyle and Clifford Williams, designed by John Napier with Martyn Bainbridge and Sue Jenkinson. The bedroom scene (act II, scene ii) with Ian Richardson as Iachimo and Susan Fleetwood as Imogen.

III *Twelfth Night*, Royal Shakespeare Theatre, 1974. Directed by Peter Gill, designed by William Dudley. Jane Lapotaire as Viola and John Price as Orsino.

IV *Twelfth Night*, act II, scene v, Nicol Williamson as Malvolio.

V *Measure for Measure*, Royal Shakespeare Theatre, 1974. Directed by Keith Hack, designed by Maria Björnson. Michael Pennington as Angelo.

VI *Measure for Measure*, Michael Pennington as Angelo, Francesca Annis as Isabella.

THE SMALLEST SEASON: THE ROYAL SHAKESPEARE COMPANY AT STRATFORD IN 1974

PETER THOMSON

The Royal Shakespeare Company has shifted its centre. Even before the completion of the Barbican Theatre, it has become a London company with a branch in Stratford. I record this progress with sadness and some sense of outrage. The British theatre is in a state of confusion, certainly, and we must expect some drawing in of horns when rising costs of materials coincide with falling attendance, an imminent increase in the actor's minimum wage, and a subsidy crisis. But at Stratford?

On 13 June 1974 *The Stage* announced in a headline 'RSC Biggest Season: Twenty-three projects in six months'. It was reporting a press-release from Trevor Nunn giving his plans for the second half of 1974, 'the most ambitious six months in the company's history'. Of these projects, the main theatre at Stratford housed three, *Twelfth Night* (opened 22 August), *Measure for Measure* (opened 4 September), and *Macbeth* (opened in November, too late for review here, and too late also for a large part of Stratford's traditional audience). Four were scheduled for performance at The Other Place, a 140-seat theatre/studio, which has offered a largely non-Shakespearian programme on occasional nights throughout the season. Of the remaining sixteen, nine were on show in London, five were 'on tour', and two were untraceable. The Arts Council subsidy for 1974–5 amounted to £450,000, 'about one-fifth', the programme told us, 'of the company's costs for that year'. For the rest, the same programme confessed, 'the company depends on loyal and long-term support (for instance, in terms of associate membership) of many who make up its audience'. Now that, from Stratford's point of view, is a joke. For the second half of August, the 'loyal' audience could see *Twelfth Night* or, on certain nights and in small numbers, Mike Leigh's improvised play *Babies Grow Old* at The Other Place. For the whole of September and October, the choice was restricted to *Twelfth Night* and *Measure for Measure* at the main theatre and to the sporadic presentations of *Babies Grow Old* or *The Tempest* at The Other Place. The promise of Nicol Williamson as Macbeth, clearly the plum of the season, and Uncle Vanya in his own production of that play at The Other Place was held over until the frosty months. The Stratford audience was not pleased, and the box-office takings recorded the displeasure. It was either a miscalculation or a deliberate insult. I spoke to leaders of several groups who will not again bring parties to Stratford. The running down of the repertoire system has destroyed their confidence. If you want to see the work of the Royal Shakespeare Company, go to London. The Company's annual costs are, evidently, over £2,000,000, a sum which reflects a mixture of boldness, perfectionism, incapacity to resist the pull of a designer's theatre, Parkinsonian disorganization, and sheer extravagance. (What has happened to the lifts installed at Stratford for the 1972 season? Can it be true that some of them are not only unused but already unusable?

What is the implied relationship between conspicuous expenditure and standards of performance, or the actual relationship between conspicuous expenditure and an assured subsidy?) I do not believe that a subsidy of £450,000 is too small to allow Stratford a full and rewarding season of plays; but I have to record the impression that 1974, the Royal Shakespeare Company's 'biggest season', was Stratford's smallest for over a decade.

It began in March, with *King John*, a production which, to be generous, may have been more acceptable at another theatre – at Marowitz's Open Space, perhaps. I am not a purist, as my previous *Survey* reviews will have made clear, but it cannot be *ignored* that the audience at the Stratford theatre will assume that the *King John* they are seeing is Shakespeare's, and that no amount of programme notes will erase that impression. The free Cast List confessed at the bottom right-hand corner that 'The text for this production incorporates lines from *The Troublesome Reign* and Bale's *King Johan*, and some additions by John Barton', but such 'honesty' is like those small-print disavowals on manufacturers' guarantees, which indemnify the deceiver without enlightening the deceived. This production by John Barton included a lot of direct quotation from Shakespeare, but framed it in such a way as to deprive it of its Shakespearian tone. An original fascinating in part for its mediaeval residues had been glossed over by a sophisticated political cynicism, and illustrated by a selection of theatrical images which seemed to me undiscriminating. It was Barton's intention, as it had been Nahum Tate's intention with *King Lear*, to make the play better. This is a quite different intention from that of a Marowitz, who leaves the original text where it is and then composes a critical exploration of it; and it is less reputable. In this production, Barton foisted onto Shakespeare notions about politicians he would not have had and language

of which he could never have been guilty. I found the occasion distressing.

The play was set on a raked stage, narrowed towards a point at the upstage horizon by an inversely sloping 'ceiling', pitted with stars like an Elizabethan 'heavens', and broken at the centre by a perspective cross. The lights around the acting area were displayed to the audience, and there was a practical curtain which would allow the staging of a number of front scenes to cover the scene-shifting. It was a set designed to remind us that we were in a theatre, and the actors were constantly reinforcing the point, for all the world like doctrinaire Brechtians. But why? Barton's patterned work on *Richard II* had here been formalised into something not far short of theatre-by-numbers. If John is to hold a warder at the play's interpolated opening, he must hold one at the end. If the effigy of Richard I is to be carried solemnly into a trap downstage left at the start, John's body, bandaged into the rigidity of an effigy, is sure to be lowered into a trap downstage right at the final curtain. If Arthur's literal fall is to be represented in a slow-motion stagger, so must John's metaphorical fall be. If the ubiquitous Peter of Pomfret is to 'read' an interpolated prologue from Shakespeare's Folio to set the play in motion, Faulconbridge must 'read' the famous last five lines to put it to rest. If the reading of Richard's will is to be the prologue, and Constance's reading of the alternative will in Arthur's favour a feature, then Faulconbridge must read John's will as a last evidence of the way history repeats itself. If John is to be crowned and swathed in a golden cloak, obviously Arthur must be, Lewis must be, John must be again (it was an oversight of Shakespeare's to omit the second coronation!), and Henry in mock-conclusiveness must be too. The unruly original has been turned, by directional interference, into a well-made play!

This method of imposing unimposing

patterns on the text is even carried from play to play. The golden cloak worn by the various claimants to the English throne is emphatically the one Richard II splendidly wears as 'glistering Phaethon' in the production repeated from last season, and Cymbeline too, at the moment of his recovered royalty, in John Barton's third contribution to the Stratford repertoire. It is a vivid costume item designed to reinforce the notion of the king's two bodies by diminishing the *man* who dares to wear it; but determination to use it in plays so dissimilar does also suggest the super-imposition of a directorial idea that pre-dates a new encounter with each text. That Barton took a major part in re-shaping the early history plays in order to provide the continuous momentum for the Wars of the Roses at Stratford in 1964 is well known. A disadvantage of the method was its over-simplification of political and human motivation and its necessary disregarding of the perimeter of a particular play. With this production of *King John*, Barton has o'erflown the measure. Six weeks after its opening, Alan Howard was playing for the Royal Shakespeare Company in London the part of the epileptic spastic, Carlos II of Spain, in Peter Barnes's *The Bewitched*. Emrys James's English John had had a transfusion of Hapsburg blood in the Company's hospital for sick plays. When he didn't grin, he fretted, and whenever possible, like Edmund Kean's Richard III,[1] he did both. He was a nursery king, a mother's boy without an inkling of adult responsibility. Three 'laughs' from the first three acts will illustrate the point. John is badgered by the Citizen of Angiers, who thinks too quickly for him. 'Mother, a word', he says (courtesy of John Barton), and leads Elinor downstage with a confidential smile to everyone else. Now, with only the audience as witness, he mouths in a comically exaggerated stage-whisper, 'What shall I do?' It's a familiar routine which, properly timed, produces one of those com-

pulsory laughs which is no necessary reflection of the audience's good humour. Add to the mixture Hilda Braid's endearingly bright-eyed, lower-middle-class Elinor, off to war with a handbag on her arm, and the picture of Freudian ineptitude grows fuller. The second example is more ingenious. Noticing the disparity in the description of Blanch's dowry in lines 487 and 527–8 of Act II, Barton made a comic feature of John's inability to find on his map the initially omitted Volquessen. The chopping up of the map was hilariously casual, and the detailed scissor-work on the tiny fragment of Volquessen was childishly inconsistent. (There always is that mad Monopoly player who'd rather have the Old Kent Road than Mayfair.) It was a good 'turn', though I was interested in Emrys James's failure to get a laugh (on the night I saw the play) out of Shakespeare's own voicing of the idiocy of territorial bargaining:

> France, shall we knit our powers
> And lay this Angiers even with the ground;
> Then after fight who shall be king of it?
> (II, i, 398–400)

If the actors are playing on the director's side of the text, the playwright loses. The third example is without justification, but illustrates most clearly the level at which this interpretation of John was pitched. Pandulph has entered (at III, i, 134) to make the Pope's demand of John:

> Why thou against the church, our holy mother,
> So wilfully dost spurn; and, force perforce,
> Keep Stephen Langton

John's by-play of ignorance interrupts him. Who's Stephen Langton? And Pandulph has to explain:

> chosen Archbishop
> Of Canterbury, [pause for laughter] from that holy see?

[1] Kean's 'grinning' and 'fretting' are recorded by James H. Hackett on his annotated edition of Cibber's *Richard III*, reproduced in facsimile by the Society for Theatre Research, and edited by A. S. Downer (1959).

A John who does not know – or who pretends not to know (and how are *we* to distinguish?) – who Stephen Langton is does not deserve Philip Faulconbridge's company, Hubert's love, or the enmity of France and Rome. The play is thrown awry by it. But there is, we are invited to believe, a terrifying *relevance* about all this. General Amin may not remember whom he last killed, nor Richard Nixon whom he last corrupted. King John, Carlos II, William Shakespeare, Peter Barnes, John Barton, *Oh What a Lovely War. Plus ça change!* Meanwhile, the extent to which *King John* is an inappropriate vehicle for the conveyance of Barton's ideas about rule is suggested by the magnitude of the changes he has made in the text.

The greatest of these changes came after the interval; which is to say that Shakespeare's fourth and fifth acts were unrecognizable. The first half of the play gave us a tame Bastard from that excellent, but on this occasion bewildered, actor Richard Pasco. John ignored him and distracted us and himself with state business during the brothers' quarrel. I take it that the presence of an effective politician would have undermined the directorial masterplan. Pasco accepted John's inanities like a gentle older cousin, never threatening to 'deaf our ears', and much too passionless to *hate* Austria. However you read John's part in the first three acts – and it may be that he is wickedly unconcerned – there is no mistaking the animosity of the Bastard and Austria or Elinor and Constance. It was a mere misreading to play these conflicts down to nothing. The first three acts were devoid of pressure and urgency. I sat up briefly on Constance's 'Lewis marry Blanch!' (III, i, 34), but almost at once John and Philip skipped in holding hands, as if an alliance were no more than a Barn Dance, and Constance the embarrassing product of over-writing. If an actor had something serious to say, the director was likely to deflate

it. Thus, when Pandulph pronounced John excommunicate, John shrugged and sprinkled wine over himself like holy water; the Bastard began the great 'Commodity' soliloquy in a downstage left corner, and was given a lightly mocking follow-spot for his cross to centre; and finally, having 'read' the last patriotic lines of the play, the same actor was asked to exit whistling. Against the general nonchalance (an attack not only against politicians, but ultimately against art as well) could be set, during these first three acts, only the melancholy Salisbury (holding his counsel like a wise uncle), Constance (softened but not silenced), Pandulph (too heavily made up, falling somewhere between a Morality 'Death' and King Rat in the Christmas pantomime), and Hubert.

The creation of Hubert resists a director's urge to distort. David Suchet is strongly built and can stand still. The savage birth-mark across one eye and cheek belonged to a child's nightmare, and made more notable Arthur's trust in him. Some family resemblance between John and Arthur was suggested at the opening of the 'murder' scene (played in front of the curtain, and neither strengthened nor destroyed by that). It was almost the last we saw of Shakespeare's play. The second coronation was interpolated to follow it, so that 'Here once again we sit, once again crown'd' became an almost superfluous mid-scene line. The Peter of Pomfret scene was much extended, for Peter was to pursue John, as a figure of Nemesis, in various guises from interpolated prologue to interpolated murder. After Arthur's death (still in innocent white, without 'shipboy's semblance'), and the discovery of his body, an intrusive front-scene carried us forward to Ascension Day, and had John, as risible as a Gilbertian Lord High Executioner, leading on Peter of Pomfret by tugging the noose around the tight-lipped prophet's neck. After sending Peter off to be hanged, John addressed to us in the audience a soliloquy of comic self-pity. (I jotted into my notebook, 'cf. Reg Dixon: "I'm not well. I'm poorly. I'm *proper* poorly"', and can no longer remember enough of the scene to check my response.) This front-scene gave time for the preparation of another interpolated scene, but this time a spectacular one. The curtains parted, and John turned upstage to be confronted by Pandulph and a mass of monks, who stripped him to loin-cloth and crown, spreadeagled him prone on the floor, and humiliated him into repentance. Those who saw his production of *Richard II* will be familiar with John Barton's use of stage-monks, but Shakespeare's *King John* is remarkable for its scarcity of religious reference.[1] Both here, and in John's later entrance (v, iii) dressed as a monk, Barton was listening to himself rather than to the play. This whole grotesque interpolation was a prelude to the opening words of Act v. There was worse to come. Before allying themselves with the Dauphin, Salisbury and five other Barons stood in a line centre-stage to explain themselves to us in obvious imitation of the prose inset in *Murder in the Cathedral*. They looked very unhappy about it, and who can blame them? Should I go on? I was confused by now, but I think v, iii, v, iv, and v, v stood in sequence before Peter of Pomfret, translated into a Swinstead monk, welcomed us in the audience to Swinstead, where there was a Christmas feast arranged according to Leonardo's 'Last Supper', with John as Christ. The white-clad monks sang a carol, John replied with a solo, 'Come home again sweetheart', Peter of Pomfret poisoned John and himself died finely on the table, and the scene closed with John helped off in pain. In v, vi, Hubert made it clear to the Bastard (they were both disguised as monks) that John's will bestowed the crown on him, and in the final scene, John having died kneeling, the Bastard misread that will to the assembled court so that Prince Henry would have untroubled access to the

throne. It was a far, far better thing than he had ever done, but I don't think I was intended to be much impressed. Almost anybody *could* have gone out whistling.

I hope that account is not merely flippant, because seriousness like John Barton's deserves something more than flippancy from a reviewer. Nevertheless, this rewriting of *King John* seems to me presumptuous. Barton is not a great writer (neither was Bale), and it would have been wiser to invite a better dramatist to do the radical reworking he eventually undertook himself *if he felt such reworking necessary*. Or again, if John's reign is to be subjected to modern scrutiny, why not pair Shakespeare's play with Arden's *Left-Handed Liberty?* Impossible after the quarrels between author and Company over *The Island of the Mighty*, but is that kind of juxtaposition adequately investigated? Something very dangerous is happening if the leading Shakespearian company in the world (and as I write that, it sounds like flattery) encourages one of its directors to turn improving playwright. *King John* is not an isolated case. Ten years after 'The Wars of the Roses', Barton has also retouched *Doctor Faustus* for a production I have not yet seen; and it's easy enough to visualize how *Edward II* might be improved, or *All's Well that Ends Well*, or *Camino Real*, or *The Seagull*. Or *Cymbeline*.

Cymbeline was the third play in the 1974 repertoire – the second was the *Richard II* which I reviewed last year – and the third to be directed by John Barton. It was not rewritten, but some lack of confidence in the text is suggested by the cutting of 1150 lines, and an anxiety about the clarity of the plot by the turning of Cornelius into a kind of magical master of ceremonies with access to the play's

[1] W. H. Clemen has noted five uses of 'God' in the play against thirty-seven in *Richard II*, twenty-five in *1 Henry IV*, and seventy-five in *Richard III*. (*A Commentary on Shakespeare's Richard III* (1968), p. 78n.)

sources and the Folio stage directions. The abiding memories are of the staging of the bedroom scene, the audience's applause at the descent of Jupiter's eagle, and the kneeling downstage centre of Imogen and Posthumus Leonatus in a reunion that was genuinely touching. The first and last of these are high points which will only be effective if they are prepared for, and the highest achievement of this production was that, in some sort, they were.

With considerable assistance from the bold design of John Napier, Barton based the performance on strong visual contrasts. Cymbeline's Queen was costumed in rainbow brilliance and crested like a cock. Relishing her witchcraft, she crowed before the potion scene, and the announcement of her death was saluted by the voice of an off-stage cock. Cloten was an overgrown bully-boy in leather, a Hell's Angel for want of a better brain. It was a pity that he was so obviously not dangerous. Guiderius and Arviragus had nothing to be afraid of. The part is not an easy one for an actor. Charles Keating enjoyed most the invention of a physical image of the pain of attempted thought, and looked aptly sheepish when caught in II, iii with flowers in his hefty hands; but need Cloten be clumsy as well as stupid? I do not know whether Barton had intended to link him physically with his mother through the image of the cock ('They dare not fight with me because of the queen my mother. Every Jack-slave hath his bellyful of fighting, and I must go up and down like a cock that nobody can match' II, i, 22–5), but there was no other visible link between the two. Like David Suchet's powerfully honest Pisanio, they provided one-dimensional aspects of Cymbeline's complex court. The contrast with Rome on the one hand and Wales on the other was evidently ecological. Rome was wine-drinking, urbane, cerebral and mercantile, a business society in which Ian Richardson's knowing Iachimo was a wholly plausible

confidence trickster. The two dialogue scenes in Rome were finely spoken, and carefully argued. Richardson's ability to reveal the gap between the line, even as he speaks it, and the mental processes that inform it is an unqualified asset in Iachimo (until Act V – and there were problems there!). There were two fine exchanges between him and Tim Piggott-Smith's honest English Posthumus: 'I should get ground of your fair mistress, make her go back, even to the yielding, had I admittance and opportunity to friend', says Iachimo. 'No', says this Posthumus, laughingly part of the company, and then suddenly alone, 'No!' (I, iv, 119–22). A few lines later, recognizing the dominion of the argument over his own wishes in a way that the civilized urgency of the scene made acceptable, Posthumus ventured again, 'What lady would you choose to assail?' 'Yours', said Richardson, blowing out the spill that had just lit Posthumus's pipe. This was a quick-thinking Italy, with the combination of artistic hedonism and financial acumen that the Medici family exemplified. Lucius's smartly uniformed army looked out of place in England, and even more so in Wales. Napier's design for Wales was lunar. Mushroom growths spread over the stage (Cloten would stumble over them) and the loops and curves of the cave entrance might have resulted from a Queen of Hearts' determination to use the Loch Ness monster as a croquet hoop. Since the interval was taken after III, ii, there was ample time to prepare this set, and the 'Welsh' trio, within the severe theatrical scope of their roles, played acceptably on it. It was a token wilderness whose mountain back-cloth was called up by Cornelius when his reading of the stage-directions revealed the need for it.

The contrasts, then, were clear, and the major effect of the cutting was to pare down all but the Imogen/Posthumus theme. Susan Fleetwood did not dominate the play, as Vanessa Redgrave did in 1962, but neither did she undersell it. Imogen has an unusual number of solo entrances (more, I suspect, than even Viola), and Barton exploited them unashamedly. There was music for her entrance – without Pisanio – through the half-closed upstage curtains at the opening of I, iii, and this giving her the whole depth or width of the stage to cross alone was characteristic. It takes some grace of movement to accomplish this without antagonizing an audience, and mutual trust between director and actress to envisage it. This was a developing Imogen, who met with increasing energy each new disaster. I was not convinced by her underplayed delivery of the terribly difficult lines over Cloten's headless corpse, but there was a shocking vehemence in the subsequent cursing of Pisanio. Nothing gives more weight to Shaw's advice to Ellen Terry to 'cut the part so as to leave the paragon out and the woman in' than this speedy jumping to the wrong conclusion. Susan Fleetwood's utter inability to answer Lucius's 'What art thou?' (IV, ii, 367) was more than mere confusion. She had lost herself. Imogen's identity is invested in Posthumus, not in Fidele. With her husband dead, she can answer no more than, 'I am nothing'. There was gentleness and passion enough in this Imogen to make the reunion with Posthumus a moment of real joy, rivalled only by the wonderfully worded,

> O, my gentle brothers!
> Have we thus met? O, never say hereafter
> But I am truest speaker.
>
> (V, v, 375–7)

This is an almost unfailingly effective stage event, with far more impact than could be easily predicted from a reading.

Of the production's special effects, I have already mentioned the spectacular descent of Jupiter's great golden egg, which opened out to form an eagle's wings and reveal the gold-painted god. (The descent of the Duke as *deus ex machina* in Keith Hack's *Measure for Measure* might almost have been a parody of this eye-catching device.) The final trick, when the great gold ring in the Heavens tilted over to form a white halo over Cymbeline's restored court, was too evidently theatrical. The transformation has occurred earlier in the text, and there was some inconsistency between this 'marvel' and the cutting of Act V to make the rush of recognitions more psychologically plausible. The fairy-tale in this performance ended with the announcement of the Queen's death and Cymbeline's shedding of the white smock that masked the glory of his golden cloak, so that there was little to justify this scenic whim. The staging of the battle in V, ii, was a happier enterprise. Cornelius, whose approach to the action was consistently humorous, read us a mixture of stage directions and additional explanations whilst the actors slowly mimed upstage the incidents he was describing. There is nothing probable about this battle, and much to be said for recounting the incidents as lucidly as possible. There remains to be described the encounter of Imogen and Iachimo. To begin with the trunk; it was adorned with painted figures whose colour and detail reminded me initially of Andrea del Sarto, and it was an insistent scenic feature of the first meeting of Imogen and Iachimo. The Imogen of this encounter was never greatly threatened by Iachimo's lies. When Pisanio tells her of Posthumus's accusation much later, she will reply 'False to his bed! What is it to be false?' If an actress is to meet the challenge of that line at III, iv, 42, she cannot afford to be too upset by Iachimo's more-than-hints in I, vi. The dialogue is a confrontation of two intellects, and Ian Richardson, as you would expect, relished it. The clarity of opposition in argument was, anyway, the outstanding feature of this production, and this scene is its high point. So impressed is he by Imogen's resistance that this Iachimo can hardly believe his one success.

There is a long pause after Imogen has promised to give 'safe stowage' to his plate and jewels 'in my bedchamber', and then a sudden staccato gesture, 'They are in this trunk.' And 'this trunk' becomes a feature in the bedchamber too. A big white bed is wheeled down to dominate the centre of the stage. Imogen reads and sleeps, and the lid of the trunk is pushed up to form a headboard upstage of the bed. The picture is of a headless, hairy, male nude, and suddenly Richardson's head is on the neck. The violation of the white room is obscene.

Cymbeline, then, marked a recovery of balance in Barton's Shakespearian work. It was not a great production, but it was sensitive and properly concerned with the communication of its fable. *Twelfth Night*, the season's other acceptably traditional production, cut less than fifty lines, and allowed its actors greater freedom. It was Peter Gill's first directing assignment for the Royal Shakespeare Company, and is unlikely to be his last. Stratford needs this kind of work, easy of access to a theatrically uninquisitive audience, and eager to display the talents of its leading actors. The Company had changed completely now that the first three plays had moved to London. That fine Stratford stalwart David Waller was Sir Toby Belch, but Jane Lapotaire (Viola), Frank Thornton (Sir Andrew Aguecheek), Patricia Hayes (Maria), and Ron Pember (Feste) were as new to the Company as their director. Where is the proud 'sixties talk of a company style? There is none. Each play must establish its particular style during the rehearsal period. Outside that and the players' prior skills, there is no resource. When the work of a single playwright is so persistently performed, this 'one-off' quality is regrettable. There is an undeniable sense that some possibility is being missed, a sense that is deepened by the nagging presence of Peter Brook's name among the Directors of the Company.

The designer, William Dudley, had surrounded the *Twelfth Night* stage with slatted, wood-textured walls, constructed in isolable blocks. A pale portrait of Narcissus decorated the central block of the back wall, which slid forward to create two upstage entrances very much in the position of the Elizabethan stage doors. The long entrances and exits, especially of Nicol Williamson's Malvolio, were made a feature of the production, whose physical norm was choreographed movement on a bare stage. As a variant on this, there were the pretty set-pieces – two box-hedges, three potted trees, a quaintly small wall as background for the drinking scene (II, iii), benches – and the cushions on which Orsino and his favourites dallied and fondled. Orsino's bisexuality and the unexplained involvement of Antonio in the dénouement were the production's most dangerous statements. Given his fondness for petting, it seemed unlikely that Orsino would not have felt through Viola's disguise, but Jane Lapotaire's nicely mixed response in I, iv and II, iv made the point worthwhile. The director's concern to emphasize the play's sexual confusion was exemplified in the timing of Viola's soliloquy after Malvolio has brought her Olivia's ring:

> She loves me sure; the cunning of her passion
> Invites me in this churlish messenger.
> None of my lord's ring! why, he sent her none.
> I am the man.
>
> (II, ii, 20–3)

She paused there in obvious confusion, then recovered with a smiling shrug, and the audience laughed delightedly. She was such a lively, boyish boy – the kind of fourth-former the heterosexual prefect has a crush on (I was adored once too!). Jane Lapotaire is, indeed, a Shakespearian actress of the highest quality. Her vocal range and her sensitivity to mid-speech shifts of emphasis reminded me of the young Dorothy Tutin in the part; and she backed up her director's concept by reaching the audience's bisexuality. Mary Rutherford's Olivia, busy and thoroughly middle-class, with an almost northern bluntness and a cuddly body, was an adequate foil, but neither Orsino nor Sebastian could sustain the idea at this Viola's high level. 'O thou dissembling cub' ought more strongly to have embodied Orsino's fury, not only that Cesario should marry *his* Olivia, but also that *his* Cesario should marry at all.

It was largely through individual performances that this production recommended itself. Nicol Williamson's Malvolio was a studied grotesque – a pinched, Scottish elder of the kirk with the distorted sexual aspirations of the 'unco' guid'. He held his voice in the back of his throat, and only his bottom lip was mobile. The walk was a heron's prance, and, at times of supreme self-satisfaction, his head leant towards his shoulder and his eyes glinted like an alert bird's. The run was an absurd lope, which carried his legs as far sideways as forwards and left the top half of his body almost static. His black costume was striped with white lines of various thickness and density and topped with a ruff. It had a *trompe-l'œil* effect, seeming to hold a tiny head an impossible distance from the bottom of the long, mean legs. He was happiest in this costume. Comically night-shirted in II, iii, and villainously cross-gartered in III, iv, he was willing to let the absurdity of the dress usurp his comic force. But in the gulling scene he was brilliant. He explained 'play with my – some rich jewel' (II, iv, 67–8) by a gesture sharper than a footnote, lifting his chain of office then slapping it down with self-annoyance. His attempts to twist his mouth into a meaningful pronunciation of M, O, A, I, were as hilarious as his sudden, irrational conclusion that they said 'Malvolio'. Remembering his dignity, he just resisted the invitation to 'revolve' contained in the letter, but 'smile' he would, and did. First he had to remember how to do it, and

then, almost imperceptibly, force his lips wider and slowly wider into a look of such joyless jollity as might have been worn by Miss Hotchkiss at the ITMA office party. His subsequent entrance to Olivia, pushing Maria aside and 'smiling' as he smeared his body along a property tree, was perfect, but the scene declined into ungainly knockabout and was only saved by the soliloquy. Twice, then, he stood to acknowledge with reverent hypocrisy Jove's hand in his well-merited glory, but for the rest of the time he sprawled beside a table in gangling self-love.

The tone of Frank Thornton's Aguecheek was set by the long face and longer silence that preceded his lifeless question, 'Shall we set about some revels?' (I, iii, 146–7). He was thin and melancholy, devoid of energy, dyspeptic and consumptive. There was a consciousness of real loneliness beneath the surface of the comic scenes, that affected not only Aguecheek but also Feste and Sir Toby. David Waller was, on his first entrance with Maria, dignified and relaxed, but drink depressed and depraved him. He made his reading of the character clear to his *Guardian* interviewer:

Toby's first line is: 'What a plague means my niece to take the death of her brother thus? I am sure care's an enemy to life.' That suggests to me a man who is, as it were, protesting too much. He is protecting himself, a wounded man – hence the drinking... Nearly his last words are 'I hate a drunken rogue'. And it seems quite clear to me that he's referring quite consciously to himself.[1]

That, expressed with admirable clarity, was the key to Waller's playing of Sir Toby. Patricia Hayes's perky Maria was a decade older and too happy below stairs to give credibility to her standing in Olivia's household. And Feste? How fascinating that it can be played so variously. Ron Pember spoke like a Londoner, dressed like a faded Harlequin now reduced to busking, and hinted always at a

[1] *The Guardian* (18 September 1974), 10.

radical's social distaste for the antics of privilege. He despised the effeteness of Orsino's court, and his angry assumption that Viola considered him a beggar (III, i, 9) had all the spikiness of class-pride. But there was more than this. One member of the audience interestingly compared him with Bosola, another joker who declines to laugh at his own jokes. He was discomforting, an outsider, almost malevolently saturnine, defying the sentimental response to Malvolio's plight by pressing home his final accusations with heartless accuracy in Act v. (Yet he, with Fabian, guided Sir Andrew off the stage after Sir Toby's cruel last rebuff.) The majority of George Fenton's music for the production had a 'Victorian Elizabethan' tone. Against that, Pember sang his songs with the gritty voice of the modern, unaccompanied folk-singer. He was a working man among the leisured classes, deeply critical of their behaviour and bitterly dissatisfied with his own. The rough-and-ready air of the curtain-call was, perhaps, his triumph over the formality of Illyria. The four lovers had whirled and weaved their way around, involving Antonio in their dance, but leaving him bemused and lonely when they went out and the stage wall slid shut behind them. And there Antonio stood, upstage alone, while Ron Pember sang his song of mutability to us. I shall never forget this Feste.

Measure for Measure, which opened in early September, was directed by another man new to Stratford. Keith Hack's work at the Glasgow Citizens' Theatre has had a Brechtian reference and a consistent determination to change society. The programme for the present production carried a terse analysis of the play by Edward Bond, which adumbrated a 'new' approach:

It is ironic that the academic theatre and the critics take the Duke at his face value, and remain caught up in the whole pretence of 'seeming' that Shakespeare attacked. In fact, our politics are still run by Angelos, made publicly respectable by Ducal figure-heads and theories, supported by hysteria (Isabella), and mindlessly obeyed by dehumanised forces (the Provost and Abhorson).

Bond here underrates the divergence of critical opinion on the play, and except in its view of the Duke, the production owed less to his ideas than might have been assumed by the prominence of their display. There was a more overt debt to the Prospect Theatre Company's recent *Pericles*, which set the play in a male brothel whose inmates and visitors chose to perform it for their own delight. I did not see this Prospect production, so that my comparisons are speculative; but there was, I suspect, an essential difference. The Prospect 'players' were theatrical amateurs enjoying themselves. Keith Hack's 'players' were jaded professionals going through the necessary motions of a performance they would willingly have avoided. The production was given a bare, shabby, theatrical fit-up setting by its designer Maria Björnson. On the right of the stage stood a figure of Christ the King in baroque decay, surrounded by festoons of jewellery and a huge red curtain that was no longer fine – there was whitewash along its fringe, and it half-hung, sagged and sprawled, forced into simultaneous service as backcloth, masking-piece and stagecloth. It was a splendid relic, the emblem of a stock company that had seen better days. Stage left was bare, and the acting area was surrounded at the back by a wire grid and downstage of the proscenium by unadorned scaffolding. Through the grid, extras and onlookers would gaze at the encaged action. The resultant ambiguity was intentional. Who was in the cage – onlookers or actors (or audience)? There was a disconcerting ambiguity about the figure of Christ too. Its vulgar artistry was almost sacrilegious, an association of the religious and the obscenely grotesque which would be highlighted by the prelude to I, iv. The part of Mistress Overdone had been given to a very large actor, Dan Meaden, and it was he, after a parodic strip-tease and switch of costume, who played the nun Francisca with the mock femininity of a pantomime dame. In Keith Hack's Vienna, a garishly perverted sexuality was in league with an established church; and the chief ally of the corruption was the Duke.

The idea in itself was witty. We were, as the desultory openings of the production made clear, watching a *performance* of the events of *Measure for Measure*. And the performers were recognizably members of a discontented stock company, making do with available scenery (Mariana could not be afforded the splendour of a moated grange – she sat, instead, at the top of a high step-ladder) and timeworn costumes. The musicians were untidily concealed at stage right, the overstage lighting was open to the audience, the technical work (black-outs, sound-cues, costume changes) was intentionally sluggish, and the play began with its actors strolling onto the stage out of character to await the cue. The Duke was among them, in a splendid robe-of-office (the company's other precious property), with his back to us. The lethargic opening music went on too long, and the actors fidgeted until the Duke turned to address to us the opening word. But what a Duke! Barrie Ingham was made up black-haired and sleek as the heavy villain of melodrama, and his voice and air-sawing gesture were in keeping. In such a company, Michael Pennington's Angelo was the juvenile lead, Escalus the first old man, and Lucio the comic man. But there was an extra twist to all this. The actors hated their overweening actor-manager. The suggestion of the costuming is, on the one hand, that everyone in Vienna is poor, and on the other, that the Vincent Crummles who plays the Duke underpays his actors, earning for himself an unpopularity that is more theatrical than social. That, I take it, was the idea; and it was a potential asset of this produc-

tion that its director brought to it more passion than had been evident in the rest of the season. There was a desperate need for something to excite the audience's imagination even where it offended. It was a severe blow to the Royal Shakespeare Company that the critical reaction was unanimously hostile. The reaction was not surprising, though it might have been ungracious. Whereas the theatrical imagination that had conceived the production was impressive, it operated at a distance from the text (take as evidence the cutting of the Duke's lines to allow villainous intention to replace sincere bewilderment), and it had not adequately communicated itself to the actors. A director who imposes on his actors an idea of whose validity he fails to convince them is the modern theatre's equivalent of the egocentric actor–manager, so that, despite the energy of his interpretation, Keith Hack must stand condemned by his own theatrical image.

Some of the effects of his proposal about the play might have been predicted. There was no psychological exploration of character, and therefore no pretence that the changes of heart were predictable from earlier in the text. The actors had been given no licence to look for a 'sub-text', and the plot was communicated with a picaresque sparseness of inference. Against the figure of so villainous a Duke, Angelo seemed strangely innocent, and Pennington played him without the ice-in-the-blood strength of, for example, Ian Richardson's 1970 performance. Subversion in a society governed so evilly might have been admirable, but the low-life characters, with the exception of Lucio, were charmless. Even Claudio, sporting unexpectedly a single ear-ring, was too ugly and wretched to wring a tear. But the outrageous hypocrisy of the Duke overwhelmed the lesser hypocrisy of Angelo and of an Isabella who not only wore black lace in the convent, but also touched Angelo before he touched her. The audience sniggered at his reference to 'the love I have in doing good' (III, i, 202), and laughed aloud at his comically inappropriate 'Benedicite' to Juliet (II, iii, 39). In disguise, the Duke wore a single black glove, and, in criticism of the Elizabethan convention, took the further precaution of hiding his face from all who might recognize it. Eventually (in IV, ii) he would reveal himself to the Provost (a solid performance by a black actor Jeffery Kissoon), in unnecessary anticipation of the fine unmasking in Act V. His change of heart was mocked by having him descend from the flies off-cue on a crudely constructed bar, and transformed now into a golden-haired god (the gold-effect was the same as that used for Jupiter in *Cymbeline*). The over-acting of the Duke in Act V was intended to undermine our belief in the happy ending he contrives. All the world's a tatty stage, and no one in authority is to be trusted.

Nothing in this production interested me more than Barry Stanton's Lucio. Here, certainly, was a *picaro*, his fashionable finery reduced to scabby tatters. Stanton is big, even fat (though without flabbiness), but astonishingly light-footed. His strut was as dainty as a bird's, and his fastidiousness was feline. Whether consciously or not I do not know, but there was a fascinating reminiscence of Frederick Lemaître's Robert Macaire in the presentation. And he spoke with such assurance.

Perhaps I should end there. I have written very little in my reviews of the seasons since 1970, of the Royal Shakespeare Company's speaking of Shakespeare. It is an aspect of which I have too little knowledge and few preconceptions. There is no point in endlessly mourning Robert Atkins, or wishing that every male voice were Sir John Gielgud's. Modern speech-training has succeeded more and more in linking voice-production with the body's movement, and it would be foolish to judge a young actor by the older criteria of 'elocution'. An anxiety fully to understand the lines is a necessary basis for good speaking, but it is not enough to mean what you say. Michael Pennington *meant* Angelo's soliloquies, but he spoke them as if meaning were separable from rhythm. On the contrary, in so breaking up the metrical discipline of the lines, he totally damaged their syntax. The use of the pause, whether conjunctively or disjunctively, is an important aspect of the actor's craft, but there are times when the pentameter is forgotten. It was not forgotten in one fine exchange between Hubert and King John, when the divided line was spoken by the two voices with an exact respect for its single cadence:

John: Death.
Hubert: My Lord?
John: A grave.
Hubert: He shall not live.
                              (III, ii, 65)

It was the absence of an actor's pause that made this terrifyingly quick contact truthful. There is, of course, no right way and several wrong ones. An actor who reaches an understanding of his lines may relax enough to let those lines speak through him, as Jane Lapotaire did in Viola. The poetry must be neither sought nor sacrificed.

© PETER THOMSON 1975

THE YEAR'S CONTRIBUTIONS TO SHAKESPEARIAN STUDY

1. CRITICAL STUDIES

reviewed by D. J. PALMER

In the subtlety of its critical argument and the richness and scope of the learning that informs it, *Shakespeare's Living Art*[1] is by any standards a distinguished work of literary scholarship; sadly, those qualities are also the measure of our loss in Rosalie Colie's death shortly after she had completed this book. Its concern is with Shakespeare's treatment of genres and literary conventions, with the ways in which he 'used, misused, criticized, recreated, and sometimes revolutionized the received topics and devices, large and small, of his artful craft'. Far from reducing the complexity of Shakespeare's work by merely identifying the conventional, this approach finds that Shakespeare's 'interest in the traditional aspects of his art lay precisely in their problematical nature, not in their stereotypical force', and that what is 'problematical' in matters of form and style has to do also with the problems of living that are dramatised.

From this point of view we are invited to consider, for instance, the competing stylistic roles that are assumed and discarded in *Love's Labour's Lost*, the new dramatic reality that is given to conventional metaphors from the sonnet tradition in *Romeo and Juliet* and *Othello*, and the reassessments of pastoralism that underlie *As You Like It*, *King Lear* and the last plays. Among the most brilliantly suggestive chapters in the book are those on the Sonnets and their relationship to the conventions of the classical epigram, on *Antony and Cleopatra* seen in terms of the traditional rhetorical antithesis between the Attic and Asiatic styles,

and on the Renaissance conception of intellectual melancholy as it helps to shape the self-reflective form as well as the substance of *Hamlet*. This is a book which greatly extends our understanding of Shakespeare's attitude to artistic problems, and illuminates the integration of form and meaning in his work.

T. McAlindon[2] is also concerned with Shakespeare's use of the controlling norms of style and behaviour, as they were defined by Renaissance tradition. His interest is not in the pluralistic decorums of artistic genres, however, but in the central issue of propriety of speech and action in the situation as presented. The basis of his approach to the plays as 'a controlled and significant vision of disorder on the stage of life' is that, in writing for a popular theatre that was essentially indecorous by received standards, 'Shakespeare resolved the problem of enforced indecorum and even made it the source of enormous artistic gain' by presenting 'those defects, lapses or perversions of judgment which are the source of tragic or comic action'. Whether or not Ben Jonson would have been convinced by this ingenious inversion of the fallacy of imitative form, McAlindon clearly demonstrates the relevance of the principle of decorum in diagnosing linguistic and logical confusion and the breakdown of public and private relationships. Recognising that it is

[1] *Shakespeare's Living Art* (Princeton University Press, 1974).
[2] *Shakespeare and Decorum* (Macmillan, 1973).

149

essentially a relative principle, requiring what Quintilian called 'a wise adaptability', McAlindon nevertheless uses it somewhat rigidly in his early chapters; he is particularly severe with Richard II (for instance, 'narcissistic pleasure' is surely not the whole truth about Richard's behaviour in the Deposition scene), and sympathetic but hardly admiring towards Hamlet. But the later chapters are full of sensitive and intelligent commentary, including a fine essay on *Antony and Cleopatra* ('in no other play does he probe quite so deeply or provocatively into our thinking about what is proper and graceful'), in which we are shown how subtle and comprehensive the concept of decorum can be.

Sharing a similar interest in Shakespeare's treatment of linguistic disorder and the collapse of social relationships, but from a completely different angle, T. Hawkes[1] argues that the plays reflect the values of an oral, pre-literate culture in which speech is man's distinctive feature, and communication involves a fuller human engagement than is possible through the written word. In reminding us that a play is not simply a printed text, with all that implies for critical interpretation, this is a useful argument, but there is little evidence or probability that the Elizabethans made a significant distinction between oral and written language when they referred to 'speech' as a civilising force, still less that they shared the primitivist attitude which leads Hawkes, for instance, to suggest that the poisoning of King Hamlet through the ears 'seems to hint symbolically at the murder of the aural counterpart of talking', with Ramus cast in the villain's part. The book inevitably prompts one to reflect, 'How well he's read, to reason against reading.'

Hawkes's polemic against the restrictive implications of treating Shakespeare as 'literature' is matched by the radicalism of John Russell Brown's *Free Shakespeare*,[2] which advocates dispensing with the idea of unified thematic interpretation and returning to what he regards as the Elizabethan sense of the play as variable, open-ended, and an opportunity for encounter and exploration. Brown protests against the processed pre-packaged Shakespeare that is so often presented to us by the directorial theatre as well as by academic criticism. But *Free Shakespeare* is more than a reiteration of the truism that there is no substitute for the personal encounter with the play: it urges upon us the need to start from an understanding of what Wellek and Warren would call 'the ontological status' of the text.

To approach the texts, as Brown would have us do, in terms of their 'variable potential in theatrical realization', is to recognise with M. Charney[3] that many of Shakespeare's most effective and dramatically resonant lines have no intrinsic rhetorical or poetic interest, but depend on context, physical gesture and expression. Moreover the emblematic Elizabethan stage is also an 'interior theatre', described by A. B. Kernan[4] as a 'small intense man-made space where the imagination realizes itself, even if only for a brief time'. Both these points are apposite to the first two volumes of a new series for students, *In Shakespeare's Playhouse*, by R. Watkins and J. Lemmon, whose aim is 'to keep the reader constantly in mind of the theatrical ambience in which Shakespeare worked'. The introductory volume[5] reconstructs the physical conditions of the Elizabethan playhouse, drawing attention to those features which distinguish it from the modern

[1] *Shakespeare's Talking Animals: Language and Drama in Society* (Edward Arnold, 1973).

[2] *Free Shakespeare* (Heinemann Educational Books, 1974).

[3] 'Shakespeare's Unpoetic Poetry', *Studies in English Literature*, XIII (1973), 199–207.

[4] 'This Goodly Frame, The Stage: The Interior Theater of Imagination in English Renaissance Drama', *Shakespeare Quarterly*, XXV (1974), 1–5.

[5] *In Shakespeare's Playhouse: The Poet's Method* (David and Charles, 1974).

theatre, illustrating ways in which the text demands more of the actor besides character-impersonation, and stressing the nature of a poetic drama 'in which language is the chief instrument for the creation of dramatic illusion'. The second volume,[1] a running commentary on the unfolding action of *Macbeth*, is a difficult and not wholly successful exercise in keeping the mind focused on what is supposed to be happening on stage at the same time as it refers to the wider structural and thematic implications to which a student, if not a spectator, is expected to pay close attention.

The most useful chapters in *Shakespeare's Religious Background*[2] demonstrate Shakespeare's familiarity with the Book of Common Prayer, the Geneva Bible and the Homilies, evidence which P. Milward does not convincingly reconcile with his supposition that Shakespeare's upbringing and faith were Roman Catholic. The biographical speculations, however, drawn from 'a penumbra of innumerable hints and possibilities', are not as extravagant as the revelations about Shakespeare's covert allegiance found in the plays. According to Milward, 'what he cannot express openly in a cruel and dangerous time... he is forced to convey indirectly by means of hints and analogues'. Macbeth's murder of Duncan is thus identified with Elizabeth's execution of Mary Queen of Scots; Richard III 'would have reminded many in an Elizabethan audience of the hated Earl of Leicester'; Polonius turns out to be Cecil, and so does Ulysses; while another figure for Elizabeth is found in Cleopatra, 'who succeeds so completely in seducing Antony from his path of duty and his ties with Rome'. Of Lear we are told that 'after having rejected the old faith, personified in Cordelia, he comes to suffer the bitter consequences of this rejection', and after this it is not difficult to anticipate what is shadowed forth in the various royal separations and reconciliations of the last plays. Cranmer's

prophecy of Elizabeth's reign must, of course, be the work of 'a lesser dramatist'. The nature of Milward's interpretive methods may be recognised as an advanced case of what R. Levin[3] dubs 'Fluellenism', following the fashion in which that Welsh captain compares Henry V to Alexander the Great.

The temptation to over-schematise the plays, to make them fit a theme, is as Brown suggests the fatal Cleopatra of modern criticism. M. B. Garber's[4] study of dreams in Shakespeare, for instance, begins with some perceptive chapters on the distinction in the early plays between Shakespeare's conventional use of dream as a formal device and his developing interest in the creative processes of the dreamer; but in her discussion of the major tragedies the idea of dream is grossly over-extended, by reliance on Freudian theory, to 'encompass the entire world of the play', so that the tragic action becomes located within the consciousness of the protagonist. A. L. Burney's[5] application of her theory of satiric catharsis also produces some strange and arbitrary distortions: Queen Margaret, for instance, may be granted the status of primitive satirist in *Richard III* (though one might argue that the hero's own vein of malicious mockery also qualifies him as some kind of satirist), but what is Falstaff doing in the sour company of Jaques, Thersites and Apemantus? 'Because the brand of hatred and censure that has been stirred up by Falstaffian satire is denied final outlet on stage', we are told *à propos* the

---

[1] In *Shakespeare's Playhouse: 'Macbeth'* (David and Charles, 1974).

[2] *Shakespeare's Religious Background* (Sidgwick and Jackson, 1973).

[3] 'On Fluellen's Figures, Christ Figures, and James Figures', *Publications of the Modern Language Association of America*, LXXXIX (1974), 302–11.

[4] *Dream in Shakespeare: From Metaphor to Metamorphosis* (Yale University Press, 1974).

[5] *Satiric Catharsis in Shakespeare: A Theory of Dramatic Structure* (University of California Press, 1973).

rejection of Falstaff, 'the audience *should* [my italics] come back into Elizabethan society (or any society) with the bitter taste of satire still on their tongues and the exposing satiric light in their eyes.' Does this even remotely correspond to the feelings of any audience at the end of *2 Henry IV*?

A reasoned defence of schematic interpretation is made by W. L. Godshalk,[1] who rightly insists that unifying structural patterns exist in the plays. A general concern with 'polarities' and with the theme of the social bond runs through the essays in this volume, but it is not allowed to obscure the individual characteristics of the particular plays that are discussed.

Turning to studies whose focus is tragedy, there are several new attempts to accommodate the tragedies within a single perspective. B. McElroy[2] relates theme and character in the four major tragedies by examining how in each case 'the tragedy which befalls the hero is predicated upon the way in which he views the world and the effect which that world view has upon his actions'. Shakespeare's tragic heroes, he observes, have in common a tendency to universalise their experience, self-awareness, and a hatred of false seeming; each of them suffers the destruction of his subjective world, and each has to come to terms with an antithetical set of values. The dualism of 'mutually exclusive but co-existent world views' which McElroy finds in the tragedies proves a fruitful approach to the hero's experience, but some admirable insights are achieved at the cost of implying that a Shakespearian tragedy presents only two alternative attitudes to life.

A different conception of character in the tragedies is elaborated by J. L. Barroll,[3] who bases his 'cultural approach to psychological theory' on the Elizabethan belief in man's fallen condition yet his aspiration for unity with 'higher Being'. Unfortunately, the cum-brous circumlocutions of Barroll's style neither clarify nor enliven his argument, and the going is equally heavy in his essay[4] on tragic structure, which, after questioning the notion that Shakespearian tragedy developed from the traditional idea of the Wheel of Fortune, makes the point that while Shakespeare sometimes used the rise-and-fall plot his preference was for a type of action in which the protagonist's character is illustrated through his response to external agency. R. E. Fortin[5] proposes 'the possibility of acknowledging religious experience in the tragedies without compromising the integrity of secular experience' by the application of what he calls 'inductive theology'. The issue that Fortin raises is similar to the problem which M. Taylor[6] defines in his valuable essay on Bradley: the failure of the great critic to reconcile or distinguish clearly an empirical attitude to tragedy as explicable in terms of natural experience and a vaguer transcendent view which borders on the religious. The difficulty of reconciling the spiritual with the physical, the sense of living in divided worlds (which McElroy also explores), and the representation of different levels of reality by different styles, in the tragedies of Shakespeare and his contemporaries, are found by C. Hoy[7] to be characteristic of 'Mannerism' as defined by Hauser (though some better versed than I am in art

---

[1] *Patterning in Shakespearean Drama* (Mouton, 1973).

[2] *Shakespeare's Mature Tragedies* (Princeton University Press, 1973).

[3] *Artificial Persons: The Formation of Character in the Tragedies of Shakespeare* (University of South Carolina Press, 1974).

[4] 'Structure in Shakespearean Tragedy', *Shakespeare Studies*, VII (1974), 345–78.

[5] 'Shakespearean Tragedy and the Problem of Transcendence', *Shakespeare Studies*, VII, 307–25.

[6] 'A. C. Bradley and Shakespearean Tragedy', *Modern Language Review*, LXVIII (1973), 734–40.

[7] 'Jacobean Tragedy and the Mannerist Style', *Shakespeare Survey 26* (1973), 49–67.

history would contend that Hauser's 'definitive account', as Hoy calls it, has been superseded by that of Shearman). Finally, among these general discussions of Shakespearian tragedy, are two companion pieces by C. Leech on the relationship between fiction and truth in the plays: his British Academy lecture[1] reflects on their creative use of history, while the other essay[2] argues that the horrors and evils in Jacobean tragedy are incredible but not untrue to life in taking us to the limits: 'the major work can in a sense be morally fortifying because it makes us see more truly, makes us credit the incredible, and it will do this because it takes us to the ultimate term'.

Two articles on *Romeo and Juliet* illuminate different aspects of its structure. R. V. Utterback[3] notes that the death of Mercutio is the crucial turning-point which makes a tragic outcome inevitable, and also points out that in its combination of accident and personal responsibility it anticipates the succeeding events. V. F. Petronella[4] discusses the dramatic function of the rather strange comic scene between Peter and the musicians, and clarifies something of its significance by suggesting that the references to gold, silver and iron reflect a transition from the romantic tone of the first two acts to the new harshness of the final tragic realities.

Hamlet unsurprisingly continues to draw varied interest. H. Jenkins,[5] who knows the play as well as anybody, makes some intriguing conjectures about Shakespeare's changes of mind in shaping the roles of Fortinbras and Laertes, observing that the talk of preparations for war in the opening scene raises expectations that are not fulfilled: 'can it be that the troops who ultimately do no more than march across Denmark were originally designed to do battle?' Jenkins suggests that the 'lawless resolutes' sharked up by Fortinbras were transformed into the rebellious mob that accompanies Laertes on his return to Elsinore,

because Shakespeare decided to make the threat to the state internal instead of external. An equally ingenious hypothesis is advanced by K. Brown,[6] who discovers a number of parallels between scenes equidistant from the centre of the play: could it be that this peculiarity of the dramatic structure has something to do with the Elizabethan association of centrality with sovereignty? Such satisfying spatial symmetry, however, does not appeal to J. G. Barry,[7] who employs a musical analogy to treat the death of Polonius in the play's central scene as a 'false resolution' which 'deepens the pattern of human experience with the sudden short circuiting of energies and the concomitant realization that a goal which had seemed within sight is now indefinitely postponed'. The distracting element in the play's structure also receives attention from B. O. States,[8] who explores the ways in which it constantly looks out from immediate and urgent concerns towards other times and places.

Shifting the focus from the dramatic structure of *Hamlet* to its hero, R. A. Foakes[9] illustrates Hamlet's tendency to project the horror and cruelty of murder and revenge into

[1] 'Shakespeare's Tragic Fiction', Annual Shakespeare Lecture, *Proceedings of the British Academy*, LIX (1973), 3–18.

[2] 'The Incredible in Jacobean Tragedy', *Rice University Studies*, LX (1974), 109–22.

[3] 'The Death of Mercutio', *Shakespeare Quarterly*, XXV, 105–16.

[4] 'The Musicians' Scene in *Romeo and Juliet*', *Humanities Association Bulletin*, XXIII (1972), 54–6.

[5] 'Fortinbras and Laertes and the Composition of *Hamlet*', *Rice University Studies*, LX, 95–107.

[6] '"Form and Cause Conjoin'd": *Hamlet* and Shakespeare's Workshop', *Shakespeare Survey 26*, 11–20.

[7] 'Shakespeare's "Deceptive Cadence": A Study in the Structure of *Hamlet*', *Shakespeare Quarterly*, XXIV (1973), 117–27.

[8] 'The Word-Pictures in *Hamlet*', *Hudson Review*, XXVI (1973), 510–22.

[9] 'The Art of Cruelty: Hamlet and Vindice', *Shakespeare Survey 26*, 21–31.

forms of fiction and play-acting, instead of carrying out the deed, while Vindice takes an artistic delight in the reality of killing. P. Gottschalk[1] also understands Hamlet in terms of his role-playing and 'trying on of identities', so that 'in every action of Hamlet's we distinguish between what momentarily he *is being* and what potentially he *is*'. R. E. Fortin,[2] on the other hand, regards this 'frustrated quest for heroic identity' not as a means of displacing dangerous and destructive energies but as a symptom of Hamlet's failure to give life to the 'mythic task' of renewing the kingdom. 'His tragedy, precisely, is that his life, and death, are meaningless', writes Fortin, with the absoluteness that befits the proponent of 'inductive theology'.

Several articles take up the question of ambiguities in Hamlet's perspective on the action of the play. E. T. Schell,[3] for instance, remarks that Hamlet's goading of Polonius over his willingness to use Ophelia as a pawn seems to contradict the fact that Hamlet has no knowledge of Polonius's intentions, an apparent contradiction which Schell resolves by attributing the accusations to 'the mind of the play rather than the mind of Hamlet'. And while C. S. Emden[4] stresses the importance which Shakespeare generally attached to the agency of the eye in interpreting character, H. Skulsky[5] finds that in *Hamlet* there is no art to find the mind's construction from outward appearance, and that Hamlet's confidence that the Mousetrap will unkennel Claudius's guilt is totally unwarranted. V. F. Petronella[6] reopens the critical debate about the meaning of the 'To be or not to be' soliloquy, and comes down on the side of those who see it as a serious contemplation of suicide, arguing that Hamlet consistently expresses an attitude of *contemptus mundi* throughout the play. Hamlet's graveyard meditation on Alexander and Julius Caesar, by implicitly recalling the young Caesar's envy of Alexander's youthful

exploits, seems to G. Reedy[7] a light-hearted 'academic joke' in which Hamlet mocks his own earlier self-reproaches for inaction. The staging of the Ghost's comings and goings is discussed by D. M. DeLuca,[8] who makes the point that the trap could not be used in the Closet scene because Gertrude's room must be upstairs, 'meaning that the Ghost must rise through the floors and walls of several stories'. 'Twere to consider too curiously to consider so, particularly for the Elizabethan stage.

Writing on *Othello*, S. Rogers[9] explores the tragedy's adaptation of materials traditionally belonging to comedy, J. R. Curtis[10] maintains that the love of Othello and Desdemona is not at odds with reason, and P. C. McGuire[11] regards 'the assay of reason', the act of knowing and judging, a more important concern of the play than love, jealousy or honour. K. S. Stockholder[12] is critical of the hero's desire for absolutes in a world subject to chance and

[1] 'Hamlet and the Scanning of Revenge', *Shakespeare Quarterly*, XXIV, 155–70.

[2] '*Hamlet* and the Mythic Hypothesis', *Tennessee Studies in Literature*, XVIII (1973), 49–61.

[3] 'Who Said That – *Hamlet* or Hamlet?', *Shakespeare Quarterly*, XXIV, 135–46.

[4] 'Shakespeare and the Eye', *Shakespeare Survey 26*, 129–37.

[5] '"I know my Course": Hamlet's Confidence', *Publications of the Modern Language Association of America*, LXXXIX, 477–86.

[6] 'Hamlet's "To be or not to be" Soliloquy: Once More unto the Breach', *Studies in Philology*, LXXI (1974), 72–88.

[7] '"Alexander Died": *Hamlet*, v. i. 216–40', *Shakespeare Quarterly*, XXIV, 128–34.

[8] 'The Movements of the Ghost in *Hamlet*', *Shakespeare Quarterly*, XXIV, 147–54.

[9] '*Othello*: Comedy in Reverse', *Shakespeare Quarterly*, XXIV, 210–20.

[10] 'The "Speculative and Offic'd Instrument": Reason and Love in *Othello*', *Shakespeare Quarterly*, XXIV, 188–97.

[11] '*Othello* as an "Assay of Reason"', *Shakespeare Quarterly*, XXIV, 198–209.

[12] '"Egregiously an Ass": Chance and Accident in *Othello*', *Studies in English Literature*, XIII, 256–72.

change, while M. C. Andrews[1] defends Othello against the tendency of modern criticism to distrust and try to detract from his noble nature. J. C. Rice,[2] on the other hand, casts a censorious eye on Desdemona, and sees in her idealism 'her refusal to face the reality of her fallen nature', to which are added charges of pride, folly, ignorance and self-righteousness, until the image is beyond recognition.

S. L. Goldberg's[3] study of *King Lear* is a close and sensitive, if somewhat tortuously articulated, engagement with the tragic experience as an irreducible conflict between the desire for justice and the acknowledgment of true feeling. Rejecting approaches to the play which treat it in terms of the hero's experience rather than our own, or which reduce it to competing philosophies of Nature, Goldberg stresses that it is precisely because the play does not exhibit some law or offer any certain answers that it compels our imagination: the need to justify or make sense of the experience, with ourselves as with the characters of the play, cannot finally be reconciled with the full personal realisation or response that is demanded. Therefore we must 'speak what we feel, not what we ought to say'. Goldberg does not so much intepret the play as wrestle with it, and the encounter produces much that is valuable. The effect of the play in stretching the capacities of drama and of its audience to the limit is also considered by R. D. Fly,[4] who maintains that 'we cannot silence our doubts about Shakespeare's achievement in this play until we have faced and accounted for his impulse to extend the boundaries of his art "beyond the outermost mark" of the dramatic'. M. Holly[5] believes that, since *King Lear* 'treats dramatically the personal fragmentation and social disintegration which is [*sic*] so evident in the twentieth century', its concern with identity can be seen in the light of Sartre's psychology of self-transcendence. M. Lascelles[6] discerns in the storm scenes, in the reunion

with Cordelia, and in the final scene allusions to the depiction of Doomsday in church-wall paintings.

In his essay on *Macbeth*, J. Ramsey[7] examines the different conceptions of manliness in terms of which the hero is presented, a theme also discussed in the books by McAlindon, Hawkes and McElroy.

M. Payne's[8] dissertation on the Roman plays is a highly abstract and diagrammatic exercise in structural analysis, which is concerned with the use of myth to give an ironic perspective on the action, but which is so forbiddingly jargon-ridden and so remote from the text that it has little to offer of what usually passes for critical insight. At the other extreme, A. L. and M. K. Kistner[9] do not venture far in informing us that the despair, desire for revenge, and madness of Titus Andronicus conform to a Senecan pattern. More interestingly, L. N. Danson[10] approaches *Titus Andronicus* as a play about 'the inability to achieve adequate expression for overwhelming

[1] 'Honest Othello: The Handkerchief Once More', *Studies in English Literature*, XIII, 273–84.

[2] 'Desdemona Unpinned: Universal Guilt in *Othello*', *Shakespeare Studies*, VII, 209–26.

[3] *An Essay on 'King Lear'* (Cambridge University Press, 1974).

[4] '"Beyond Extremity": A Reading of *King Lear*', *Texas Studies in Literature and Language*, XVI (1974), 45–63.

[5] '*King Lear*: The Disguised and Deceived', *Shakespeare Quarterly*, XXIV, 171–80.

[6] '*King Lear* and Doomsday', *Shakespeare Survey* 26, 69–79.

[7] 'The Perversion of Manliness in *Macbeth*', *Studies in English Literature*, XIII, 285–300.

[8] *Irony in Shakespeare's Roman Plays*, Salzburg Studies in English Literature: Elizabethan Studies 19 (Institut für Englische Sprache und Literatur, Universität Salzburg, 1974).

[9] 'The Senecan Background of Despair in *The Spanish Tragedy* and *Titus Andronicus*', *Shakespeare Studies*, VII, 1–9.

[10] 'The Device of Wonder: *Titus Andronicus* and Revenge Tragedies', *Texas Studies in Literature and Language*, XVI, 27–43.

emotional needs', and about the struggle to turn words into actions.

Commentators on *Julius Caesar* find little to admire in the play's image of humanity. J. R. Rice,[1] for instance, discusses 'the centality of the theme of irrationality', and finds that the tragedy presents a Pyrrhonic view of the fallibility of the senses and judgment. M. Taylor[2] and R. A. Yoder[3] offer two very different accounts of the play's sense of history, both of which are surely wide of the mark. Taylor, for whom Shakespeare's Rome is 'very like contemporary London' and his Romans 'recognisable English types', concludes that 'the play validates the supernatural view of history'. Yoder, on the other hand, following in the footsteps of Jan Kott, argues that the historical process revealed in the dramatic action is 'circular and absurd'. What both these interpretations share is a reductive attitude to the individuality of character and event. Yoder's remark that 'there are no redeeming or sustaining personal relationships' in the play is complemented by M. Vawter's[4] analysis of the ways in which 'the bonds of community are posited and broken at many levels'. In another essay,[5] Vawter expresses an unqualified antipathy to Brutus, whom he sees as 'a dramatic illustration of the hollowness, presumption, and moral sickness inherent in the secular concept of virtue-reason's sufficiency'.

There is considerably more sympathy, and even enthusiasm, in responses to *Antony and Cleopatra*. V. K. Whitaker,[6] however, is quite out of step with the prevailing evaluation of the play in his suggestion that it lacks unity because 'Shakespeare followed the story for its own sake without clarifying the relationship of Cleopatra's death to Antony's.' Most of the studies here under review read like refutations of this judgment. On the latter point, for instance, A. Barton[7] puts forward a closely-argued case for the 'divided catastrophe', in which Cleopatra's death is seen as a resolution of the suspense and ambiguity intensified by the death of Antony, and as a transfiguration of the earlier stages of the story. The 'unremitting attempt at valuation' of the two protagonists by other characters, to which Barton draws attention, is also discussed by J. Adelman[8] in her admirably comprehensive and perceptive study of the play. She notes that the constantly shifting focus and broad scope of the action both dramatises the relativity of judgments and diffuses and dissipates our attention in a way that resembles the techniques of comedy: 'the entire tragic vision of the play is subjected to the comic perspective'. In demonstrating the coherence and complexity of the dramatic structure, Adelman's most illuminating chapters are those on Shakespeare's use of emblematic and mythological traditions, including the allusions to Dido and Aeneas, Mars and Venus, and Hercules; she makes some very interesting points about the lovers' aspiration to mythical status. A link with Goldberg's attitude to *King Lear* is also provided in the critical humility of her observation that 'Shakespeare's art usually functions to suggest that our experiences are larger than the intellectual formulations in which we attempt to embody them.'

[1] '*Julius Caesar* and the Judgment of the Senses', *Studies in English Literature*, XIII, 238–55.

[2] 'Shakespeare's *Julius Caesar* and the Irony of History', *Shakespeare Quarterly*, XXIV, 301–8.

[3] 'History and the Histories in *Julius Caesar*', *Shakespeare Quarterly*, XXIV, 309–27.

[4] '*Julius Caesar*: Rupture in the Bond', *Journal of English and Germanic Philology*, LXXII (1973), 311–28.

[5] '"Division 'tween our Souls": Shakespeare's Stoic Brutus', *Shakespeare Studies*, VII, 173–95.

[6] 'Shakespeare the Elizabethan', *Rice University Studies*, LX, 141–51.

[7] '*Nature's piece 'gainst fancy*': The Divided Catastrophe in '*Antony and Cleopatra*' (Inaugural Lecture, Bedford College, University of London, 1973).

[8] *The Common Liar: An Essay on 'Antony and Cleopatra'* (Yale University Press, 1973).

Several of Adelman's insights are paralleled in other approaches to the play. D. B. Hamilton[1] surveys the literary tradition in which Antony and Cleopatra were associated with other famous lovers, especially Dido and Aeneas, as 'exemplars of truth and faithfulness'. A. H. Bell[2] examines the 'spectrum of conventional postures through which Antony moves', as courtly lover, Homeric hero, man of 'policy', and Stoic sage, with reference to his adjustment to time, and Bell concludes that 'Antony is the suggestion of a humanness that no single world view can wholly accommodate.' R. D. Hume[3] adduces a mass of detail about the speech traits of the dramatic characters, though he comes to disappointingly generalised and impressionistic conclusions. A more precise article by J. Shaw,[4] focusing on the mysterious scene in which the soldiers hear music and comment that Hercules is leaving Antony, suggests that behind the stage-direction referring to 'every corner of the stage' there is another echo of the apocalyptic imagery of the Book of Revelation which occurs elsewhere in the play.

Relating Antony and Cleopatra to Coriolanus, J. L. Simmons[5] refers 'the horror of Cleopatra and Coriolanus in contemplating their representation before a vulgar crowd' to the divergence of aristocratic and popular sympathies in the Jacobean theatre. The interrelation of war and sex in Coriolanus is the subject of R. Berry's essay,[6] which disturbingly observes that if the play presents war as a displacement of sex, as 'a communal therapy and a communal bond', then 'it is, on the whole, rather more depressing than anything in King Lear'. H. Levin,[7] however, is of the opinion that Shakespeare did not find cynical misanthropy a congenial topic, to judge from the artistic limitations of Timon of Athens.

The tendency to see in Shakespeare a reflection of our own modern disillusion with politics is exemplified by M. Manheim's[8] book on the history plays. Manheim takes the plays to be more about the emergence of Machiavellism in Shakespeare's own day than about the dynastic struggles of the fifteenth century. Thus he argues that the early histories, in which a legitimate but ineffectual king is 'no match for the treacherous and brutal tactics of those around', were 'written in anger at political realities as Shakespeare and his audience knew them'; while the later histories, in which Hal attempts to reconcile 'some sense of personal honour with political effectiveness', represent 'a carefully reasoned, objective, detailed dramatic treatment of the coming to terms with Machiavellianism which dominated political life at the close of the sixteenth century'. Whether or not this 'pattern of rather bitter political maturation' has 'deep and immediate significance' for the modern crisis of leadership, by Elizabethan standards some important distinctions are blurred in regarding Hal as even a half-hearted disciple of Machiavelli.

Shakespeare's treatment of concepts of time in Richard III, Macbeth and King Lear is the subject of a learned iconographical study by the Japanese scholar, S. Iwasaki,[9] providing

[1] 'Antony and Cleopatra and the Tradition of Noble Lovers', Shakespeare Quarterly, XXIV, 245–51.

[2] 'Time and Convention in Antony and Cleopatra', Shakespeare Quarterly, XXIV, 253–64.

[3] 'Individuation and Development of Character Through Language in Antony and Cleopatra', Shakespeare Quarterly, XXIV, 280–300.

[4] '"In Every Corner of the Stage": Antony and Cleopatra, IV. iii', Shakespeare Studies, VII, 227–32.

[5] 'Antony and Cleopatra and Coriolanus: Shakespeare's Heroic Tragedies: A Jacobean Adjustment', Shakespeare Survey 26, 95–101.

[6] 'Sexual Imagery in Coriolanus', Studies in English Literature, XIII, 301–16.

[7] 'Shakespeare's Misanthrope', Shakespeare Survey 26, 89–94.

[8] The Weak King Dilemma in the Shakespearean History Play (Syracuse University Press, 1973).

[9] The Sword and the Word: Shakespeare's Tragic Sense of Time (Shinozaki Shorin Press, 1973).

further evidence of the light which a knowledge of emblematic traditions can throw upon the plays: the book is amply illustrated. The 'dynamic' idea of time, as opposed to the 'static' idea of order, in the early histories, is a theme suggestively developed by the Czech scholar Z. Stříbrný,[1] who traces it from York's sense of 'the growing tendencies of the whole historical period', through his son Richard's Machiavellian time-serving, to the Bastard's 'acute awareness of the drifts of time', which anticipates that of Bolingbroke and Hal.

There are considerable differences of opinion and approach to the issues of rebellion and deposition in the early histories. F. L. Kelly[2] examines at some length the making and breaking of oaths in the *Henry VI* plays, until it is not only Shakespeare who 'relentlessly drives home the theme'. R. E. Burkhart[3] believes that, contrary to received opinion, the early histories do not uphold the Tudor doctrine of obedience and the evils of rebellion, but treat it inconsistently, since the kings in the plays are presented as 'either suited or unsuited for kingship': 'rebellions in the plays were against kings who deserved it, and the Tudors, a line founded by a man who acted as God's agent, clearly did not'. The circumstances in which the rule of Shakespeare's Richard III is ended also elicit the attention of B. A. Doebler,[4] who, supported by the confidence of knowing just how an Elizabethan audience would have responded, ascribes Richard's downfall to his despair: 'his death, in the larger sense, has been brought about by the wickedness of his own past'. A. Gurr[5] cannot accept either Providence or conscience as adequate explanations of Richard's end; according to Gurr's reading of the play, because Richard's legal claim to the crown is at least as good as Richmond's, the issue can only be decided by force of arms, and 'what decides the battle *in the play* is neither God's hand nor Richard's despair, but the human agency of a subject who

changes sides', namely Stanley, who is 'the symbolic representative of popular feeling'. Another aspect of Richard III, his favourite invocation of St Paul, is carefully investigated by J. B. Harcourt,[6] who finds that it is not merely a trick of speech, but that on each occasion there is in the context a meaningful allusion to either the scriptural or the apocryphal Paul.

The question of Shakespeare's attitude to the doctrine of obedience is resumed in R. Battenhouse's[7] discussion of *Richard II*, where the emphasis on the king's abuse of his responsibilities is taken as an indication that 'the dramatist is testing and exposing latent deficiencies in the premises of Tudor thinking'. The Homilies, however, from which Battenhouse derives his description of the Tudor idea of kingship, were intended to remind subjects of their responsibilities: they were not addressed to kings. Other kinds of latent deficiencies are implied in the numerous Biblical allusions to 'man's fall and first fratricide' which S. C. Maverty[8] pursues through the play, to suggest that, like Adam and Cain, Richard and Bolingbroke bring a curse upon their own heads, upon the land, and upon future generations. But symbolic values are also open to

---

[1] 'The Idea and Image of Time in Shakespeare's Early Histories', *Shakespeare Jahrbuch*, CX (1974), 129–38.

[2] 'Oaths in Shakespeare's *Henry VI* Plays', *Shakespeare Quarterly*, XXIV, 357–71.

[3] 'Obedience and Rebellion in Shakespeare's Early History Plays', *English Studies*, LV (1974), 108–17.

[4] '"Dispaire and Dye": The Ultimate Temptation of Richard III', *Shakespeare Studies*, VII, 75–85.

[5] 'Richard III and the Democratic Process', *Essays in Criticism*, XXIV (1974), 39–47.

[6] '"Odde Old Ends, Stolne"…: King Richard and Saint Paul', *Shakespeare Studies*, VII, 87–100.

[7] 'Tudor Doctrine and the Tragedy of *Richard II*', *Rice University Studies*, LX, 31–53.

[8] 'A Second Fall of Cursed Man: The Bold Metaphor in *Richard II*', *Journal of English and Germanic Philology*, LXXII, 175–93.

question in the play, as H. F. Folland[1] reminds us in treating the Deposition scene as a 'competition of ceremony', in which Richard wins a 'wry victory' over his antagonist 'because he understands better both its weakness as an idol and its strength as a shadowing forth'.

The indebtedness of *Henry IV* to the tradition of the morality play has long been recognised, but A. C. Dessen[2] refines our understanding in an essay that distinguishes between the structure of the early moralities, unified in a central character, and that of the later moralities which turn upon contrast and parallelism between two characters or attitudes to life. It is this structural duality, according to Dessen, that serves as a model for Shakespeare's play. The parallels and contrasts between Hotspur, Hal and Falstaff are considered by N. Council[3] in terms of their attitudes to honour, in an essay which seems to have been overtaken by his recent book on the same theme (reviewed in *Shakespeare Survey* 27). Council contends that, instead of forming an Aristotelian paradigm with Prince Hal as the mean between excess and deficiency, the play shows Hotspur to be 'the perfect mirror of honour', while Falstaff rejects honour and Hal exploits it pragmatically. This is a point of view that not only involves a shift in the play's centre of interest from one Harry to another, but also calls for some justification of Hotspur's rebellion against his King. It is difficult to feel that the play endorses Hotspur's 'virtuous and honorable duty' to make Mortimer king, or that Shakespeare ever made any character 'the perfect mirror' of anything. Nevertheless, as J. Black[4] observes, Hotspur is sorely missed in Part II, where his heroic idealism is 'stolen and counterfeited by Falstaff, Pistol, and even Shallow, uttered again in Feeble, and restored by Hal'. K. Aoki[5] tackles the thorny question of why Hal reappears in the tavern in Part II after apparently emerging in his true colours at the Battle of Shrewsbury,

and points out that his defeat of Hotspur is not revealed to the King, though this does not quite solve the problem as completely as Aoki believes. Much has been written on the literary and dramatic antecedents of Falstaff, but P. N. Siegel[6] provides him with an Elizabethan social milieu among the 'declassed down-and-outs of the London underworld', and pairs him with another declining gent in Samuel Rowlands' burlesque description of *The Melancholy Knight*.

What little critical interest there is currently in *Henry V* is reflected in V. F. Petronella's essay,[7] which would have us believe that the scene of Henry's encounter with the soldiers on the eve of Agincourt is 'a psychological journey' of memory, will and understanding based on the pattern of the formal meditation.

Turning to the comedies, new light is thrown on the development of comedy in Shakespeare's day by M. Pfister's study[8] of structural perspectives, which includes chapters on *The Comedy of Errors*, *Twelfth Night* and *The Tempest*. A. Leggatt[9] gives us a balanced, intelligent and stylish account of the sequence that culminates in *Twelfth Night*. The book is somewhat mistitled, for Leggatt's main topic

[1] 'King Richard's Pallid Victory', *Shakespeare Quarterly*, XXIV, 390–9.

[2] 'The Intemperate Knight and the Politic Prince: Late Morality Structure in *1 Henry IV*', *Shakespeare Studies*, VII, 147–71.

[3] 'Prince Hal: Mirror of Success', *Shakespeare Studies*, VII, 125–46.

[4] 'Counterfeits of Soldiership in *Henry IV*', *Shakespeare Quarterly*, XXIV, 372–82.

[5] *Shakespeare's 'Henry IV' and 'Henry V': Hal's Heroic Character and the Sun–Cloud Theme* (Showa Press, 1973).

[6] 'Falstaff and his Social Milieu', *Shakespeare Jahrbuch*, CX, 139–45.

[7] 'Shakespeare's *Henry V* and the Second Tetralogy: Meditation as Drama', *Costerus*, IV (1972), 169–82.

[8] *Studien zum Wandel der Perspectivenstruktur in Elisabethanischen und Jakobäischen Komödien* (Wilhelm Fink Verlag, 1974).

[9] *Shakespeare's Comedy of Love* (Methuen, 1974).

is not love but the shifts of style and dramatic idiom within each play. He rides no hobby-horses, however, and his own critical predisposition is to be gathered from such phrases as 'reassuringly ordinary and familiar', 'sober, common-sense, homely virtues' and 'the restraints of humanity and common-sense'. Not surprisingly, though he always has something valuable to say, he is at his best on the prose comedies, particularly on *Much Ado About Nothing* and *As You Like It* (a play on which he writes with elegance, tact and penetration, while using the word 'pastoral' only once, on my reckoning). Leggatt extricates himself from the duty of discussing *The Merry Wives of Windsor* here by promising a future study of citizen comedy: it is to be looked forward to.

P. Swinden's[1] brisk and invigorating trot through the comedies is unduly modest in calling itself an 'Introduction', if that term suggests a cautious or elementary level of approach. In fact, Swinden is not in the least afraid to take the plunge, by committing himself to the view that some plays were originally designed for special occasions, by reproving over-sophistication in other critics, and even by being ready to accept that Shakespeare was capable of negligence and inconsistency. The only fashionable indulgence that Swinden allows himself is an attraction towards C. L. Barber's association of comedy with festive game. But if a fresh and personal response, going directly to the central issues of the plays and constantly aware of the practical conditions of the theatre, constitutes an 'Introduction', then it is surely not a bad kind of introduction to have.

The posthumous collection of J. Smith's[2] essays, many of them previously unpublished, reveal that for more than thirty years he was preparing a book on Shakespearian comedy. His interest in comedy seems to confirm Dryden's view that it suits the melancholic

disposition of the English, for the ruminations of these essays are neither lighthearted nor easy-going, though they are occasionally lit by a dry and disapproving humour. The reflection on Jaques in *As You Like It*, for instance, that melancholy is the great danger of pastoral inactivity, is quite Johnsonian; so, too, is the quip that Bassanio's speech in the Caskets scene of *The Merchant of Venice* 'displays the spirit of resignation and self-sacrifice proper to a bridegroom'. People in the comic worlds seem to get away with undeserved happiness too easily: the fact strikes him again and again, like a challenge to his deepest moral convictions. The necessity and availability of good luck to bring about the happy endings seem to trigger his critical energies: 'without favour from fortune the convention remains inapplicable'. Equally characteristic is the remark in his essay on *The Tempest* about 'the folly, and even...the wickedness of fantasies of an earthly paradise'.

Studies of the early comedies include V. F. Petronella's[3] investigation of the recurrent patterns of binding and loosing in the language and action of *The Comedy of Errors*, a new Spanish translation of this play by the Costa Rican scholar J. B. Acuña,[4] and M. West's[5] venture into the folk traditions of song-and-dance mating-games which he relates to Petruchio's treatment of Kate in *The Taming of the Shrew*: 'criticism has generally misconstrued the issue of the play as women's rights, whereas what the audience delightedly respond

[1] *An Introduction to Shakespeare's Comedies* (Macmillan, 1973).
[2] *Shakespearian and other essays* (Cambridge University Press, 1974).
[3] 'Structure and Theme through Separation and Union in Shakespeare's *The Comedy of Errors*', *Modern Language Review*, LXIX (1974), 481–8.
[4] *La Comedia de las Equivocaciones* (Ciudad Universitaria 'Rodrigo Facio', 1973).
[5] 'The Folk Background of Petruchio's Wooing Dance: Male Supremacy in *The Taming of the Shrew*', *Shakespeare Studies*, VII, 65–93.

to are sexual rites'. In *The Two Gentlemen of Verona*, T. E. Scheyer[1] draws 'a paradigm for future comedies' from the two comic worlds of Milan and the forest where Valentine loses and recovers his identity. S. K. Heninger, Jr[2] undertakes 'a careful and extensive explication' of the pattern of opposing attitudes in *Love's Labour's Lost*, epitomised in the pair of concluding songs, which are somewhat extravagantly described as 'an abstract of eternity, the integer of infinity, the microcosmic icon of human experience'. A less flatulant appraisal of the songs in relation to the play's 'complex apprehension of life, love and time' is made by R. G. Hunter,[3] who sees the play in terms of a conflict between Lent and Carnival, implying different attitudes to time as rectilinear and circular.

Writing on *A Midsummer Night's Dream*, R. Henze[4] distinguishes between Theseus's conception of the poetic imagination and that which emerges from the play as a whole; Shakespeare, according to Henze, was concerned not with ideal truth or with frenzy but with credibility, 'the workmanlike ability to deliver an image analogous to the images of most men yet unique as an artistic expression of that image'. If 'workmanlike' is a term that calls to mind the artistic aspiration of Bottom, then appropriately J. D. Huston[5] finds in the waking of Bottom an analogue to Shakespeare's own creative processes: 'first he raises him up from a formless mass on an empty stage, an action which symbolically suggests the very act of dramatic creation itself...' This, to adduce yet another analogue, is the silliest stuff that ever I heard. M. Doran[6] treads on firmer ground in exploring the rich literary and traditional associations underlying Shakespeare's wood, the fairies, and the moonlight, in which nature is translated into art. T. Clayton[7] restores an original piece of staging from years of editorial obfuscation, showing from the bawdy innuendo of the text itself that Wall

discharges his part, not simply by holding out two fingers, but by spreading his legs: the significance is fundamental. Comparing the Pyramus and Thisbe interlude with the masque in *The Tempest*, R. F. Willson, Jr[8] finds that 'burlesque and parody are fitting techniques of comedy when the essential structure of nature is not in danger', while the darker presence of evil in the later play is set off against the 'formal and stylized depiction of blessed nature' in the masque.

L. Rockas's[9] elegant but oblique essay on *The Merchant of Venice* seems to be without a focal point, but comments on several aspects of the play, including the motif of missing fathers and their substitutes. J. A. Barish[10] writes on the prose style of *Much Ado About Nothing*, remarking with subtle insight how 'excessive patterning seems to be a symptom of repression', and how the patterns break down in crisis and are 'reassembled to serve as emblems and ornaments of sociable man in society'. Discussing the same play from the point of view of an antithesis between 'wit' and

[1] 'Two Gentlemen of Milan', *Shakespeare Studies*, VII, 11–23.

[2] 'The Pattern of *Love's Labour's Lost*', *Shakespeare Studies*, VII, 25–53.

[3] 'The Function of the Songs at the End of *Love's Labour's Lost*', *Shakespeare Studies*, VII, 55–64.

[4] '*A Midsummer Night's Dream*: Analogous Image', *Shakespeare Studies*, VII, 115–23.

[5] 'Bottom Waking: Shakespeare's "Most Rare Vision"', *Studies in English Literature*, XIII, 207–22.

[6] 'Titania's Wood', *Rice University Studies*, LX, 55–70.

[7] '"Fie What a Question's That If Thou Wert Near a Lewd Interpreter": The Wall Scene in *A Midsummer Night's Dream*', *Shakespeare Studies*, VII, 101–13.

[8] 'The Plays Within *A Midsummer Night's Dream* and *The Tempest*', *Shakespeare Jahrbuch*, CX, 101–11.

[9] 'A "Dish of Doves": *The Merchant of Venice*', *English Literary History*, XL (1973), 339–51.

[10] 'Pattern and Purpose in the Prose of *Much Ado About Nothing*', *Rice University Studies*, LX, 19–30.

'intuitive modes of understanding', C. Dennis[1] argues that 'the drama of the play resides in the protagonists' moving from one way of seeing to the other; and their practical and moral success is determined by their willingness to lay down their wits and approach the world through faith, through irrational belief'. It is not clear what we should therefore make of the fact that Benedick and Beatrice seem as witty as ever in the play's last scene. J. Doebler's[2] identification of the athletic hero of *As You Like It* with Hercules and David as 'iconographical ideals of youthful virtue overthrowing vice' leaves Orlando, one feels, a little o'erparted. Two essays on *Twelfth Night* both discover a quasi-religious dimension in the accidents that befall in the play: C. Dennis[3] maintains that these call for an attitude of 'religious awe before the unearned bounty which the world bestows on man, an awe akin to man's perception of God's grace'; and J. Hartwig[4] perceives a 'contest between human will and suprahuman control' that is implied in the play's alternative title: '"what you will" may be realized, but under conditions which the human will cannot manipulate'.

The divergence of critical responses to *All's Well That Ends Well* is reflected in two studies: W. L. Godshalk[5] finds the play an ironic confirmation of 'the Morality ethic', since Helena gains her desired end through questionable means, while F. M. Pearce[6] argues that it does indeed end well: 'the recognition that failure may be redeemed by grace, that each one who loves has the power to bestow grace, and that each one who loves is himself dependent on another for grace enabled Shakespeare to contrive a truly comic harmony at the close'. With *Troilus and Cressida* the problem is to discover the form of the play: M. T. Jones-Davies,[7] for instance, approaches 'the discordant elements in this story of love and war' in the light of the myth of Mars and Venus and its philosophical interpretation as

a union of contrary qualities, a *discordia concors*. C. Slights,[8] on the other hand, contends that the juxtaposition of 'antithetically parallel scenes' determines the play as a tragic satire. Stylistic discontinuity in *Measure for Measure*, in the view of J. Altieri,[9] reflects the play's fragmented society. L. Owen[10] takes us further into this play's problematic mode with her study of its dramatic treatment of forgiveness in relation to the way in which the characters reach an understanding of their experience: 'repentance is not just expressed remorse, nor forgiveness a spoken pardon, but both are part of this process of coming to terms with oneself as a human being and a creature of God'. J. Black,[11] in an essay of considerable scope and insight, also examines the dramatisation of the characters' moral experience, drawing attention to the enclosed worlds of the play, the inadequacy and ambiguity of words in moral contexts and the pattern of substitutions in the action, to show that the play is 'about human beings who in an uncertain world are shut up against themselves and from one another. They

[1] 'Wit and Wisdom in *Much Ado About Nothing*', *Studies in English Literature*, XIII, 223–37.

[2] 'Orlando: Athlete of Virtue', *Shakespeare Survey 26*, 111–17.

[3] 'The Vision of *Twelfth Night*', *Tennessee Studies in Literature*, XVIII (1973), 63–74.

[4] 'Feste's "Whirligig" and the Comic Providence of *Twelfth Night*', *English Literary History*, XL, 501–13.

[5] '*All's Well That Ends Well* and the Morality Play', *Shakespeare Quarterly*, XXV, 61–70.

[6] 'In Quest of Unity: A Study of Failure and Redemption in *All's Well That Ends Well*', *Shakespeare Quarterly*, XXV, 71–88.

[7] 'Discord in Shakespeare's *Troilus and Cressida*; or, The Conflict between "Angry Mars and Venus Queen of Love"', *Shakespeare Quarterly*, XXV, 33–41.

[8] 'The Parallel Structure of *Troilus and Cressida*', *Shakespeare Quarterly*, XXV, 42–51.

[9] 'Style and Social Disorder in *Measure for Measure*', *Shakespeare Quarterly*, XXV, 6–16.

[10] 'Mode and Character in *Measure for Measure*', *Shakespeare Quarterly*, XXV, 17–32.

[11] 'The Unfolding of *Measure for Measure*', *Shakespeare Survey 26*, 119–28.

find release and fulfilment in "going forth" through self-abnegation and forgiveness.'

The recent critical tendency to relate a growing number of Shakespeare's Jacobean plays directly to the person and policies of King James reaches what might be its ultimate stage in G. Wickham's[1] bold claim that virtually the whole of Shakespeare's work in the second half of his career is to be understood in the light of the advent of the new monarch: 'the drift away from revenge tragedy and towards regenerative tragi-comedy in the first decade of James's reign...has its true origin in the political consciousness of the British peoples saved from foreign invasion and civil war by the peaceful accession of James I in 1603, by the timely discovery of the Gunpowder Plot in 1605, and the final ratification of the Union of the two Crowns by Act of Parliament in 1608'. Wickham does not maintain, as others have, that the plays were designed for particular Court occasions or special audiences, 'an extreme of particularity' against which R. Levin[2] assembles a formidable battery of argument and evidence. Nevertheless it is difficult not to sense that some of Levin's fire falls, and should fall, on a broader spectrum of the approach to topicality in the later Shakespeare: 'this approach inevitably tends to distort the plays so that they will fit the preconceived thesis, and to substitute external for internal interpretations of their components and overall meaning, and to distract us from their universal aspects which have preserved them as such an important part of our artistic heritage'. It is a pity that Levin's important contribution to a major critical debate on Shakespeare is not published where Shakespearians would be more likely to encounter it.

Among new essays on the last plays, J. S. Colley[3] discusses the emblematic use of disguise in *Cymbeline*, with particular reference to the phases of Posthumus's moral development, J. E. Siemon[4] brings out the parallels

between the two halves of *The Winter's Tale*, embodying 'two aspects of a single conception of human nature and human society', and K. A. Semon[5] explores the different senses of 'wonder' in *The Tempest*. D. W. Pearson[6] roundly declares that 'recognizing Prospero as a type of the potentially damned sorcerer is essential to any realization of the full scope of *The Tempest*', but one doubts whether Miranda, or anyone else, would recognise her father, even 'within the pneumatological framework of the period', as 'a type of Satan' driving his enemies to despair.

Turning to the poems, C. Hoy[7] imaginatively illustrates his proposition that 'what exists in the Sonnets as subjective feeling issues in the plays as objectified dramatic event', giving a new twist to the search for parallels between them, while H. Asals[8] develops a Neoplatonic interpretation of *Venus and Adonis* in which Adonis is identified with Beauty and the action of the poem represents the goddess's progression from sensual desire to a higher kind of love. R. A. Underwood's[9] dissertation on *The Phoenix and Turtle* is a comprehensive but rather pedestrian summary of the wide-ranging arguments about the

[1] 'From Tragedy to Tragi-Comedy: *King Lear* as Prologue', *Shakespeare Survey 26*, 33–48.

[2] 'The King James Version of *Measure for Measure*', *Clio*, III (1974), 129–63.

[3] 'Disguise and New Guise in *Cymbeline*', *Shakespeare Studies*, VII, 233–52.

[4] '"But it Appears She Lives": Iteration in *The Winter's Tale*', *Publications of the Modern Language Association of America*, LXXXIX, 10–16.

[5] 'Shakespeare's *Tempest*: Beyond a Common Joy', *English Literary History*, XL, 24–43.

[6] '"Unless I Be Reliev'd by Prayer": *The Tempest* in Perspective', *Shakespeare Studies*, VII, 253–82.

[7] 'Shakespeare and the Revenge of Art', *Rice University Studies*, LX, 71–94.

[8] '*Venus and Adonis*: The Education of a Goddess', *Studies in English Literature*, XIII, 31–51.

[9] *Shakespeare's 'The Phoenix and Turtle': A Survey of Scholarship*, Salzburg Studies in English Literature: Elizabethan Studies 15 (Institut für Englische Sprache und Literatur, Universität Salzburg, 1974).

authenticity, form and meaning of this puzzling poem.

Finally, a welcome should be extended to two well-edited and eminently useful works of reference. The bibliographical guide prepared under the editorship of S. Wells[1] is intended for students, and divided into chapters on the plays and poems, some of which are treated individually, others in groups. The contributor of each chapter describes the range of important textual and critical scholarship on his topic without imposing a rigid or limited orthodoxy, and appends a reference list of the studies referred to. B. Vickers[2] has undertaken the daunting task of selecting and editing more than three centuries of Shakespeare criticism in six volumes. In the first volume, which covers the seventeenth century, he has decided not to include contemporary allusions in the text proper (though some of them are quoted in the Introduction) on the grounds that they do not 'amount to sustained criticism of any value': Ben Jonson's private and public assessments, however, are included. Deciding that it would have 'falsified the total picture to limit the selections to formal criticism', Vickers draws the bulk of Shakespeare's critical heritage in this volume from the theatre itself, by giving us samples from the Restoration adaptations. One is sustained by the expectation of better things to come in future volumes.

[1] *Shakespeare: Select Bibliographical Guides* (Oxford University Press, 1973).
[2] *Shakespeare: The Critical Heritage*, vol. 1: 1623–1692 (Routledge and Kegan Paul, 1974).

© D. J. PALMER 1975

2. SHAKESPEARE'S LIFE, TIMES, AND STAGE

reviewed by N. W. BAWCUTT

Literary scholarship is not an exact science, and there are few occasions on which a scholarly argument is so powerfully set out that we cannot possibly refuse assent to it. But this does not mean that all arguments are equally valid, and one of the most valuable qualities of a good scholar is a strongly developed awareness of the difference between provable fact, reasonable hypothesis, and mere speculation. These remarks are prompted by two book-length studies of aspects of Shakespeare's life, both written by academics, which seem to the present reviewer to be seriously lacking in balanced judgement.

The first of these is W. Nicholas Knight's *Shakespeare's Hidden Life: Shakespeare at the Law 1585–1595*.[1] The aim of Knight's book is to prove that Shakespeare was a lawyer's scribe during the late 1580s and early 1590s,

and that he had a deep personal interest in the administration and reform of the law. Knight looks first at the legal troubles which overtook Shakespeare's father from 1577 onwards and which caused the loss of property Shakespeare might have expected to inherit from his mother. Then Knight discusses what he considers to be an authentic Shakespeare signature in a law-book by William Lambarde now in the Folger Shakespeare Library. He concludes with a consideration of Shakespeare's legal attitudes as exhibited in his plays and in his will.

Unfortunately Knight's use of evidence is surprisingly careless for someone so concerned with legal matters. (He never seems to have asked himself whether his case would stand up to severe cross-examination in a court of

[1] (Mason and Lipscomb, 1973).

law.) Even if we accept that the Lambarde signature is genuine, and then combine it with the undoubted use of legal phraseology in Shakespeare's writings, this does not *prove* for a moment that Shakespeare was at any time professionally connected with the law, even though we may think it, according to our taste, possible, plausible, or highly probable. The only irrefutable proof would be documentary evidence, and here Knight has nothing to offer. Even on his own ground Knight's assumption that a writer's vocabulary necessarily reflects his profession seems somewhat naïve; there are plenty of Elizabethan writers with undisputed connections with the law who do not pack their writings with legal terms.

Repeatedly Knight builds up an elaborate argument on the flimsiest basis. Knight assumes, for example, that Lambarde and Shakespeare were personal friends, and that Shakespeare put his signature in the book not as a sign of ownership but because Lambarde had lent it to him and he was reminding himself to return it. This logic is not very compelling in itself, but for Knight it provides a springboard into an exhilarating flight of fancy:

A reasonable speculation is that the volume might have been returned to William Lambarde and remained in his private library, until sometime before 1915, where such a similar volume (warped vellum cover) remained until the library was broken up in 1924. If this is entertained as a possibility, then the information about Shakespeare's address could have been inserted between 1776 and 1796 by a member of the Lambarde family from some legal source, or possibly even from the private judicial papers of their famous ancestor. If indeed Shakespeare had to return the volume, then it might have been to Lambarde's private library at Lincoln's Inn, then Shakespeare may have come in contact there with other books and manuscripts Lambarde had in his possession pertaining to law and literature.

Every effort is made to expand Shakespeare's connections with the Inns of Court, and we are even told that Mr W. H. was almost certainly a member of Gray's Inn 'as the three leading candidates for the honor of addressee (William Hatcliffe, or the Earls of Southampton or Pembroke) were all members of that Inn'.

In discussing the plays themselves Knight completely ignores twentieth-century textual scholarship. He blithely assumes that Shakespeare frequently re-wrote his plays, and claims without any attempt to prove his case in detail that various bad quartos or possible source-plays like *King Leir* and *The Taming of a Shrew* are early versions which Shakespeare later improved. It is hardly complimentary to Shakespeare to assert that he began his career by writing rubbish, yet on p. 98 we find a casual allusion to 'Shakespeare's early bad dramatic poetry'.

It is perhaps inevitable that Knight should read the plays in autobiographical terms. *Hamlet* is a tribute to Shakespeare's father (though Knight does not discuss what the play may be supposed to tell us about Shakespeare's mother). *Timon of Athens* is an artistic failure because it is too closely bound up with John Shakespeare's difficulties (though there is no evidence that his problems were caused by excessive generosity). Yet Knight seems curiously unaware that his picture of a Shakespeare who never managed to escape from the family troubles of his boyhood, and who brooded for years over the loss of some property, is decidedly unattractive and does nothing to enhance Shakespeare's greatness.

The second book is Peter Milward's *Shakespeare's Religious Background*.[1] This includes chapters on Shakespeare's family background and early education, on his attitude towards the clergy, both Protestant and Catholic, of the time, and on various theological and liturgical influences on his work. There is a chapter on Shakespeare's attitude to King Henry VIII and Queen Elizabeth, and the

[1] (Indiana University Press, 1973).

book concludes with an assessment of Shakespeare's philosophical and religious outlook. There is certainly room for a book of this kind, and Milward shows clearly that Shakespeare repeatedly used terms from religion or with potentially religious associations. It is hard, however, not to have serious reservations about Milward's treatment of this material.

In the first place, Milward is obviously anxious to present Shakespeare as sympathetic towards Catholicism, and uncritically accepts any evidence, no matter how flimsy, that points in that direction. The 'tradition', mentioned at the beginning of chapter 2, that the young Shakespeare was educated by 'an old Benedictine monk, Don Thomas Combe' is surely worthless (Chambers does not bother to mention it). Milward is favourably disposed towards the theory that Shakespeare was the William Shakeshafte mentioned in Alexander Houghton's will, but in the light of Douglas Hamer's vigorous discussion it seems highly improbable.[1] What most scholars have accepted as hostile references to Jesuits (in, for example, the Porter scene in *Macbeth*) are awkwardly explained away, and it is unconvincingly asserted that Shakespeare in fact admired the Jesuits. Much use is made of parallel passages as evidence of Shakespeare's reading, but the parallels quoted between his plays and the writings of Robert Southwell, Henry Smith, and Robert Persons are much too vague and general to prove a genuine indebtedness on Shakespeare's part.

Milward's bias is evident in other ways. Religious assertions in the plays are treated as coming directly from Shakespeare, while expressions of scepticism or despair are regarded as simply belonging to the character who utters them. The allegorising of the plays in order to give them a religious meaning is sometimes carried to fantastic lengths. One after another of Shakespeare's evil or misguided rulers turns out to be a type of Henry VIII, tragically responsible for destroying England's connection with Catholicism, and the reunion celebrated in the last plays indicates Shakespeare's longing that England should rejoin the Catholic communion. The description of the ceremony at Apollo's temple at the beginning of Act III of *The Winter's Tale* refers in its 'underlying Christian meaning' to Mass as it might be celebrated at St Peter's in Rome, and both Polixenes and Posthumus, 'by some hidden analogy', as Milward puts it, stand for the Pope himself. Despite some obviously respectful allusions to her Shakespeare really disliked Queen Elizabeth, and his portrayal of the death of Prince Arthur in *King John* shows us his feelings towards the execution of Mary Stuart.[2]

The final result of all this is to present us with a Shakespeare who was never seriously disturbed by life and who went on repeating the same rather dull orthodoxies throughout his career. It may well be that Shakespeare had deeper theological interests than most modern critics will allow, but to assert this without crudely simplifying the plays will demand a more subtle and thoughtful approach than that offered us by Milward.

Recent work on Shakespeare's sources suggests that few major discoveries remain to be made in this field, and scholars seem to be increasingly turning their attention to possible source-material which Shakespeare could certainly have read but which offers only a very vague or general analogy to his writings. Articles of this kind are Wallace Graves's 'Plutarch's *Life of Cato Utican* as a Major

[1] 'Was William Shakespeare William Shakeshafte?, *Review of English Studies*, n.s. XXI (1970), 41–8.

[2] It might be added here that in 'On Fluellen's Figures, Christ Figures, and James Figures', *Publications of the Modern Language Association of America*, LXXXIX (1974), 302–11, Richard Levin has made a vigorous attack on modern attempts to present certain Shakespearian characters as types of Christ or James I.

Source of *Othello*'[1] and Donna Hamilton's 'Some Romance Sources for *King Lear*', which argues that the play was influenced by the popular story of Robert the Devil, easily available in Lodge's prose version of 1591.[2] With both articles the reader ends by feeling that there are indeed some similarities between the play and proposed source, but that they are not detailed and specific enough to prove Shakespeare's indebtedness. It is perhaps significant that Edith Williams, writing 'In Defense of Lady Macbeth',[3] spends her time in a refutation of W. L. Godshalk's suggestion that Tarquin's wife Tullia, as portrayed by Livy, was a prototype for Lady Macbeth.[4] This approach may seem merely negative, but it could have the beneficial effect of forcing scholars to make up their minds on the issue. On a point of detail, T. Sipahigil suggests that IV, i, 260–4 of *Othello* was influenced by a passage in Montaigne's *Essays*, I, 54.[5]

M. L. Wine's full and scholarly edition of *Arden of Faversham* is a useful contribution to the study of apocryphal plays attributed to Shakespeare.[6] The introduction sets the play firmly in its historical background, and the critical discussion is sympathetic and persuasive. Wine admires the play and would like to assign it to Shakespeare, but he offers no new or persuasive evidence on this point, and his case is made more problematic by the fact that (as he convincingly asserts) the only text we have is a bad quarto in which the original version has been seriously mutilated.

The analysis of image-clusters has become a useful technique in dealing with problems of attribution. Karl P. Wentersdorf, in 'Linkages of Thought and Imagery in Shakespeare and *More*',[7] strengthens the case for Shakespeare's participation in *Sir Thomas More* by extending the patterns of imagery first noted by R. W. Chambers in his classic essay on the play, and James O. Wood, in 'Shakespeare and the Belching Whale',[8] argues that II, i, 29–62 of

Pericles, with its elaborate references to whales, is authentically Shakespearian and that Shakespeare uses in various plays an image-cluster based on the sea, whales, and the idea of belching or throwing-up.

Much useful work continues to be done on the Elizabethan stage, the range and variety of which can be assessed from Philip C. Kolin and R. O. Wyatt's helpful 'Bibliography of Scholarship on the Elizabethan Stage Since Chambers'.[9] One of the most attractive of recent books is C. Walter Hodges's *Shakespeare's Second Globe: The Missing Monument*.[10] Its aim is clear and simple: to reconstruct the second Globe theatre, built after the first Globe burnt down in 1613, exclusively on the basis of Hollar's drawing of the theatre in his panorama of London. Hodges's skill as an artist is celebrated, and his book is full of sketches and diagrams, culminating in a splendid double-page cut-away illustration in colour of the reconstructed interior. We must not expect, however, a history of the theatre or a collection of information about it (for that the reader must turn to vol. VI of G. E. Bentley's *The Jacobean and Caroline Stage*), and it is perhaps a little surprising that Hodges makes hardly any use of stage-directions from plays known to have been performed at this theatre.

Hodges does make some assumptions which cannot be proved from Hollar's drawing – for example, that there were no pillars between the

---

[1] *Shakespeare Quarterly*, XXIV (1973), 181–7.
[2] *Studies in Philology*, LXXI (1974), 173–91.
[3] *Shakespeare Quarterly*, XXIV (1973), 221–3.
[4] 'Livy's Tullia: A Classical Prototype of Lady Macbeth', *Shakespeare Quarterly*, XVI (1965), 240–1.
[5] 'Montaigne's *Essays* and *Othello*', *Notes and Queries*, n.s. XX (1974), 130.
[6] The Revels Plays (Methuen, 1973).
[7] *Modern Language Quarterly*, XXXIV (1973), 384–405.
[8] *English Language Notes*, IX (1973), 40–4.
[9] *Research Opportunities in Renaissance Drama*, XV–XVI (1972–3), 33–59.
[10] (Oxford University Press, 1973).

stage and the gabled structure above it. It is not clear beyond doubt that the hatching on the front of the gabled superstructure is intended to represent a timber framework. There is an unfortunate misprint at the beginning of chapter 3, where the dimension of the theatre in the etching is given as $\frac{3}{8}$ in. instead of $2\frac{3}{8}$ in., and scholars might have found it useful to have slightly more detailed information about the nature and location of some of the illustrations. Some readers may be surprised to find that although Hodges would like a modern reconstruction of the Globe to be built, he would use it as a museum rather than as a live theatre. But these are only minor reservations, and all those interested in the Elizabethan stage will consult this book with pleasure.

Two substantial collections of essays on the stage deserve attention. The first of these, *Renaissance Drama*, n.s. IV, *Essays Principally on the Playhouse and Staging*, appeared some while ago but has not been reviewed in these pages.[1] Marion Trousdale opens with an article on 'The Question of Harley Granville-Barker and Shakespeare on Stage'.[2] This is not a full survey of Granville-Barker as a Shake-spearian critic. It starts from Granville-Barker's assertions, made in the early 1920s, that Shakespeare's plays have meaning only in performance, and that reading them is like reading the score of a symphony. Miss Trous-dale shows that Granville-Barker did not in fact take up such a simple and one-sided attitude while producing and criticising Shakespeare, and even seems to have moved away from it towards the end of his life. She notes that the Elizabethans themselves regarded the poet as author much more highly than the mere actor, and argues that we must base our interpreta-tions primarily on our experience of the text as poetry. D. F. Rowan's 'The English Play-house: 1595–1630' is not as inclusive as its title might suggest.[3] He discusses chiefly the drawings for a private playhouse from the Inigo

Jones/Webb collection in Worcester College Library which he has considered in various places elsewhere, including *Shakespeare Survey* 23 (1970). (He now believes, incidentally, that the drawings have nothing to do with Barber-Surgeons' Hall.) Rowan claims that the draw-ings are 'unmistakably' by Jones himself, though this is not quite the same as Rudolf Wittkower's phrase, in a private letter to Rowan, that 'it is not at all unlikely' that they are. The evidence of these drawings, together with other pictorial evidence, leads Rowan to assert that there was a standard pattern for all Elizabethan playhouses, though perhaps some other scholars will not share his confidence that the major problems of the Elizabethan stage have now been settled conclusively.

What effect did the opening of an Elizabe-than theatre have on the surrounding district? Were there complaints of rowdiness and disturbance? In '"Neere the Playe House": The Swan Theater and Community Blight', the next contributor, William Ingram, tries to answer these problems in terms of the Swan theatre, built in 1595–6.[4] He shows that accord-ing to local records the immediate neighbour-hood was not noticeably affected. There were complaints about Francis Langley, builder of the Swan, but this was because he neglected his duties as Lord of the Manor. Werner Habicht links several plays together by looking at 'Tree Properties and Tree Scenes in Eliza-bethan Theater';[5] he finds that they are used flexibly in both literal and emblematic signi-ficances. David J. Houser, in 'Armor and Motive in *Troilus and Cressida*', studies the way in which characters in the play arm and unarm themselves as an exhibition of visual symbolism.[6]

[1] Edited by Samuel Schoenbaum (Northwestern University Press, 1972).
[2] *Ibid.*, pp. 3–36.   [3] *Ibid.*, pp. 37–51.
[4] *Ibid.*, pp. 53–68.   [5] *Ibid.*, pp. 69–92.
[6] *Ibid.*, pp. 121–34.

Other contributors discuss the staging of Marlowe's *The Jew of Malta*[1] and *Tamburlaine*.[2] Stephen Orgel identifies a little pamphlet by Aurelian Townshend called simply *The Ante-Masques* as belonging with the French pastoral play *Florimène* performed before Charles I and Henrietta Maria on 21 December 1635, and reprints it together with the English summary of the play published in 1636.[3] Orgel regards the whole of Townshend's contribution as an epilogue, but it is in several sections which might possibly have been inserted into the play at different points. Finally, T. J. King provides a review-article assessing the major twentieth-century contributions to knowledge of the Elizabethan stage.[4]

The same scholar provides the opening paper in the second set of essays, *The Elizabethan Theatre III*, edited by David Galloway.[5] It is called 'Shakespearian Staging, 1599–1642', and is basically a summary of King's book with the same title published in 1971.[6] King obviously wants to establish rigorous standards of validity for evidence concerning the Elizabethan stage, and for him there are only three acceptable sources of evidence: contemporary drawings and engravings, surviving buildings where Elizabethan plays are known to have been acted, and plays, printed or manuscript, which show clear signs of use as prompt-books. We may, however, feel at times that King is too rigorous. He is entitled to disregard obvious closet-drama written by amateur playwrights, but he seems rather too dismissive of foul-papers texts. If the play in question is by an experienced professional dramatist like Shakespeare, surely he would not ask for stage effects which he knew were difficult, if not impossible, to achieve? King argues that most Elizabethan plays require a very simple stage, and deduces from this that all Elizabethan theatres had very rudimentary equipment. But we know that *some* plays by professional dramatists required elaborate stage-effects, and

it follows by simple logic that there must have been *some* theatres capable of producing them. It might be an interesting exercise to take the opposite approach from King and look for the most extreme and difficult stage-effects the Elizabethan theatre was capable of when stretched to the uttermost.

Clifford Leech's intriguingly titled 'Three Times *Ho* and a Brace of Widows: Some Plays for the Private Theatre' discusses *Westward Ho*, *Eastward Ho*, and *Northward Ho*, and emphasises their literary relationships with each other and with later plays of the period.[7] In 'The Boar's Head Again' Herbert Berry continues his investigation into the public playhouse at the Boar's Head Inn in Whitechapel.[8] In this section the stress falls on the people involved in the lawsuits which are our main evidence for the existence of this theatre, and the essay concludes with an attempt to determine the precise location of the inn. J. A. Lavin's 'Shakespeare and the Second Blackfriars' is a robust and well-argued attack on G. E. Bentley's 'Shakespeare and the Blackfriars Theatre', first published in *Shakespeare Survey* 1 (1948).[9] Lavin denies that the acquisition of the Blackfriars theatre by the King's Men in 1609 had any effect on Shakespeare as a dramatist, and he can detect no proof whatever that the company held conferences or discussions in 1608 over its future policy. Plausible assumptions can too easily harden into accepted fact, and it is a good thing when challenges like this are made.

The remaining essays in the collection are less directly concerned with the stage. Glynne Wickham interprets *The Winter's Tale* as an

[1] J. L. Simmons, 'Elizabethan Stage Practice and Marlowe's *The Jew of Malta*', *ibid.*, pp. 93–104.
[2] Nancy T. Leslie, '*Tamburlaine* in the Theater: Tartar, Grand Guignol, or Janus?', *ibid.*, pp. 105–20.
[3] *Ibid.*, pp. 135–53.   [4] *Ibid.*, pp. 199–235.
[5] (Macmillan, 1973).   [6] *Ibid.*, pp. 1–13.
[7] *Ibid.*, pp. 14–32.   [8] *Ibid.*, pp. 33–65.
[9] *Ibid.*, pp. 66–81.

emblematic celebration of the union of England and Scotland brought about by the efforts of James I.[1] He treats the play as a political allegory (Paulina, for example, is 'perhaps' Sir Francis Bacon), and supports his argument from contemporary art and literature which has an unmistakably emblematic intention. To the present reviewer, however, Wickham gives no compelling reasons that oblige us to read an allegorical meaning into Shakespeare's play. W. R. Gair shows how James I and Charles I distrusted antiquarians because their researches into the English past might prove politically subversive, and argues that the figure of the antiquarian Veterano, in Shackerly Marmion's *The Antiquary*, is partly based on Sir Robert Cotton, whose library of ancient manuscripts was put under royal control in 1630.[2] According to Gair, Marmion was on Cotton's side against the King and Privy Council.

George R. Kernodle uses the art-historians' concept of 'mannerism' to help to define certain characteristics of Shakespeare's middle-period plays.[3] The essay is wide-ranging and richly allusive, but the separate details do not perhaps always fuse together into a convincing general argument. The last item in the collection is John Lawlor's 'Continuity and Innovation in Shakespeare'.[4] How, he asks, should we read Shakespeare, as an Elizabethan or as a contemporary? There is no easy answer, but Lawlor suggests that we ought to study single plays in the light of Shakespeare's work as a whole, and not look for 'ideas' or 'themes' in isolation but consider the whole content of the play as it comes to life in performance.

Other articles on the stage deal with a miscellaneous range of topics. A. B. Kernan has made a short but suggestive attempt to define the symbolic significance of the theatre for Elizabethan dramatists by examining the device of a play-within-a-play and the common use of theatrical metaphors.[5] Joseph Weixlmann offers

a conjectural solution to the vexed problem of how the Romans were '*beat back to their trenches*' in *Coriolanus*, I, iv, 29.[6] John Doebler provides a more accurate version of the 'Constitutions' established for the Revels Office by Sir Thomas Cawarden in 1545 than that given in Chambers's *Elizabethan Stage*.[7] In two complementary articles F. E. Snyder discusses the underlying significance of the pageants performed during the progresses of Queen Elizabeth,[8] and Richard L. DeMolen surveys Mulcaster's contributions to Elizabethan pageantry and tries to work out his purposes in writing pageants.[9]

Inigo Jones seems to have had no direct connection with Shakespeare, but his importance as a stage-designer is such that it would be churlish not to record the celebration in 1973 of the quatercentenary of his birth. A splendid exhibition of drawings, paintings, and photographs was mounted in the newly decorated Banqueting Hall at Whitehall from 12 July to 2 September 1973, and the catalogue for the event, *The King's Arcadia: Inigo Jones and the Stuart Court*, by John Harris, Stephen Orgel, and Roy Strong, is so substantial that it can be regarded as a book in its own right.[10] Two of these scholars, Stephen Orgel and Roy Strong, are also responsible for a work of major importance, *Inigo Jones: The Theatre of the Stuart Court*, in which all the surviving

[1] *Ibid.*, pp. 82–99. [2] *Ibid.*, pp. 100–18.
[3] *Ibid.*, pp. 119–34. [4] *Ibid.*, pp. 135–44.
[5] 'This Goodly Frame, The Stage: The Interior Theater of Imagination in English Renaissance Drama', *Shakespeare Quarterly*, XXV (1974), 1–5.
[6] 'How the Romans Were Beat Back to their Trenches: An Historical Note on *Coriolanus*, I, iv', *Notes and Queries*, n.s. XX (1974), 133–4.
[7] 'A Lost Paragraph in the Revels Constitution', *Shakespeare Quarterly*, XXIV (1973), 333–4.
[8] 'Composition des fêtes et cortèges d'apparat élizabéthains', *Revue d'Histoire du Théâtre*, XXV (1973), 244–56.
[9] 'Richard Mulcaster and Elizabethan Pageantry', *Studies in English Literature*, XIV (1974), 209–21.
[10] (Arts Council of Great Britain, 1973).

drawings relating to stages, scenery, and costumes are freshly reproduced.[1] The drawings have been carefully re-examined and some identifications have been altered from those previously accepted. The editors provide a series of introductory essays, and reprint full texts of all the relevant masques. No-one interested in the Stuart masque can ignore this book; it is, however, extremely expensive, and a separate and cheaper reprint of the drawings alone would be very welcome.

Recent studies of famous Shakespearian actors and productions may be listed in approximate historical order. Don B. Wilmeth gives a full account of the last years of G. F. Cooke, the English actor who performed numerous Shakespearian roles in America from 1810 to 1812 and died in New York on 26 September 1812.[2] John A. Mills writes on Charles Fechter, the French-born actor whose performances of Hamlet in England in 1861 and America in 1870 were regarded as revolutionary in presenting a more vigorous and self-assured Hamlet than was customary at the time.[3] Hans Schmid discusses Henry Irving's Shylock of 1879, and notes that in 1907 Irving made a gramophone record of the 'Hath not a Jew eyes?' speech at the beginning of Act III which is still in existence.[4] An amusing sidelight on early nineteenth-century theatre-history is cast by J. W. Robinson, who reprints a street ballad of circa 1838 by James Bouton recounting the tribulations (possibly mythical) of an amateur actor in the role of Othello.[5]

To move to more modern times, Michael Mullin describes Komisarjevsky's production of Macbeth at Stratford-upon-Avon in 1933,[6] and Patrick J. Sullivan discusses the Jonathan Miller production of The Merchant of Venice, with Olivier as Shylock, first performed in 1970 by the National Theatre.[7] Three interesting items can be found in the same journal: Dame Peggy Ashcroft briefly describes her conception of the role of Margaret of Anjou

as it develops through Henry VI and Richard III;[8] A. C. Sprague provides an account of Robert Atkins as a Shakespearian producer which is simultaneously entertaining and serious;[9] and Marvin Rosenberg gives a scene-by-scene commentary on the development during rehearsals of Peter Hall's Stratford production of Macbeth with Paul Scofield in the title role.[10]

The Fall 1973 issue of Literature/Film Quarterly is completely devoted to film versions of Shakespeare's plays, and discusses the work of several famous modern directors.[11] All the contributors respect the art of the cinema, and yet, as one of them remarks, 'no one seems

[1] (Sotheby Parke Bernet Publications and University of California Press, 1973).
[2] 'Cooke Among the Yankee Doodles', Theatre Survey, XIV (1973), 1–32.
[3] Ibid., XV (1974), 59–78.
[4] 'Held und Bösewicht: Irvings Shylock', Deutsche Shakespeare-Gesellschaft West Jahrbuch 1973, pp. 97–110.
[5] 'An Amateur among Professionals, "When I performed Othello"', Theatre Notebook, XXVIII (1974), 6–8.
[6] 'Augures and Understood Relations: Theodore Komisarjevsky's Macbeth', Educational Theater Journal, XXVI (1974), 20–30.
[7] Ibid., pp. 31–44.
[8] 'Margaret of Anjou', Deutsche Shakespeare-Gesellschaft West Jahrbuch 1973, pp. 7–9.
[9] 'Robert Atkins as a Shakespearian Director', ibid., pp. 19–30.
[10] 'Macbeth in Rehearsal – A Journal', ibid., pp. 111–30.
[11] The contents are as follows: Normand Berlin, 'Macbeth: Polanski and Shakespeare', pp. 291–8; R. H. Ball, 'On Shakespeare Filmography', pp. 299–306; Jack J. Jorgens, 'Image and Meaning in the Kozintsev Hamlet', pp. 307–15; Jay L. Halio, 'Three Filmed Hamlets', pp. 316–20; J. E. Fisher, 'Olivier and the Realistic Othello', pp. 321–31; Michael Mullin, 'Macbeth on Film', pp. 332–42; K. S. Rothwell, 'Hollywood and Some Versions of Romeo and Juliet', pp. 343–51; John Gerlach, 'Shakespeare, Kurosawa, and Macbeth: A Response to J. Blumenthal', pp. 352–9; James Naremore, 'The Walking Shadow: Welles's Expressionist Macbeth', pp. 360–6; and John Reddington, 'Film, Play, and Idea', pp. 367–71.

quite sure how to respond to films of Shakespeare's plays'; we do not receive much help in working out what differences there are, or ought to be, between a screen production and a stage production. Elsewhere one of the contributors, R. H. Ball, provides fresh information about the extract from *King John* filmed by Beerbohm Tree in 1899.[1]

Shakespeare's reception in Germany, Holland, and Switzerland is studied in several recent books and articles. In 'A Hapsburg Letter' Irene Morris reprints the German text, with an English translation, of a letter written in February 1608 from Archduchess Maria Magdalena to her brother, later Emperor Ferdinand II, describing a visit of the English players to the court at Graz.[2] This was the famous troupe led by John Greene, and among the plays they performed was one 'about the Jew' (*von dem Jude*), which may have been *The Merchant of Venice*. In the same journal Joseph H. Stodder argues for an influence of *Othello* on Büchner's *Woyzeck*, but some of the parallels he quotes do not seem particularly convincing.[3] Annie van Nassau-Sarolea shows that a play by the Dutch actor Abraham Sybant, *De dolle Bruyloft*, performed in 1654, is in fact a translation of *The Taming of the Shrew*.[4] Martin Bircher and Heinrich Straumann have provided us with an annotated bibliography of studies relating to Shakespeare's influence in German-speaking Switzerland up to the end of the eighteenth century,[5] and Balz Engler has examined the work of R. A. Schröder, the leading modern Swiss translator of Shakespeare.[6] Much of the *Deutsche Shakespeare-Gesellschaft West Jahrbuch 1973* is taken up with studies of important German Shakespearian actors from the eighteenth century to the present day.[7]

The Folger Shakespeare Library has published the catalogue of its Shakespeare collection in two large volumes.[8] The first lists editions of the works and separate plays, and the second contains works on Shakespeare. Vol. I is quite useful, though it would have been helpful to indicate in the table of contents that the section on the non-dramatic poems begins on p. 651 and the section on doubtful or spurious plays on p. 691. Vol. II is in two parts, a subject-index classification of miscellaneous books and an alphabetical list of all books whose titles begin with the word 'Shakespeare'. This seems a rather arbitrary arrangement; no index is provided and it must be said that the book will not help the inexperienced reader as much as it might have done.

Finally, two items are inserted here because they do not obviously seem to belong anywhere else. Judith C. Levinson has attempted to explain a puzzling phrase in *1 Henry IV*, III, i, 239,[9] and D'Orsay W. Pearson has argued that Shakespeare intended the audience

---

[1] 'Tree's *King John* Film: An Addendum', *Shakespeare Quarterly*, XXIV (1973), 455-9.

[2] *Modern Language Review*, LXIX (1974), 12-22.

[3] 'Influences of *Othello* on Büchner's *Woyzeck*', *ibid.*, pp. 115-20.

[4] 'Abraham Sybant, strolling player and first Dutch Shakespeare translator', *Theatre Research*, XIII (1973), 38-59.

[5] *Shakespeare und die deutsche Schweiz bis zum Beginn des 19. Jahrhunderts* (A. Francke, 1971).

[6] *Rudolf Alexander Schröders Übersetzungen von Shakespeares Dramen*, The Cooper Monographs, 18 (A. Francke, 1974).

[7] Leopold Lindtberg, 'Die Qual der Wahl und ihr Ergebnis: Josef Meinrad als Fluellen in König Heinrichs Armee', pp. 10-18; Martin Brunkhorst, 'Natur und Wahrheit: Probleme der Hamlet-Rolle im 18. Jahrhundert', pp. 38-52; Eike Pies, 'David Borchers (1744-1796). Ein Shakespeare-darsteller des 18. Jahrhunderts', pp. 53-61; Heinz Kindermann, 'Josef Kainz in seinen Shakespearerollen', pp. 62-77; Ernst Th. Sehrt, 'Der Shylock Fritz Kortners', pp. 78-96; and K. G. Kachler, 'Leopold Biberti als Darsteller des Othello', pp. 131-43.

[8] *Folger Shakespeare Library: Catalog of the Shakespeare Collection* (G. K. Hall, 1972).

[9] ''Tis a Woman's Fault', *English Language Notes*, IX (1973), 38-40.

of *A Midsummer Night's Dream* to remember the evil side of Theseus's character and not to idealise him.[1] He gives us an interesting survey of Renaissance attitudes to Theseus, but the argument is rather strained, and it is very odd that he should completely omit to mention *The Two Noble Kinsmen.* Several volumes from the University of Salzburg series of Elizabethan and Jacobean studies have recently come to hand; the items of Shakespearian interest will be discussed in next year's issue of *Shakespeare Survey.*

[1] '"Unkinde" Theseus: A Study in Renaissance Mythography', *English Literary Renaissance,* IV (1974), 276–98.

© N. W. BAWCUTT 1975

3. TEXTUAL STUDIES

reviewed by RICHARD PROUDFOOT

Publication of the American *Riverside Shakespeare,*[1] whose text has been edited throughout from the early editions by G. Blakemore Evans, has been long awaited with keen interest, nor are expectations disappointed by the handsome and substantial book which has now appeared. Never before can a single-volume edition of Shakespeare have managed to combine so reliably edited a text presented in such a readable form with so rich a digest of ancillary and explanatory materials. John Heminge and Henry Condell addressed themselves and the First Folio of 1623 to 'the great Variety of Readers', a phrase which the publishers of this new Shakespeare translate as covering 'in the plainer language of today...the general reader, the student, and the scholar'. The general reader may find more grounds for speculation about the plan of the volume than others with a professional interest in the subject. He will find obvious sense in the chronological grouping of the plays and distinct convenience in the placing of the brief but helpful commentary unobtrusively at the foot of each page of text. In the text itself, he may wonder why words sometimes appear in a spelling which departs from modern usage and why square brackets enclose not only many stage directions but words, phrases or more extended passages in the speeches themselves. He may reflect that the textual notes, although decently postponed to the end of each text, occupy enough space to suggest comprehensiveness, and it may occur to him to question the relative prominence given to the general textual introduction (which precedes the works) and the stage history (which follows them). He should be grateful for the numerous illustrations, selected with a discriminating eye from sixteenth- and seventeenth-century sources, which combine pleasure with profit in the best tradition of Shakespeare's own age and he will learn all that is to be known of the author and much about his age from the chronological tables and the substantial excerpts

[1] (Houghton Mifflin Company, 1974).

from documentary sources reprinted in the Appendices.

The introductory essays will rapidly reveal the professional and academic bias of Shakespeare studies in our time, but the reader who will attend Professor Harry Levin's tactful and magisterial induction course will find Shakespeare related to his age and to our own in terms which combine the respect implied by a description of his works as 'virtually canonized as humanistic scriptures' with a wide range of information on all aspects of his life, times and art. He may, indeed, be left wondering whether ten pages of general introduction devoted to 'The Linguistic Medium', 'The Stylistic Technique' and 'The Theatrical Setting' in a volume of nearly 2,000 pages is not a lean portion of bread to the surrounding gallons of critical and textual sack. Following the further courses provided by Professors Anne Barton, on the comedies, Herschel Baker, on the histories, Frank Kermode, on the tragedies, and Hallett Smith, on the poems and the romances (sensibly allowed the standing of a separate group, which includes *The Two Noble Kinsmen*), our general reader will again be reassured by their various combinations of historical scholarship and critical balance, not only in the introductions to the works but in the commentary, which they have also supplied (except for Professor Barton, the comedies having been annotated by Professor Evans and collaborators). Perhaps the most challenging part of the course will be Professor Evans's own graduate seminar on 'Shakespeare's Text', while the relegation of Professor Charles Shattuck's lively stage history to an appendix will sufficiently indicate the low priority which this course accords to the study of the plays as texts for performance. The general reader, in short, will find himself transformed into a student under the influence of the edition's emphasis on those aspects of academic Shakespeare studies which have predominated in the mid-twentieth century, the history of ideas, formal and thematic analysis of the works and the bibliographical approach to the problems of the texts and their transmission. In time, it may be that these emphases will come to seem the most outdated aspect of the book.

A few internal inconsistencies which should have been resolved, or at least faced as points of controversy, result from the collaborative nature of the enterprise. Thus Anne Barton's introduction to *The Two Gentlemen of Verona* supports an early dating, even before 1592, seeing it as possibly Shakespeare's 'first professional play', while the table of chronology lists it under 1594 (and further differs from Professor Barton in retaining the common error of calling its source *Diana Enamorada*, rather than simply *Diana*). Similar vagueness surrounds the anonymous play of *Edward III*, which is excluded from the edition without more than passing (and conflicting) references to the possibility that Shakespeare wrote it, and the date of the earthquake perhaps alluded to in *Romeo and Juliet*, which is rightly given as 1580 on p. 1055 but misdated 1584 on p. 51. Less serious is a tendency to devote too much space to issues now topical, such as D. F. McKenzie's views on Elizabethan proofreading or Roman Polanski's film of *Macbeth*. The inclusion, in an appendix, of an Elizabethan court epilogue 'possibly by Shakespeare' may also owe more to the recent date of its discovery than to any impressively Shakespearian quality in the lines recovered by W. A. Ringler, Jr, and S. W. May from the commonplace book of Henry Stanford. One strange omission seems to be the result of the presentation of the preliminary pages of the First Folio in facsimile (from the Harvard copy). They are the only contemporary documents reprinted in the edition without introduction or commentary – a serious lack, especially for the epistles and for Jonson's verses.

The text of the *Riverside Shakespeare* is as

soundly established, in terms of the materials used and of the general editorial principles, as that of any popular Shakespeare yet published. Those principles are conservative and bear a strong resemblance to McKerrow's recommendations in his *Prolegomena for the Oxford Shakespeare*.[1] A single 'copy-text' is chosen for each of the works and is adhered to as closely as possible. 'Every effort consistent with critical sense has been made to adhere to the declared copy-text', though other readings have been admitted where it 'resisted all reasonable attempts to make sense of it'. The edition reflects its principles throughout, though without that degree of austerity which would banish a familiar Falstaff who '[babbl'd] of green fields' (F Table), a Macbeth stranded 'upon this bank and [shoal] of time' (F Schoole) or an Antony deserted by 'The hearts / That [spannell'd] me at heels' (F pannelled). The brackets and spellings in these quotations are those of the edition: they are among the tools of interpretation used by Professor Evans to mediate between the differing demands of his intended readers and his own integrity as an editor – they are also the features of his text which are likely to cause readers most trouble. Their purposes are described in the general textual introduction. Brackets are to warn the reader of departures from the copy-text (defined as 'the printed edition or manuscript upon which an editor bases his text' rather than in Greg's more particular sense, which would be irrelevant to a modern-spelling edition), whether these are emendations, additions or variants from another early edition. Spelling is handled with a freedom not always claimed by modernizing editors, in that copy-spellings are sometimes retained, either on phonetic grounds (though no general account of what these grounds may be is attempted) or, more vaguely, to suggest 'the kind of linguistic climate in which [Shakespeare] wrote'. Some dangers are appa-

rent, even in the familiar lines already quoted. Not only has each of the rejected F readings had its defenders (it is here after all that an editor's 'critical sense' will be the arbiter), but the use of brackets is revealed as extending to readings which interpret the copy-text rather than strictly replacing it. 'Shoal' is rightly bracketed as a disputed reading, but the modern form is an available interpretation of F's 'Schoole'. Elsewhere, the rule is not to use brackets for readings which result from the editor's choice between two available modernizations of his copy, such as 'travel/travail' or 'human/humane'. The spelling 'spannell'd' seems likewise to result, not from the stated phonetic principle, but from a desire to account for what is held to be an error in F; 'spaniel' is invariably used elsewhere in the edition.

The use of brackets becomes even more questionable in those plays where collateral substantive texts exist. For *Lear* and *Othello*, Evans adopts the Folio as his copy-text, which is reasonable, even if the case against Quarto *Lear* is slightly overstated in the process and its status as simply a 'bad Quarto' too easily assumed. In *Lear* he accepts some 100 readings from Q, in *Othello* nearly twice as many. Each of these Q readings is duly bracketed and the unbiassed reader will take the relative infrequency of the brackets as presumptive evidence of the general superiority of F. What he will learn only by consulting the textual notes is how often conservatism is controversial, as nothing in the text designates as doubtful those places where a difficulty has been resolved by the retention of the copy-text reading. In responding to a proper desire to show his editorial hand and to reveal the status of his text, Evans has hit on a method which is as likely to confuse as it is to enlighten. He might have been wiser to have limited his textual apparatus to the notes and confined brackets to their conventional

[1] (Clarendon Press, 1939).

role of indicating editorial additions. His chosen practice has the awkward effect of drawing equal attention to trivial or certain corrections and to difficult readings involving true variants, while at the same time failing to distinguish places where doubt exists about the text and where conservatism involves either retaining a crux, such as 'moon used', *A Midsummer Night's Dream*, v, i, 206, or 'make rope's in such a scarre', *All's Well*, IV, ii, 38, or preferring a copy-text reading to a variant often adopted by other editors, such as 'Being (Q Bring) oil to fire', *Lear*, II, ii, 77, or 'Traitors ensteep'd (Q enscerped) to enclog (Q clog) the guiltless keel', *Othello*, II, i, 70.

The question of spellings has a further dimension. In many of the notes on the texts, certain spelling forms are adduced (though without the support of any general discussion) as evidence that the early editions were printed from Shakespeare's 'foul papers'. Once again, the conservative principles of the edition seem to have induced, or drawn strength from, a slightly too optimistic view. Nowhere is it suggested that a handful of idiosyncratic spellings might well have survived scribal transcription, nor is it ever demonstrated that the forms used can safely be identified as distinctive (indeed one of them, 'a leven' for 'eleven', is not uncommon in other writers of the period). Furthermore, if Q2 *Hamlet* and Q1 *Merchant of Venice* were both set from Shakespeare's 'foul papers', as Evans believes, then some ingenuity will be required to account for the very different results produced by the two compositors in James Roberts's shop who set both.

The effect of the retention of some copy-text spellings is mixed. Above all, it seems obtrusive in an edition which elsewhere shows little interest in historical linguistic matters. That it is arbitrary will be sufficiently indicated by some examples: 'mounch'd' is preserved in *Macbeth*, 'smoile' rejected from *Lear*; else-where in *Macbeth*, 'spungy' and 'germains' (*germens*) are kept, but 'herbenger' becomes 'harbinger' and 'intombe', 'entomb', which indicates that no consistent phonetic principle is at work. Even odder is the treatment of proper names, which gives us, again in *Macbeth*, Rosse, Enverness, Birnan (as in F and Holinshed), Menteth and Cathness but balks at Foris (F Soris), Glamys, Banquoh, Seyward and Lenox, all of which are regularized. The resulting oddity seems a high price to pay for the possible reinstatement of such presumptively authentic forms as 'triumphery' and 'triumpherate'. In the matter of spelling, compromise between full conservatism and full modernization, whatever its apparent attractions, can only lead to anomaly.

The features of Evans's text which I have mentioned so far are noticeable because they are innovations. In some other particulars his edition stands closer than might be expected to the eighteenth- and nineteenth-century editorial tradition. Thus, he silently capitalizes titles and words referring to god. More important still is his acceptance of full power to make silent alterations in punctuation and verse-lining. His handling of these aspects of the text reveals assumptions which many will share: he believes in a Shakespeare who wrote verses that scanned and he will let no historical niceness prevent him from punctuating intelligibly. Nevertheless readers should be told whether the verse-lining of the text they are reading is that of the copy-text, at least in passages where there has been much controversy. The metrical value of final '-ed' is decided by printing '-'d' for the unstressed syllable in verse and invariably in prose: the verse practice is defensible, but the departure from modern usage in prose is fussy and pre-empts decisions about the speaking of such lines as Lady Macbeth's 'Out, damn'd spot.'

Misprints and errors are rare, but a few may be noted; note 1 on p. 80 should refer to

Appendix B and should give a page-reference; there is no King Oswald in *A Knack to Know a Knave* (p. 1020); it is hard to see in what sense Hamlet's deliberate hyperbole 'Doubt that the sun doth move' can 'anticipate Galileo's demonstration that the earth revolves around the sun' (p. 5); Shakespeare's reference to 'this solid globe' in *Troilus and Cressida* can only have involved a 'side-glance' at the Globe playhouse if the play was ever performed there, which is disputed (p. 7); the connotation of 'fellow' was not always insulting in Shakespeare's day, or Heminge and Condell would hardly have used it of him in their dedication of the First Folio to the Herbert brothers (p. 9); the distinction between the comic styles of William Kempe and Robert Armin was not so absolute as to prevent Armin from playing Dogberry (p. 18); the equation of Theobald's *Double Falsehood* with the lost play of *Cardenio*, though possible and attractive, is not proven (p. 31, n. 14); the author of *A Marriage between Wit and Wisdom* was Francis Merbury, not Medbury (p. 1865); references (p. 1093) to textual notes on *Romeo and Juliet*, II, vi, 1 and III, i, 103, do not lead to the Shakespearian spellings said to be found there as no note is given on either line; 'shard-borne', *Macbeth*, III, ii, 42, does not mean 'carried on scaly wings' (p. 1325); at *Macbeth*, III, iii, 7, where the text rightly emends to 'and', F 'end' is not collated (p. 1340); *Lear*, III, ii, lacks the initial F stage direction 'Storm still' (p. 1274); at *The Winter's Tale*, V, iii, 20 s.d., F reads 'Paulina', not, as the textual note says, 'Paulia' (p. 1605); *The Birth of Merlin*, which shows knowledge of Shakespeare's *Henry VIII*, is unlikely to have been written as early as 1608 (p. 1887).

Of the general excellence of the *Riverside Shakespeare* there can be no doubt. It deserves to become a standard college text, as much for its generous supply of ancillary material as for the responsibility of its text and commentary.

It is for this reason that it seems particularly to invite comment on the more questionable details of its presentation and interpretation of the text.

One branch of the recent strong growth of Shakespeare concordances blossoms with the publication of *The Harvard Concordance to Shakespeare*, edited by Marvin Spevack,[1] which appeared a year ahead of its parent edition, *The Riverside Shakespeare*. Its claims to be the first complete and reliable one-volume concordance to all the plays and poems of Shakespeare are necessarily linked with those of the edition itself, but the wide utility of such a concordance, in modern spelling (so far as the edition is), is self-evident, whatever the scholarly needs that can only be satisfied by the Oxford old-spelling concordances to the First Folio and Quarto texts of the plays.

Completeness is claimed on the basis both of the inclusion of texts not concorded by Bartlett, namely *The Two Noble Kinsmen* and the fragments from *Sir Thomas More*, and of the provision of full entries for all but forty-three of the commonest words. In addition, each entry specifies whether the passage is in verse or prose and all readings (of whatever origin) which are not those of 'the declared copy-texts' of the parent edition are separately listed and distinguished by a slash. The provision of statistics of the absolute and relative frequency of occurrence of each form is among the features inherited by this volume from its six-volume precursor,[2] although the figures can hardly have much significance, unless all editorial emendations are right. The reduction of the concordance to a single volume and the substitution of a roman type-face for the typewriter face of the original are clear advantages, although the computer's need to suppress upper-case letters turns Shakespeare into an antetype of e. e. cummings.

[1] (Harvard University Press; Oxford University Press, 1974).　[2] (Georg Olms, 1969–70).

The eccentricities already noticed in the *Riverside* text recur in the concordance, where cross-references are needed to warn the user, for example, to refer also under 'heckfer' if he wishes to survey Shakespeare's views on heifers. Despite the claim in the introduction that homographs are distinguished when separate entries for them are found in the Oxford English Dictionary, such distinctions are at least inconsistent: a single listing covers three *OED* entries for STEM; *sb*[1], stalk or branch; *sb*[2], bow of a ship; and *v*[2], to stop or delay, while *steer*, bovine, and *to steer*, nautical, are also mixed. The record is fuller than Bartlett's: in a short section checked for this review, Spevack adds *steep* from *A Midsummer Night's Dream*, II, i, 69, which Bartlett missed. The impression that he has added even more derives from his listing of the poems together with the plays and from the inclusion of *More* and the *Noble Kinsmen* (so that Shakespeare is now credited with some distinctive touches of Fletcher's vocabulary, such as *extremely*). The least satisfactory aspect of the concordance is the provision, for electronic reasons, of contexts which often fail to complete either the sense or the syntax, such as 'STEERING steering with due course toward the isle of' or 'STEEP'D head, / steep'd me in poverty to the very lips'. At worst, the context may mislead by suggesting a sense opposite to Shakespeare's: again under STEEP'D, we find 'deserve / and yet are steep'd in favors;', where the omission of 'neither' before 'deserve' creates an apparent paradox quite foreign to the passage. As a mechanical aid, this concordance improves on its predecessors, but at the cost of making unprecedented fritters of the text it concords.

General accounts of Shakespeare's comedies (and Harry Levin's *Riverside* introduction is no exception) often either omit *The Merry Wives of Windsor* altogether or relegate it to a special class in order to avoid the need it creates of qualifying almost all broad generali-

zations. G. R. Hibbard, whose earlier contributions to the series include *The Taming of the Shrew*, has now edited *The Merry Wives* for the New Penguin Shakespeare[1] and once more demonstrates his characteristic independence of critical approach in an introductory essay which takes the play seriously as the successful comedy it is. Starting from the fact of the play's distinguished stage history, he dismisses alike the long-standing tradition of occasional composition and the identification of the alleged occasion as the Garter celebrations of 1597, arguing for a date of composition no earlier than the summer of 1599 and accounting for the Garter material in Act V as extrinsic to the play and grafted onto it from a separate show written in 1597. This view, though wholly conjectural, has the merit of allowing us to see Pistol, Nym and Bardolph as later versions of the characters in *2 Henry IV* and *Henry V* and Sir Hugh Evans as a stage Welshman less obtrusive than Fluellen because imagined after him. The plot is treated as a comic transmutation of the revenge play and of Ovidian myth, set in the familiar world of Elizabeth's England. The Quarto, which Hibbard regards as both reported and abridged, is used sparingly in establishing the text. Two new readings, 'you, you rogue' (F, you rogue), at II, ii, 25 and 'escape' (F vncape) at III, iii, 155, make excellent sense, although 'vncape' is left unaccounted for in terms of its likely origin.

The other addition to the New Penguins is *King John*, edited by R. L. Smallwood.[2] The scale of both introduction and commentary is generous, perhaps even to excess, and there is some sense of a desire to leave nothing unsaid and no word unglossed. Typical is the com-

[1] Penguin Books (Harmondsworth, 1973); *The Merry Wives*, edited by H. J. Oliver, New Arden Shakespeare, has been published in paperback (Methuen, 1973).
[2] Penguin Books (Harmondsworth, 1974).

ment on the name 'James Gurney', given by Shakespeare to Lady Faulconbridge's servant in I, i, 'The F stage direction, and the Bastard at line 230, both identify Lady Faulconbridge's follower...with apparently unnecessary precision', where the simple dramatic point is that the Bastard, in his newly-created knighthood, and having just promised to show his rank by forgetting men's names, forgets to forget the name of this servant, who is the next man he meets. A valuable contribution to the study of the play is made by an appendix in which its relation to *The Troublesome Reign of King John* is reassessed and strong and detailed arguments are presented for the orthodox view, that *The Troublesome Reign* is the source of *King John* rather than some sort of 'bad quarto' of it. The text is handled with appropriate conservatism.

J. L. Halio has added editions of *Macbeth* and *King Lear* to the Shakespeare plays included in the old-spelling Fountainwell Drama Texts.[1] These volumes exhibit the uneasy blend of textual elaboration and elementary annotation characteristic of the series as a whole. As it stands, *Macbeth*, which has perforce to follow the Folio, is the more reliable of the two, though marred by a few misprints in the text. The convention of using dashes for changes of address is inconsistently introduced and alterations to the F verse-lining are sometimes wilful or even simply wrong, e.g. IV, iii, 32–4, where F is perfectly satisfactory as it stands. *King Lear* is of greater textual interest, if partly as a cautionary exhibit for future editors. Halio has had the courage to test the hypothesis that the Quarto, far from being an inferior report, stands in close relation to Shakespeare's 'foul papers' by adopting it as the copy-text for his edition, assimilating those sections of text which have to be printed from F to the Quarto's practice in capitalization. The size of the book has not permitted the editor to argue for particular readings at any

length, but the overall effect of his text is to present an unfamiliar *Lear*, 'caterickes, and Hircanios' and all. So long as the nature of the Q text and the degree of confidence which can be extended to F's correction of it remain matters of debate, editions which attempt, as this one does, to demonstrate the consequences of an unorthodox position will make a useful contribution to that debate.

In an edition of *Arden of Feversham*[2] remarkable for its handling of historical and local evidence bearing on the murder which is the play's subject, M. L. Wine scouts the question of Shakespeare's alleged authorship of it. After reviewing such literary arguments as have been put forward in support of Shakespeare, which he shows some signs of wishing to find persuasive, he sensibly concludes that 'in dealing with a corrupt text we cannot be absolutely sure that we are isolating features individual to the writer in question' and that the suggestion must be rejected – a position which has seemed inevitable to many who have considered the question closely.

Gunnar Sorelius,[3] reporting on a skilful piece of detective work, demonstrates the common origin of cuttings containing quotations from Shakespeare which are now dispersed among two manuscripts in the Folger Library and more than sixty Halliwell-Phillipps scrapbooks at the Shakespeare Centre in Stratford-upon-Avon. All are shown to have been cut by Halliwell-Phillipps from a commonplace-book of the mid-seventeenth century (dated in the Folger manuscripts 'about A.D. 1670' and 'about A.D. 1660' respectively). He included facsimiles from the collections now in the Folger Library, from the comedies only, in his edition of Shakespeare, 1853–65,

[1] *Macbeth* (Oliver and Boyd, 1972); *Lear* (Oliver and Boyd, 1973).
[2] The Revels Plays (Methuen, 1973).
[3] 'An Unknown Shakespearian Commonplace Book', *Library*, XXVIII (1973), 294–308.

and recorded some variants from them, though without attributing any authority to these readings. A third Folger manuscript, also once in the possession of Halliwell-Phillipps, turned out to preserve the first two and final six leaves of the original collection from which all the cuttings were taken. It was entitled 'Hesperides' and ended with 'A Catalogue of the Bookes from whence these Collections were extracted'. The catalogue lists 302 titles, including 36 of Shakespeare's plays. The collection apparently belongs to the years about 1660 and once contained over 1,000 pages, the quotations in it being arranged by subject under alphabetically ordered headings. The surviving cuttings preserve 730 quotations from Shakespeare, in the text of the First Folio, but altered in a variety of different ways, from corrections anticipating later editorial conjectures to clarifications needed to make them intelligible out of context. Sorelius lists the variants in all the quotations, of which the largest groups are from *The Winter's Tale*, *Measure for Measure*, *Henry VIII*, *King John*, *Romeo and Juliet* and *Cymbeline*.

S. W. Reid[1] takes a close look at the ways in which Jaggard's compositor B handled his text when justifying his line. He begins with a timely reminder that the need to justify affects every line set, not only, as has been widely assumed in spelling-analysis, lines set to the full measure. Working from our present knowledge of B's strongest spelling preferences, Reid is able to show how he set about the job of justifying, adding spaces, often after punctuation, to fill out a loose line or adapting spelling to loosen an over-tight one. Most such adjustments, in either direction, are in the second half of the line, suggesting that he worked backwards from the end. In setting full lines of prose, he apparently began to adapt his spelling only as he neared the end of the line, whereas in full verse lines he seems to have done so from the beginning. As often, a

modest enquiry into a detail of printing practice calls in question assumptions based on over-simplification and shows the need for finer analysis. D. Allen Carroll[2] finds in James Roberts's edition of Everard Guilpin's *Skialetheia* (1598) the same two patterns of spelling as in *The Merchant of Venice* (1600), *Titus Andronicus* (1600), and *Hamlet* (1604/5), and concludes that the two compositors known as X and Y in the Shakespeare Quartos also set Guilpin's satires, but the evidence is hardly enough to warrant his conclusion 'that Roberts's personnel during this time was stable and that one ought to enter into the study of other texts with such an assumption' – only the study of those other texts can tell us more. Millard T. Jones[3] describes the press-variants in nine formes of Nicholas Okes's 1622 Quarto of *Othello* and finds in them evidence of cursory and careless proofing, without reference to copy except in outer H and inner I. The standard of accuracy seems to improve after outer H. These facts should alert editors to the possibility of undetected compositorial error as a major source of Q variation from the text as represented by F, especially in the earlier part of the play. Faint light may be thrown on Edward Knight, book-keeper of the King's Men, and therefore, perhaps, on the text of the First Folio, if Knight could have played some part in transcribing copy for it, by Fredson Bowers's analysis of the two basic texts of *Beggars' Bush*,[4] by Fletcher and Massinger, that of the 1647 Beaumont and Fletcher Folio,

[1] 'Justification and Spelling in Jaggard's Compositor B', *Studies in Bibliography*, XXVII (1974), 91–111.
[2] 'James Roberts's Compositors in 1598', *Papers of the Bibliographical Society of America*, LXVIII (1974), 52–3.
[3] 'Press-Variants and Proofreading in the First Quarto of *Othello* (1622)', *Studies in Bibliography*, XXVII (1974), 177–84.
[4] '*Beggars Bush*: A Reconstructed Prompt-Book and its Copy', *Studies in Bibliography*, XXVII, 113–36.

assumed to have been printed from fair copy in the hand of Massinger, and that of the Lambarde manuscript, derived from the same fair copy by way of a prompt-book prepared by Knight. As what is demonstrated is Knight's ability to produce a prompt-book containing 'unresolved tangles in the action and even in the casting', it may be hoped that he had little to do with the Folio, though his hand has been tentatively identified in the prompt annotations printed in the 1634 Quarto of *The Two Noble Kinsmen*.

Joseph E. Kramer[1] regards the fly-killing scene in Folio *Titus Andronicus* as a late addition and questions Shakespeare's authorship of it. In a subtle and well-argued article, Sidney Thomas[2] proposes that Mercutio's 'Queen Mab' speech, *Romeo and Juliet*, I, iv, 53–95, is more correctly preserved in the 'bad' Quarto of 1597 than in the 'good' one of 1599, where it was printed from a garbled report. He explains the need for such a report as arising from the absence of the speech from the 'foul papers' which were transcribed as copy for Q2, perhaps because the speech was only added to Mercutio's role in rehearsal. J. C. Maxwell[3] cites *Othello*, III, iii, 388–90, as a likely source for 'his blacke and grimme complexion smeerd' in Q1 *Hamlet*, II, ii, 477, and points out that if this were accepted it would date *Othello* before 1603. G. R. Proudfoot[4] proposes the adjective 'travailous' as the original behind both Q's 'trauels' and F's 'Trauellours' at *Othello*, I, iii, 139. James O. Woods[5] continues his investigation of the authorship of *Pericles* with discussions of Shakespeare's use of vegetation imagery and of whales.

[1] '*Titus Andronicus*: The "Fly-Killing" Incident', *Shakespeare Studies*, V (1969), 9–19.
[2] 'The Queen Mab Speech in *Romeo and Juliet*', *Shakespeare Survey 25* (1972), 73–80.
[3] '*Othello* and the Bad Quarto of *Hamlet*', *Notes and Queries*, n.s. XXI (1974), 130.
[4] 'Othello's History: I. iii. 139', *ibid.*, 130–1.
[5] 'The Running Imagery in *Pericles*', *Shakespeare Studies*, V (1969), 240–52; 'Shakespeare and the Belching Whale', *English Language Notes*, XI (1973), 40–4.

© RICHARD PROUDFOOT 1975

INDEX

INDEX

INDEX

INDEX